SECOND EDITION

D0219875

Animal Rights and Human Obligations

Edited by

TOM REGAN
North Carolina State University

PETER SINGER
Monash University

PRENTICE HALL, Englewood Cliffs, New Jersey 07632

Library of Congress Cataloging-in-Publication Data

Animal rights and human obligations / edited by Tom Regan, Peter
Singer. -- 2nd ed.
      p.   cm.
   ISBN 0-13-036864-4
   1. Animals, Treatment of. 2. Animals, Treatment of--Moral and
ethical aspects.   I. Regan, Tom. II. Singer, Peter.
HV4711.A56 1989
179'.3--dc19   88-13785
                                                      CIP

Editorial/production supervision: Linda B. Pawelchak
Cover design: Wanda Lubelska
Manufacturing buyer: Peter Havens

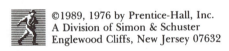 ©1989, 1976 by Prentice-Hall, Inc.
A Division of Simon & Schuster
Englewood Cliffs, New Jersey 07632

All rights reserved. No part of this book may be
reproduced, in any form or by any means,
without permission in writing from the publisher.

Printed in the United States of America
10 9 8 7

ISBN   0-13-036864-4

Prentice-Hall International (UK) Limited, *London*
Prentice-Hall of Australia Pty. Limited, *Sydney*
Prentice-Hall Canada Inc., *Toronto*
Prentice-Hall Hispanoamericana, S.A., *Mexico*
Prentice-Hall of India Private Limited, *New Delhi*
Prentice-Hall of Japan, Inc., *Tokyo*
Simon & Schuster Asia Pte. Ltd., *Singapore*
Editora Prentice-Hall do Brasil, Ltda., *Rio de Janeiro*

CONTENTS

pp. 6-22
Tues. 11/6

Tues. 11/13

Th. 11/8

PART THREE
Equal Consideration for Animals

PART FOUR
Animal Rights

PART FIVE
Killing and the Value of Life

PART SIX
The Treatment of Farm Animals

Th. 11/1

PREFACE

Preparing this second edition of *Animal Rights and Human Obligations* has made us realize just how far the discussion of ethical issues relating to nonhuman animals has progressed in the fourteen years since we began preparing the original edition. At that time, philosophers simply did not discuss the ethics of our treatment of animals. It was not considered to be a topic of any interest or importance. Hence, in compiling the first edition, our primary objective was to awaken our readers to the thought that our relations with animals raise important ethical issues. That was the essential first step.

To be sure, from a long-term historical perspective, the issue was not a new one. Earlier thinkers had been well aware of the need to justify our use of animals: we can read the attempted justifications in the book of *Genesis* and in the works of philosophers like Aristotle and Aquinas. There had also been strong critics of what we do to animals—some well-known writers like Plutarch and Bentham and other neglected figures such as Henry Salt.

The existence of this substantial historical body of thought was, from our point of view, doubly fortunate. First, it helped to establish the respectability of the issue as a subject of philosophical thought: the fact that the ethics of our treatment of animals had been discussed previously by key figures in the great tradition of Western philosophy made it much more difficult for one's conservative colleagues to object to it being taught in philosophy classes today. Second, there was so little contemporary work being done on the ethics of our relations with animals that without the wealth of historical materials, we would have had difficulty finding enough good writing to fill a book.

How things have changed! Since 1974, dozens of books and hundreds of articles have been published on the ethics of our treatment of animals. Journals like *Inquiry, Ethics, Philosophy,* and *The Monist,* which previously had published virtually nothing on the topic, have put out entire issues devoted to it. A Society for the Study of Ethics and Animals has been founded which holds regular meetings in conjunction with the meetings of the American Philosophical Association. So, in preparing the second edition, the problem has been to select from the abundance of material in order to produce a volume which, while inevitably larger than the first edition, is still of manageable size. To achieve this goal we have, reluctantly, had to cut back on the historical material included in the first edition. Though the earlier writers deserve to be remembered, and we have kept enough of them to provide a historical perspective, the balance of the book has shifted in favor of writings that confront today's issues in today's terms.

It could be said, then, that the first edition has achieved, or contributed to the achievement of, its primary objective. Philosophers and the public as a whole are now much more aware of the ethical significance of what we do to nonhuman animals. The anthologies most widely used for teaching philosophy courses in applied ethics standardly include some coverage of the issue; there can be few philosophy departments, in North America, Britain and Australia, in which the topic has not been taught. Moreover, what has happened in philosophy is beginning to happen in other disciplines—in religion, for example, where a precedent-setting international conference was held in London, in 1984, and where there is a steadily increasing amount of serious scholarship addressing the theme of human responsibility to the created order.

No less remarkable than the enormous growth of scholarship has been the creation of professional organizations devoted to animal concerns. Veterinarians for Animal Rights, the Animal Legal Defense Fund, the Physicians' Committee for Responsible Medicine, and Psychologists for the Ethical Treatment of Animals have all come into being during the past decade; before then, such groups would have been unthinkable. These groups, important as they are in focusing the interests and skills of experts on matters that concern nonhuman animals, are also noteworthy for their encouragement of professional research. When Andrew W. Rowan, Assistant Dean for Special Programs at Tufts University, School of Veterinary Medicine, remarks that "philosophers have written more on the general topic of animal rights during the past ten years than their predecessors wrote during the preceding two thousand," he speaks accurately; in *another* ten years it may be possible to make a similar remark about scholarship in religion, law, and other more or less well-defined areas of human endeavor.

All these signs—and there are many more, including the steadily expanding coverage "animal liberation" receives in the media, and its recognized legitimacy and seriousness as a political issue—indicate that there is a deep, profound reexamination underway, one that asks what we owe the animals, not merely what they can give us. For centuries we have accepted what they give to us without giving much thought to the matter. The remains of dead animals are ubiquitous. Their pelts and skins are used in our dress in such articles as shoes, belts, vests, gloves, skirts, and watchbands; in sporting goods such as baseballs, footballs, and gloves of "genuine cowhide"; in home furnishings like rugs, chairs, sofas, and hassocks—even in the chamois cloth people use to polish their cars. Animals also give their flesh, and most people who read this book will be in the habit of eating it. Only we usually don't call it "flesh." Usually we call it "hamburger," "hotdog," "beef" or "pork."

What should we think about these and related customs—for example, using nonhuman animals in scientific research or as sources of commercial entertainment? Are we justified in exploiting them as we do, or does a more enlightened, more just ethic call for radical changes in our behavior? These questions are at the very heart of the reexamination that already is well underway. It is too early to say how far this reexamination will take us, whether individually or collectively, and what effects, if any, this process will have on how we humans treat other animals. And even if it were time to predict, a prediction from our pens would be out of place here. In this volume, our overriding interest has been the same as in the first edition: to give the competing sides an opportunity to speak their minds, whether they speak for or against animal rights, for or against vegetarianism, for or against vivisection, and the like. The truth wins out in any fair debate. Or so we believe.

Our belief, then, is that we have allowed the debate to be a fair one. But our hope is that, through the educational process, this book will contribute to bringing about those changes the truth demands.

Tom Regan
Peter Singer

PART ONE
Animals in the History of Western Thought

THE BIBLE

Selections

20 And God said, "Let the waters bring forth swarms of living creatures, and let birds fly above the earth across the firmament of the heavens." ^{21}So God created the great sea monsters and every living creature that moves, with which the waters swarm, according to their kinds, and every winged bird according to its kind. And God saw that it was good. ^{22}And God blessed them, saying, "Be fruitful and multiply and fill the waters in the seas, and let birds multiply on the earth." ^{23}And there was evening and there was morning, a fifth day.

24 And God said, "Let the earth bring forth living creatures according to their kinds: cattle and creeping things and beasts of the earth according to their kinds." And it was so. ^{25}And God made the beasts of the earth according to their kinds and the cattle according to their kinds, and everything that creeps upon the ground according to its kind. And God saw that it was good.

26 Then God said, "Let us make man in our image, after our likeness; and let them have dominion over the fish of the sea, and over the birds of the air, and over the cattle, and over all the earth, and over every creeping thing that creeps upon the earth." ^{27}So God created man in his own image, in the image of God he created him; male and female he created them. ^{28}And God blessed them, and God said to them, "Be fruitful and multiply,

and fill the earth and subdue it; and have dominion over the fish of the sea and over the birds of the air and over every living thing that moves upon the earth." [29]And God said, "Behold I have given you every plant yielding seed which is upon the face of all the earth, and every tree with seed in its fruit; you shall have them for food. [30]And to every beast of the earth, and to every bird of the air, and to everything that creeps on the earth, everything that has the breath of life, I have given every green plant for food." And it was so. [31]And God saw everything that he had made, and behold, it was very good. And there was evening and there was morning, a sixth day.

Edan'. only at veggils

Genesis 1:20–31

And God blessed Noah and his sons, and said to them, "Be fruitful and multiply, and fill the earth. [2]The fear of you and the dread of you shall be upon every beast of the earth, and upon every bird of the air, upon everything that creeps on the ground and all the fish of the sea; into your hand they are delivered. [3]Every moving thing that lives shall be food for you; and as I gave you the green plants, I give you everything."

Genesis 9:1–3

All things whatsoever ye would that men should do to you, do ye even so to them; for this is the law and the prophets.

St. Matthew 7:12

To what purpose is the multitude of your sacrifices unto me? saith the Lord: I am full of the burnt offerings of rams, and the fat of fed beasts; and I delight not in the blood of bullocks, or of lambs, or of he goats . . . Bring no more vain oblations . . . Your new moons and your appointed feasts my soul hateth: they are a trouble unto me; I am weary to bear them. And when ye spread forth your hands, I will hide mine eyes from you: yea, when ye make many prayers, I will not hear: your hands are full of blood.

Isaiah 1:11–15

The wolf also shall dwell with the lamb, and the leopard shall lie down with the kid; and the calf and the young lion and the fatling together; and a little child shall lead them . . . They shall not hurt nor destroy in all my holy mountain; for the earth shall be full of the knowledge of the Lord, as the waters cover the sea.

Isaiah 11:6–9

He that killeth an ox is as if he slew a man; he that sacrificeth a lamb, as if he cut off a dog's neck; he that offereth an oblation, as if he offered swine's blood; he that burneth incense, as if he blessed an idol. Yea, they have chosen their own ways, and their soul delighteth in their abominations.

Isaiah 66:3

A righteous man regardeth the life of his beast: but the tender mercies of the wicked are cruel.

Proverbs 12:10

Open thy mouth for the dumb, in the cause of all such as are appointed to destruction.

Proverbs 31:8

Blessed are the merciful, for they shall receive mercy.

Matthew 5:7

Hurt not the earth, neither the sea, nor the trees.

Revelation 7:3

ARISTOTLE

Animals
and Slavery

It is clear that the rule of the soul over the body, and of the mind and the rational element over the passionate, is natural and expedient; whereas the equality of the two or the rule of the inferior is always hurtful. The same holds good of animals in relation to men; for tame animals have a better nature than wild, and all tame animals are better off when they are ruled by man; for then they are preserved. Again, the male is by nature superior, and the female inferior; and the one rules, and the other is ruled; this principle, of necessity, extends to all mankind. Where then there is such a difference as that between soul and body, or between men and animals, (as in the case of those whose business is to use their body, and who can do nothing better), the lower sort are by nature slaves, and it is better for them as for all inferiors that they should be under the rule of a master. For he who can be, and therefore is, another's and he who participates in rational principle enough to apprehend, but not to have, such a principle, is a slave by nature. Whereas the lower animals cannot even apprehend a principle;

Aristotle (384–322 B.C.) was one of the greatest Greek philosophers. He wrote extensively in all the major areas of philosophy and has had a lasting influence.

From Aristotle, "Politics," Book I, chapters 5 and 8, translated by Benjamin Jowett from *The Oxford Translation of Aristotle* edited by W. D. Ross. By permission of the Oxford University Press, Oxford.

they obey their instincts. And indeed the use made of slaves and of tame animals is not very different; for both with their bodies minister to the needs of life. . . .

Other modes of life are similarly combined in any way which the needs of men may require. Property, in the sense of a bare livelihood, seems to be given by nature herself to all, both when they are first born, and when they are grown up. For some animals bring forth, together with their offspring, so much food as will last until they are able to supply themselves; of this the vermiparous or oviparous animals are an instance; and the viviparous animals have up to a certain time a supply of food for their young in themselves, which is called milk. In like manner we may infer that, after the birth of animals, plants exist for their sake, and that the other animals exist for the sake of man, the tame for use and food, the wild, if not all, at least the greater part of them, for food, and for the provision of clothing and various instruments. Now if nature makes nothing incomplete and nothing in vain, the inference must be that she has made all animals for the sake of man. And so, in one point of view, the art of war is a natural art of acquisition, for the art of acquisition includes hunting, an art which we ought to practice against wild beasts, and against men who, though intended by nature to be governed, will not submit; for war of such a kind is naturally just.

SAINT THOMAS AQUINAS

Differences between Rational and Other Creatures

In the first place then, the very condition of the rational creature, in that it has dominion over its actions, requires that the care of providence should be bestowed on it for its own sake: whereas the condition of other things that have not dominion over their actions shows that they are cared for, not for their own sake, but as being directed to other things. Because that which acts only when moved by another, is like an instrument; whereas that which acts by itself, is like a principal agent. Now an instrument is required, not for its own sake, but that the principal agent may use it. Hence whatever is done for the care of the instruments must be referred to the principal agent as its end: whereas any such action directed to the principal agent as such, either by the agent itself or by another, is for the sake of the same principal agent. Accordingly intellectual creatures are ruled by God, as though He cared for them for their own sake, while other creatures are ruled as being directed to rational creatures.

Again. That which has dominion over its own act, is free in its action, because *he is free who is cause of himself:* whereas that which by some kind of

Saint Thomas Aquinas (c. 1224–1274) is generally recognized as the most important Catholic theologian.

From Saint Thomas Aquinas, *Summa Contra Gentiles,* literally translated by the English Dominican Fathers (Chicago: Benziger Brothers, 1928), Third Book, Part II, Chap. CXII.

necessity is moved by another to act, is subject to slavery. Therefore every other creature is naturally under slavery; the intellectual nature alone is free. Now, in every government provision is made for the free for their own sake; but for slaves that they may be useful to the free. Accordingly divine providence makes provision for the intellectual creature for its own sake, but for other creatures for the sake of the intellectual creature.

Moreover. Whenever certain things are directed to a certain end, if any of them are unable of themselves to attain to the end, they must needs be directed to those that attain to the end, which are directed to the end for their own sake. Thus the end of the army is victory, which the soldiers obtain by their own action in fighting, and they alone in the army are required for their own sake; whereas all others, to whom other duties are assigned, such as the care of horses, the preparing of arms, are requisite for the sake of the soldiers of the army. Now, it is clear from what has been said, that God is the last end of the universe, whom the intellectual nature alone obtains in Himself, namely by knowing and loving Him, as was proved above. Therefore the intellectual nature alone is requisite for its own sake in the universe, and all others for its sake.

Further. In every whole, the principal parts are requisite on their own account for the completion of the whole, while others are required for the preservation or betterment of the former. Now, of all the parts of the universe, intellectual creatures hold the highest place, because they approach nearest to the divine likeness. Therefore divine providence provides for the intellectual nature for its own sake, and for all others for its sake.

Besides. It is clear that all the parts are directed to the perfection of the whole: since the whole is not on account of the parts, but the parts on account of the whole. Now, intellectual natures are more akin to the whole than other natures: because, in a sense, the intellectual substance is all things, inasmuch as by its intellect it is able to comprehend all things; whereas every other substance has only a particular participation of being. Consequently God cares for other things for the sake of intellectual substances.

Besides. Whatever happens to a thing in the course of nature happens to it naturally. Now, we see that in the course of nature the intellectual substance uses all others for its own sake; either for the perfection of the intellect, which sees the truth in them as in a mirror; or for the execution of its power and development of its knowledge, in the same way as a craftsman develops the conception of his art in corporeal matter; or again to sustain the body that is united to an intellectual soul, as is the case in man. It is clear, therefore, that God cares for all things for the sake of intellectual substances.

Moreover. If a man seek something for its own sake, he seeks it always, because *what is per se, is always:* whereas if he seek a thing on account of something else, he does not of necessity seek it always but only in reference to that for the sake of which he seeks it. Now, as we proved above, things derive their being from the divine will. Therefore whatever is always is willed by God for its own sake; and what is not always is willed by God, not for its own sake, but for another's. Now, intellectual substances approach nearest to being always, since they are incorruptible. They are, moreover, unchangeable, except in their choice. Therefore intellectual substances are governed for their own sake, as it were; and others for the sake of intellectual substances.

The fact that all the parts of the universe are directed to the perfection of the whole is not in contradiction with the foregoing conclusion: since all the parts are directed to the perfection of the whole, in so far as one part serves another. Thus in the human body it is clear that the lungs belong to the body's perfection, in that they serve the heart: wherefore there is no contradiction in the lungs being for the sake of the heart, and for the sake of the whole animal. In like manner that other natures are on account of the intellectual is not contrary to their being for the perfection of the universe: for without the things required for the perfection of the intellectual substance, the universe would not be complete.

Nor again does the fact that individuals are for the sake of the species militate against what has been said. Because through being directed to their species, they are directed also to the intellectual nature. For a corruptible thing is directed to man, not on account of only one individual man, but on account of the whole human species. Yet a corruptible thing could not serve the whole human species, except as regards its own entire species. Hence the order whereby corruptible things are directed to man, requires that individuals be directed to the species.

When we assert that intellectual substances are directed by divine providence for their own sake, we do not mean that they are not also referred by God and for the perfection of the universe. Accordingly they are said to be provided for on their own account, and others on account of them, because the goods bestowed on them by divine providence are not given them for another's profit: whereas those bestowed on others are in the divine plan intended for the use of intellectual substances. Hence it is said (Deut. iv. 19): *Lest thou see the sun and the moon and the other stars, and being deceived by error, thou adore and serve them, which the Lord thy God created for the service of all the nations that are under heaven:* and (Ps. viii. 8): *Thou hast subjected all things under his feet, all sheep and oxen: moreover, the beasts also of the field:* and (Wis. xii. 18): *Thou, being master of power, judgest with tranquillity, and with great favor disposest of us.*

Hereby is refuted the error of those who said it is sinful for a man to kill dumb animals: for by divine providence they are intended for man's use in the natural order. Hence it is no wrong for man to make use of them, either by killing or in any other way whatever. For this reason the Lord said to Noe (Gen. ix. 3): *As the green herbs I have delivered all flesh to you.*

And if any passages of Holy Writ seem to forbid us to be cruel to dumb animals, for instance to kill a bird with its young: this is either to remove man's thoughts from being cruel to other men, and lest through being cruel to animals one become cruel to human beings: or because injury to an animal leads to the temporal hurt of man, either of the doer of the deed, or of another: or on account of some signification: thus the Apostle expounds the prohibition against *muzzling the ox that treadeth the corn.*

* If we are bad to them, we will be bad to eachother

SAINT THOMAS AQUINAS

On Killing Living Things and the Duty to Love Irrational Creatures

QUESTION 64, ARTICLE 1

Whether It Is Unlawful to Kill Any Living Thing

We proceed thus to the First Article:

Objection 1. It would seem unlawful to kill any living thing. For the Apostle says (Rom. xiii. 2): *They that resist the ordinance of God purchase to themselves damnation.* Now Divine providence has ordained that all living things should be preserved, according to Ps. cxlvi. 8, 9: *Who maketh grass to grow on the mountains, . . . Who giveth to beasts their food.* Therefore it seems unlawful to take the life of any living thing.

Obj. 2. Further, Murder is a sin because it deprives a man of life. Now life is common to all animals and plants. Hence for the same reason it is apparently a sin to slay dumb animals and plants.

Obj. 3. Further, In the Divine law a special punishment is not appointed save for a sin. Now a special punishment had to be inflicted, according to the Divine law, on one who killed another man's ox or sheep (Exod. xxii. I). Therefore the slaying of dumb animals is a sin.

On the contrary, Augustine says (*De Civ. Dei* i. 20): *When we hear it said, 'Thou shalt not kill,' we do not take it as referring to trees, for they have no sense, nor to irrational animals, because they have no fellowship with us. Hence it follows that the words, 'Thou shalt not kill' refer to the killing of a man.*

From Saint Thomas Aquinas, *Summa Theologica,* literally translated by the English Dominican Fathers (Chicago: Benziger Brothers, 1918), Part II, Question 64, Article 1, and Question 25, Article 3.

10

I answer that, There is no sin in using a thing for the purpose for which it is. Now the order of things is such that the imperfect are for the perfect, even as in the process of generation nature proceeds from imperfection to perfection. Hence it is that just as in the generation of a man there is first a living thing, then an animal, and lastly a man, so too things, like the plants, which merely have life, are all alike for animals, and all animals are for man. Wherefore it is not unlawful if man use plants for the good of animals, and animals for the good of man, as the Philosopher states (*Polit.* i. 3).

Now the most necessary use would seem to consist in the fact that animals use plants, and men use animals, for food, and this cannot be done unless these be deprived of life: wherefore it is lawful both to take life from plants for the use of animals, and from animals for the use of men. In fact this is in keeping with the commandment of God Himself: for it is written (Gen. i. 29, 30): *Behold I have given you every herb . . . and all trees . . . to be your meat, and to all beasts of the earth:* and again (ibid. ix. 3): *Everything that moveth and liveth shall be meat to you.*

Reply Obj. 1. According to the Divine ordinance the life of animals and plants is preserved not for themselves but for man. Hence, as Augustine says (*De Civ. Dei* i. 20): *By a most just ordinance of the Creator, both their life and their death are subject to our use.*

Reply Obj. 2. Dumb animals and plants are devoid of the life of reason whereby to set themselves in motion; they are moved, as it were by another, by a kind of natural impulse, a sign of which is that they are naturally enslaved and accommodated to the uses of others.

Reply Obj. 3. He that kills another's ox, sins, not through killing the ox, but through injuring another man in his property. Wherefore this is not a species of the sin of murder but of the sin of theft or robbery.

QUESTION 65, ARTICLE 3

Whether Irrational Creatures Also Ought to Be Loved out of Charity

We proceed thus to the Third Article:

Objection 1. It would seem that irrational creatures also ought to be loved out of charity. For it is chiefly by charity that we are conformed to God. Now God loves irrational creatures out of charity, for He loves *all things that are* (Wis. xi. 25), and whatever He loves, He loves by Himself Who is charity. Therefore we also should love irrational creatures out of charity.

Obj. 2. Further, Charity is referred to God principally, and extends to other things as referable to God. Now just as the rational creature is referable to God, in as much as it bears the resemblance of image, so too, are the irrational creatures, in as much as they bear the resemblance of a trace. Therefore charity extends also to irrational creatures.

Obj. 3. Further, Just as the object of charity is God, so is the object of faith. Now faith extends to irrational creatures, since we believe that heaven and earth were created by God, that the fishes and birds were brought forth out of the waters, and animals that walk, and plants, out of the earth. Therefore charity extends also to irrational creatures.

On the contrary, The love of charity extends to none but God and our neighbour. But the word neighbour cannot be extended to irrational creatures, since they have no fellowship with man in the rational life. Therefore charity does not extend to irrational creatures.

I answer that, According to what has been stated above (Q. XIII., A. 1) charity is a kind of friendship. Now the love of friendship is twofold: first, there is the love for the friend to whom our friendship is given, secondly, the love for those good things which we desire for our friend. With regard to the first, no irrational creature can be loved out of charity; and for three reasons. Two of these reasons refer in a general way to friendship, which cannot have an irrational creature for its object: first because friendship is towards one to whom we wish good things. While properly speaking, we cannot wish good things to an irrational creature, because it is not competent, properly speaking, to possess good, this being proper to the rational creature which, through its free will, is the master of its disposal of the good it possesses. Hence the Philosopher says (*Phys.* ii. 6) that we do not speak of good or evil befalling suchlike things, except metaphorically. Secondly, because all friendship is based on some fellowship in life; since *nothing is so proper to friendship as to live together,* as the Philosopher proves (*Ethic* viii. 5). Now irrational creatures can have no fellowship in human life which is regulated by reason. Hence friendship with irrational creatures is impossible, except metaphorically speaking. The third reason is proper to charity, for charity is based on the fellowship of everlasting happiness, to which the irrational creature cannot attain. Therefore we cannot have the friendship of charity towards an irrational creature.

Nevertheless we can love irrational creatures out of charity, if we regard them as the good things that we desire for others, in so far, to wit, as we wish for their preservation, to God's honour and man's use; thus too does God love them out of charity.

Wherefore the *Reply to the First Objection* is evident.

Reply Obj. 2. The likeness by way of trace does not confer the capacity for everlasting life, whereas the likeness of image does: and so the comparison fails.

Reply Obj. 3. Faith can extend to all that is in any way true, whereas the friendship of charity extends only to such things as have a natural capacity for everlasting life; wherefore the comparison fails.

RENÉ DESCARTES

Animals Are Machines

I

I had explained all these matters in some detail in the Treatise which I formerly intended to publish. And afterwards I had shown there, what must be the fabric of the nerves and muscles of the human body in order that the animal spirits therein contained should have the power to move the members, just as the heads of animals, a little while after decapitation, are still observed to move and bite the earth, notwithstanding that they are no longer animate; what changes are necessary in the brain to cause wakefulness, sleep and dreams; how light, sounds, smells, tastes, heat, and all other qualities pertaining to external objects are able to imprint on it various ideas by the intervention of the senses; how hunger, thirst and other internal affections can also convey their impressions upon it; what should be regarded as the "common sense" by which these ideas are received, and

René Descartes (1596–1650), sometimes called "the father of modern philosophy," is one of philosophy's most original and influential thinkers. His *Meditations* remains a philosophical classic.

Selection I is from Descartes, *Discourse on Method*, in *Philosophical Works of Descartes*, trans. E. S. Haldane and G. R. T. Ross (London: Cambridge University Press), vol. I, pp. 115–18. Selections II and III are from two letters by Descartes, to the Marquess of Newcastle (November 23, 1646) and to Henry More (February 5, 1649), in *Descartes: Philosophical Letters*, trans. and ed. Anthony Kenny. © 1970, Oxford University Press. Reprinted by permission of The Clarendon Press, Oxford.

what is meant by the memory which retains them, by the fancy which can change them in diverse ways and out of them constitute new ideas, and which, by the same means, distributing the animal spirits through the muscles, can cause the members of such a body to move in as many diverse ways, and in a manner as suitable to the objects which present themselves to its senses and to its internal passions, as can happen in our own case apart from the direction of our free will. And this will not seem strange to those, who, knowing how many different *automata* or moving machines can be made by the industry of man, without employing in so doing more than a very few parts in comparison with the great multitude of bones, muscles, nerves, arteries, veins, or other parts that are found in the body of each animal. From this aspect the body is regarded as a machine which, having been made by the hands of God, is incomparably better arranged, and possesses in itself movements which are much more admirable, than any of those which can be invented by man. Here I specially stopped to show that if there had been such machines, possessing the organs and outward form of a monkey or some other animal without reason, we should not have had any means of ascertaining that they were not of the same nature as those animals. On the other hand, if there were machines which bore a resemblance to our body and imitated our actions as far as it was morally possible to do so, we should always have two very certain tests by which to recognise that, for all that, they were not real men. The first is, that they could never use speech or other signs as we do when placing our thoughts on record for the benefit of others. For we can easily understand a machine's being constituted so that it can utter words, and even emit some responses to action on it of a corporeal kind, which brings about a change in its organs; for instance, if it is touched in a particular part it may ask what we wish to say to it; if in another part it may exclaim that it is being hurt, and so on. But it never happens that it arranges its speech in various ways, in order to reply appropriately to everything that may be said in its presence, as even the lowest type of man can do. And the second difference is, that although machines can perform certain things as well as or perhaps better than any of us can do, they infallibly fall short in others, by the which means we may discover that they did not act from knowledge, but only from the disposition of their organs. For while reason is a universal instrument which can serve for all contingencies, these organs have need of some special adaptation for every particular action. From this it follows that it is morally impossible that there should be sufficient diversity in any machine to allow it to act in all the events of life in the same way as our reason causes us to act.

By these two methods we may also recognise the difference that exists between men and brutes. For it is a very remarkable fact that there are none so depraved and stupid, without even excepting idiots, that they cannot arrange different words together, forming of them a statement by which they make known their thoughts; while, on the other hand, there is no other animal, however perfect and fortunately circumstanced it may be, which can do the same. It is not the want of organs that brings this to pass, for it is evident that magpies and parrots are able to utter words just like ourselves, and yet they cannot speak as we do, that is, so as to give evidence that they think of what they say. On the other hand, men who, being born deaf and dumb, are in the same degree, or even more than the brutes, destitute of the organs which serve the others for talking, are in the habit of themselves inventing certain signs by which they make themselves understood by those who, being usually in their company, have leisure to learn their language. And this does not merely show that the brutes have less reason than men, but that they have none at all, since it is clear that very little is required in order to be able to talk. And when we notice the inequality that exists between animals of the same species, as well as between men, and observe that some are more capable of receiving instruction than others, it is not credible that a monkey or a parrot, selected as the most perfect of its species, should not in these matters equal the stupidest child to be found, or at least a child whose mind is clouded, unless in the case of the brute the soul were of an entirely different nature from ours. And we ought not to confound speech with natural movements which betray passions and may be imitated by machines as well as be manifested by animals; nor must we think, as did some of the ancients, that brutes talk, although we do not understand their language. For if this were true, since they have many organs which are allied to our own, they could communicate their thoughts to us just as easily as to those of their own race. It is also a very remarkable fact that although there are many animals which exhibit more dexterity than we do in some of their actions, we at the same time observe that they do not manifest any dexterity at all in many others. Hence the fact that they do better than we do, does not prove that they are endowed with mind, for in this case they would have more reason than any of us, and would surpass us in all other things. It rather shows that they have no reason at all, and that it is nature which acts in them according to the disposition of their organs, just as a clock, which is only composed of wheels and weights is able to tell the hours and measure the time more correctly than we can do with all our wisdom.

I had described after this the rational soul and shown that it could not be in any way derived from the power of matter, like the other things of which I had spoken, but that it must be expressly created. I showed, too, that it is not sufficient that it should be lodged in the human body like a pilot in his ship, unless perhaps for the moving of its members, but that it is necessary that it should also be joined and united more closely to the body in order to have sensations and appetites similar to our own, and thus to form a true man. In conclusion, I have here enlarged a little on the subject of the soul, because it is one of the greatest importance. For next to the error of those who deny God, which I think I have already sufficiently refuted, there is none which is more effectual in leading feeble spirits from the straight path of virtue, than to imagine that the soul of the brute is of the same nature as our own, and that in consequence, after this life we have nothing to fear or to hope for, any more than the flies and ants. As a matter of fact, when one comes to know how greatly they differ, we understand much better the reasons which go to prove that our soul is in its nature entirely independent of body, and in consequence that it is not liable to die with it. And then, inasmuch as we observe no other causes capable of destroying it, we are naturally inclined to judge that it is immortal.

II

I cannot share the opinion of Montaigne and others who attribute understanding or thought to animals. I am not worried that people say that men have an absolute empire over all the other animals; because I agree that some of them are stronger than us, and believe that there may also be some who have an instinctive cunning capable of deceiving the shrewdest human beings. But I observe that they only imitate or surpass us in those of our actions which are not guided by our thoughts. It often happens that we walk or eat without thinking at all about what we are doing; and similarly, without using our reason, we reject things which are harmful for us, and parry the blows aimed at us. Indeed, even if we expressly willed not to put our hands in front of our head when we fall, we could not prevent ourselves. I think also that if we had no thought we would eat, as the animals do, without having to learn to; and it is said that those who walk in their sleep sometimes swim across streams in which they would drown if they were awake. As for the movements of our passions, even though in us they are accompanied with thought because we have the faculty of thinking, it is nonetheless very clear that they do not depend on thought, because they often occur in spite of us. Consequently they can also occur in animals, even more violently than they do in human beings, without our being able to conclude from that that they have thoughts.

In fact, none of our external actions can show anyone who examines them that our body is not just a self-moving machine but contains a soul with thoughts, with the exception of words, or other signs that are relevant to particular topics without expressing any passion. I say words or other signs, because deaf-mutes use signs as we use spoken words; and I say that these signs must be relevant, to exclude the speech of parrots, without excluding the speech of madmen, which is relevant to particular topics even though it does not follow reason. I add also that these words or signs must not express any passion, to rule out not only cries of joy or sadness and the like, but also whatever can be taught by training to animals. If you

emotions: fear, hope, joy

conditioning

teach a magpie to say good-day to its mistress, when it sees her approach, this can only be by making the utterance of this word the expression of one of its passions. For instance it will be an expression of the hope of eating, if it has always been given a titbit when it says it. Similarly, all the things which dogs, horses, and monkeys are taught to perform are only expressions of their fear, their hope, or their joy; and consequently they can be performed without any thought. Now it seems to me very striking that the use of words, so defined, is something peculiar to human beings. Montaigne and Charron may have said that there is more difference between one human being and another than between a human being and an animal; but there has never been known an animal so perfect as to use a sign to make other animals understand something which expressed no passion; and there is no human being so imperfect as not to do so, since even deaf-mutes invent special signs to express their thoughts. This seems to me a very strong argument to prove that the reason why animals do not speak as we do is not that they lack the organs but that they have no thoughts. It cannot be said that they speak to each other and that we cannot understand them; because since dogs and some other animals express their passions to us, they would express their thoughts also if they had any.

I know that animals do many things better than we do, but this does not surprise me. It can even be used to prove they act naturally and mechanically, like a clock which tells the time better than our judgement does. Doubtless when the swallows come in spring, they operate like clocks. The actions of honeybees are of the same nature, and the discipline of cranes in flight, and of apes in fighting, if it is true that they keep discipline. Their instinct to bury their dead is no stranger than that of dogs and cats who scratch the earth for the purpose of burying their excrement; they hardly ever actually bury it, which shows that they act only by instinct and without thinking. The most that one can say is that though the animals do not perform any action which shows us that they think, still, since the organs of their body are not very different from ours, it may be conjectured that there is attached to those organs some thoughts such as we experience in ourselves, but of a very much less perfect kind. To which I have nothing to reply except that if they thought as we do, they would have an immortal soul like us. This is unlikely, because there is no reason to believe it of some animals without believing it of all, and many of them such as oysters and sponges are too imperfect for this to be credible. But I am afraid of boring you with this discussion, and my only desire is to show you that I am, etc.

III

But there is no prejudice to which we are all more accustomed from our earliest years than the belief that dumb animals think. Our only reason for this belief is the fact that we see that many of the organs of animals are not very different from ours in shape and movement. Since we believe that there is a single principle within us which causes these motions—namely the soul, which both moves the body and thinks—we do not doubt that some such soul is to be found in animals also. I came to realize, however, that there are two different principles causing our motions: one is purely mechanical and corporeal and depends solely on the force of the spirits and the construction of our organs, and can be called the corporeal soul; the other is the incorporeal mind, the soul which I have defined as a thinking substance. Thereupon I investigated more carefully whether the motions of animals originated from both these principles or from one only. I soon saw clearly that they could all originate from the corporeal and mechanical principle, and I thenceforward regarded it as certain and established that we cannot at all prove the presence of a thinking soul in animals. I am not disturbed by the astuteness and cunning of dogs and foxes, or all the things which animals do for the sake of food, sex, and fear; I claim that I can easily explain the origin of all of them from the constitution of their organs.

But though I regard it as established that we cannot prove there is any thought in animals, I do not think it is thereby proved that there is not, since the human mind does not reach into their hearts. But when I investigate what is most probable in this matter, I see no argument for animals having thoughts except the fact that since they have eyes, ears, tongues, and other sense-organs like ours, it seems likely that they have sensation like us; and since thought is included in our mode of sensation, similar thought seems to be attributable to them. This argument, which is very obvious, has taken possession of the minds of all men from their earliest age. But there are other arguments, stronger and more numerous, but not so obvious to everyone, which strongly urge the opposite. One is that it is more probable that worms and flies and caterpillars move mechanically than that they all have immortal souls.

It is certain that in the bodies of animals, as in ours, there are bones, nerves, muscles, animal spirits, and other organs so disposed that they can by themselves, without any thought, give rise to all animals the motions we observe. This is very clear in convulsive movements when the machine of the body moves despite the soul, and sometimes more violently and in a more varied manner than when it is moved by the will.

Second, it seems reasonable, since art copies nature, and men can make various automata which move without thought, that nature should produce its own automata, much more splendid than artificial ones. These natural automata are the animals. This is especially likely since we have no reason to believe that thought always accompanies the disposition of organs which we find in animals. It is much more wonderful that a mind should be found in every human body than that one should be lacking in every animal.

But in my opinion the main reason which suggests that the beasts lack thought is the following. Within a single species some of them are more perfect than others, as men are too. This can be seen in horses and dogs, some of whom learn what they are taught much better than others. Yet, although all animals easily communicate to us, by voice or bodily movement, their natural impulses of anger, fear, hunger, and so on, it has never yet been observed that any brute animal reached the stage of using real speech, that is to say, of indicating by word or sign something pertaining to pure thought and not to natural impulse. Such speech is the only certain sign of thought hidden in a body. All men use it, however stupid and insane they may be, and though they may lack tongue and organs of voice; but no animals do. Consequently it can be taken as a real specific difference between men and dumb animals.

For brevity's sake I here omit the other reasons for denying thought to animals. Please note that I am speaking of thought, and not of life or sensation. I do not deny life to animals, since I regard it as consisting simply in the heat of the heart; and I do not deny sensation, in so far as it depends on a bodily organ. Thus my opinion is not so much cruel to animals as indulgent to men—at least to those who are not given to the superstitions of Pythagoras—since it absolves them from the suspicion of crime when they eat or kill animals.

Perhaps I have written at too great length for the sharpness of your intelligence; but I wished to show you that very few people have yet sent me objections which were as agreeable as yours. Your kindness and candour has made you a friend of that most respectful admirer of all who seek true wisdom, etc.

VOLTAIRE

A Reply to Descartes

Souls of animal

Descartes said:

What a pitiful, what a sorry thing to have said that animals are machines bereft of understanding and feeling, which perform their operations always in the same way, which learn nothing, perfect nothing, etc.!

What! that bird which makes its nest in a semi-circle when it is attaching it to a wall, which builds it in a quarter circle when it is in an angle, in a circle upon a tree; that bird acts always in the same way? That hunting-dog which you have disclined for three months, does it not know more at the end of this time than it knew before your lessons? Does the canary to which you teach a tune repeat it at once? do you not spend a considerable time in teaching it? have you not seen that it has made a mistake and that it corrects itself?

Is it because I speak to you, that you judge that I have feeling, memory, ideas? Well, I do not speak to you; you see me going home looking disconsolate, seeking a paper anxiously, opening the desk where I remember having shut it, finding it, reading it joyfully. You judge that I have experienced the feeling of distress and that of pleasure, that I have memory and understanding.

Voltaire (1694–1778), French philosopher and essayist, is the author of the *Philosophical Dictionary* and, among other moral tales, *Candide*.

From Voltaire, *Philosophical Dictionary,* "Animals."

Bring the same judgment to bear on this dog which has lost its master, which has sought him on every road with sorrowful cries, which enters the house agitated, uneasy, which goes down the stairs, up the stairs, from room to room, which at last finds in his study the master it loves, and which shows him its joy by its cries of delight, by its leaps, by its caresses.

Barbarians seize this dog, which in friendship surpasses man so prodigiously; they nail it on a table, and they dissect it alive in order to show the mesenteric veins. You discover in it all the same organs of feeling that are in yourself. Answer me, machinist, has nature arranged all the means of feeling in this animal, so that it may not feel? has it nerves in order to be impassible? Do not suppose this impertinent contradiction in nature.

But the schoolmasters ask what the soul of animals is? I do not understand this question. A tree has the faculty of receiving in its fibres its sap which circulates, of unfolding the buds of its leaves and its fruit; will you ask what the soul of this tree is? it has received these gifts; the animal has received those of feeling, of memory, of a certain number of ideas. Who has bestowed these gifts? who has given these faculties? He who has made the grass of the fields to grow, and who makes the earth gravitate towards the sun.

"Animals' souls are substantial forms," said Aristotle, and after Aristotle, the Arab school, and after the Arab school, the angelical school, and after the angelical school, the Sorbonne, and after the Sorbonne, nobody at all.

"Animals' souls are material," cry other philosophers. These have not been in any better fortune than the others. In vain have they been asked what a material soul is; they have to admit that it is matter which has sensation: but what has given it this sensation? It is a material soul, that is to say that it is matter which gives sensation to matter; they cannot issue from this circle.

Listen to other brutes reasoning about the brutes; their soul is a spiritual soul which dies with the body; but what proof have you of it? what idea have you of this spiritual soul, which, in truth, has feeling, memory, and its measure of ideas and ingenuity; but which will never be able to know what a child of six knows? On what ground do you imagine that this being, which is not body, dies with the body? The greatest fools are those who have advanced that this soul is neither body nor spirit. There is a fine system. By spirit we can understand only some unknown thing which is not body. Thus these gentlemen's system comes back to this, that the animals' soul is a substance which is neither body nor something which is not body.

Whence can come so many contradictory errors? From the habit men have always had of examining what a thing is, before knowing if it exists. The clapper, the valve of a bellows, is called in French the "soul" of a bellows. What is this soul? It is a name that I have given to this valve which falls, lets air enter, rises again, and thrusts it through a pipe, when I make the bellows move.

There is not there a distinct soul in the machine: but what makes animals' bellows move? I have already told you, what makes the stars move. The philosopher who said, *"Deus est anima brutorium,"* was right; but he should go further.

IMMANUEL KANT

Duties
in Regard to
Animals

Baumgarten speaks of duties towards beings which are beneath us and beings which are above us. But so far as animals are concerned, we have no direct duties. Animals are not self-conscious and are there merely as a means to an end. That end is man. We can ask, "Why do animals exist?" But to ask, "Why does man exist?" is a meaningless question. Our duties towards animals are merely indirect duties towards humanity. Animal nature has analogies to human nature, and by doing our duties to animals in respect of manifestations of human nature, we indirectly do our duty towards humanity. Thus, if a dog has served his master long and faithfully, his service, on the analogy of human service, deserves reward, and when the dog has grown too old to serve, his master ought to keep him until he dies. Such action helps to support us in our duties towards human beings, where they are bounden duties. If then any acts of animals are analogous to human acts and spring from the same principles, we have duties towards the animals because thus we cultivate the corresponding duties towards

Immanuel Kant (1724–1804) was a German philosopher of great brilliance and originality. His important works in ethics include *Groundwork for the Metaphysic of Morals* and *Lectures on Ethics*.

From Immanuel Kant, "Duties to Animals and Spirits," in *Lectures on Ethics*, trans. Louis Infield (New York: Harper and Row, 1963), pp. 239–41.

human beings. If a man shoots his dog because the animal is no longer capable of service, he does not fail in his duty to the dog, for the dog cannot judge, but his act is inhuman and damages in himself that humanity which it is his duty to show towards mankind. If he is not to stifle his human feelings, he must practice kindness towards animals, for he who is cruel to animals becomes hard also in his dealing with men. We can judge the heart of a man by his treatment of animals. Hogarth depicts this in his engravings. He shows how cruelty grows and develops. He shows the child's cruelty to animals, pinch the tail of a dog or a cat; he then depicts the grown man in his cart running over a child; and lastly, the culmination of cruelty in murder. He thus brings home to us in a terrible fashion the rewards of cruelty, and this should be an impressive lesson to children. The more we come in contact with animals and observe their behavior, the more we love them, for we see how great is their care for their young. It is then difficult for us to be cruel in thought even to a wolf. Leibnitz used a tiny worm for purposes of observation, and then carefully replaced it with its leaf on the tree so that it should not come to harm through any act of his. He would have been sorry—a natural feeling for a humane man—to destroy such a creature for no reason. Tender feelings towards dumb animals develop humane feelings towards mankind. In England butchers and doctors do not sit on a jury because they are accustomed to the sight of death and hardened. Vivisectionists, who use living animals for their experiments, certainly act cruelly, although their aim is praiseworthy, and they can justify their cruelty, since animals must be regarded as man's instruments; but any such cruelty for sport cannot be justified. A master who turns out his ass or his dog because the animal can no longer earn its keep manifests a small mind. The Greeks' ideas in this respect were highminded, as can be seen from the fable of the ass and the bell of ingratitude. Our duties towards animals, then, are indirect duties towards mankind.

JEREMY BENTHAM

A Utilitarian View

IV. What other agents then are there, which, at the same time that they are under the influence of man's direction, are susceptible of happiness? They are of two sorts: (1) Other human beings who are styled persons. (2) Other animals, which, on account of their interests having been neglected by the insensibility of the ancient jurists, stand degraded into the class of *things*.

Under the Hindu and Mahometan religions, the interests of the rest of the animal creation seem to have met with some attention. Why have they not, universally, with as much as those of human creatures, allowance made for the difference in point of sensibility? Because the laws that are have been the work of mutual fear; a sentiment which the less rational animals have not had the same means as man has of turning to account. Why *ought* they not? No reason can be given. If the being eaten were all, there is very good reason why we should be suffered to eat such of them as we like to eat: we are the better for it, and they are never the worse. They have none of those long-protracted anticipations of future misery which we have. The death they suffer in our hands commonly is, and always may be,

Jeremy Bentham (1748–1832) was an English philosopher and one of the most famous advocates of the moral theory called *utilitarianism*.

From Jeremy Bentham, *The Principles of Morals and Legislation* (1789), Chapter XVII, Section 1.

a speedier, and by that means a less painful one, than that which would await them in the inevitable course of nature. If the being killed were all, there is very good reason why we should be suffered to kill such as molest us: we should be the worse for their living, and they are never the worse for being dead. But is there any reason why we should be suffered to torment them? Not any that I can see. Are there any why we should *not* be suffered to torment them? Yes, several. The day has been, I grieve to say in many places it is not yet past, in which the greater part of the species, under the denomination of slaves, have been treated by the law exactly upon the same footing as, in England for example, the inferior races of animals are still. The day *may come,* when the rest of the animal creation may acquire those rights which never could have been withholden from them but by the hand of tyranny. The French have already discovered that the blackness of the skin is no reason why a human being should be abandoned without redress to the caprice of a tormentor. It may come one day to be recognized, that the number of the legs, the villosity of the skin, or the termination of the *os sacrum,* are reasons equally insufficient for abandoning a sensitive being to the same fate. What else is it that should trace the insuperable line? Is it the faculty of reason, or, perhaps, the faculty of discourse? But a full-grown horse or dog is beyond comparison a more rational, as well as a more conversable animal, than an infant of a day, or a week, or even a month, old. But suppose the case were otherwise, what would it avail? the question is not, Can they *reason?* nor, Can they *talk?* but, Can they *suffer?*

CHARLES DARWIN

Comparison of the Mental Powers of Man and the Lower Animals

We have seen in the last two chapters that man bears in his bodily structure clear traces of his descent from some lower form; but it may be urged that, as man differs so greatly in his mental power from all other animals, there must be some error in this conclusion. . . .

My object in this chapter is to show that there is no fundamental difference between man and the higher mammals in their mental faculties. Each division of the subject might have been extended into a separate essay, but must here be treated briefly. As no classification of the mental powers has been universally accepted, I shall arrange my remarks in the order most convenient for my purpose; and will select those facts which have struck me most, with the hope that they may produce some effect on the reader. . . .

The lower animals, like man, manifestly feel pleasure and pain, happiness and misery. Happiness is never better exhibited than by young animals, such as puppies, kittens, lambs, etc., when playing together, like our own children. Even insects play together, as has been described by that

Charles Darwin (1809–1882) was an English biologist whose theory of evolution has had a profound impact on ideas in science, theology, and philosophy.

From Charles Darwin, *The Descent of Man*, Chapters III and IV.

excellent observer, P. Huber, who saw ants chasing and pretending to bite each other, like so many puppies.

The fact that the lower animals are excited by the same emotions as ourselves is so well established, that it will not be necessary to weary the reader by many details. Terror acts in the same manner on them as on us, causing the muscles to tremble, the heart to palpitate, the sphincters to be relaxed, and the hair to stand on end. Suspicion, the offspring of fear, is eminently characteristic of most wild animals. It is, I think, impossible to read the account given by Sir E. Tennent, of the behaviour of the female elephants, used as decoys, without admitting that they intentionally practice deceit, and well know what they are about. Courage and timidity are extremely variable qualities in the individuals of the same species, as is plainly seen in our dogs. Some dogs and horses are ill-tempered, and easily turn sulky; others are good-tempered; and these qualities are certainly inherited. Every one knows how liable animals are to furious rage, and how plainly they show it. Many, and probably true, anecdotes have been published on the long-delayed and artful revenge of various animals. The accurate Rengger and Brehm state the American and African monkeys which they kept tame, certainly revenged themselves. Sir Andrew Smith, a zoologist whose scrupulous accuracy was known to many persons, told me the following story of which he was himself an eye-witness; at the Cape of Good Hope an officer had often plagued a certain baboon, and the animal, seeing him approaching one Sunday for parade, poured water into a hole and hastily made some thick mud, which he skillfully dashed over the officer as he passed by, to the amusement of many bystanders. For long afterwards the baboon rejoiced and triumphed whenever he saw his victim.

The love of a dog for his master is notorious; as an old writer quaintly says, "A dog is the only thing on this earth that luvs you more than he luvs himself."

In the agony of death a dog has been known to caress his master, and every one has heard of the dog suffering under vivisection, who licked the hand of the operator; this man, unless the operation was fully justified by an increase of our knowledge, or unless he had a heart of stone, must have felt remorse to the last hour of his life.

As Whewell has well asked, "who that reads the touching instances of maternal affection, related so often of the women of all nations, and of the females of all animals, can doubt that the principle of action is the same in the two cases?" We see maternal affection exhibited in the most trifling details; thus Rengger observed an American monkey (a Cebus) carefully driving away the flies which plagued her infant; and Duvaucel saw a Hylobates washing the faces of her young ones in a stream. So intense is the grief of female monkeys for the loss of their young, that it invariably caused the death of certain kinds kept under confinement by Brehm in N. Africa. . . .

Most of the more complex emotions are common to the higher animals and ourselves. Everyone has seen how jealous a dog is of his master's affection, if lavished on any other creature; and I have observed the same fact with monkeys. This shows that animals not only love, but have desire to be loved. Animals manifestly feel emulation. They love approbation or praise; and a dog carrying a basket for his master exhibits in a high degree self-complacency or pride. There can, I think, be no doubt that a dog feels shame, as distinct from fear, and something very like modesty when begging too often for food. A great dog scorns the snarling of a little dog, and this may be called magnanimity. Several observers have stated that monkeys certainly dislike being laughed at; and they sometimes invent imaginary offences. In the Zoological Gardens I saw a baboon who always got into a furious rage when his keeper took out a letter or book and read it aloud to him; and his rage was so violent that, as I witnessed on one occasion, he bit his own leg until the blood flowed. Dogs show what may be fairly called a sense of humour, as distinct from mere play; if a bit of stick or other such object be thrown to one, he will often carry it away for a short distance; and then squatting down with it on the ground close before him, will wait until his master comes quite close to take it away. The dog will then seize it and rush away in triumph, repeating the same maneuvre, and evidently enjoying the practical joke.

We will now turn to the more intellectual emotions and faculties, which are very important, as forming the basis for the development of the higher mental powers. Animals manifestly enjoy excitement, and suffer from ennui, as may be seen with dogs, and, according to Rengger, with monkeys. All animals feel *Wonder,* and many exhibit *Curiosity.* They sometimes suffer from this latter quality, as when the hunter plays antics and thus attracts them; I have witnessed this with deer, and so it is with the wary chamois, and with some kinds of wild-ducks. . . .

Hardly any faculty is more important for the intellectual progress of man than *Attention.* Animals clearly manifest this power, as when a cat watches a hole and prepares to spring on its prey. Wild animals sometimes become so absorbed when thus engaged that they may be easily approached. Mr. Bartlett has given me a curious proof how variable this faculty is in monkeys. A man who trains monkeys to act in plays used to purchase common kinds from the Zoological Society at the price of five pounds for each; but he offered to give double the price if he might keep three or four of them for a few days in order to select one. When asked how he could possibly learn so soon whether a particular monkey would turn out a good actor, he answered that it all depended on their power of attention. If when he was talking and explaining anything to a monkey its attention was easily distracted, as by a fly on the wall or other trifling object, the case was hopeless. If he tried by punishment to make an inattentive monkey act it turned sulky. On the other hand, a monkey which carefully attended to him could always be trained.

It is almost superfluous to state that animals have excellent *memories* for persons and places. A baboon at the Cape of Good Hope, as I have been informed by Sir Andrew Smith, recognized him with joy after an absence of nine months. I had a dog who was savage and averse to all strangers, and I purposely tried his memory after an absense of five years and two days. I went near the stable where he lived and shouted to him in my old manner; he showed no joy, but instantly followed me out walking, and obeyed me exactly as if I had parted with him only half an hour before. A train of old associations, dormant during five years, had thus been instantaneously awakened in his mind. Even ants, as P. Huber has clearly shown, recognized their fellow-ants belonging to the same community after a separation of four months. Animals can certainly by some means judge of the intervals of time between recurrent events.

The *Imagination* is one of the highest prerogatives of man. By this faculty he unites former images and ideas, independently of the will, and thus creates brilliant and novel results. A poet, as Jean Paul Richter remarks, "who must reflect whether he shall make a character say yes or no—to the devil with him; he is only a stupid corpse." Dreaming gives us the best notion of this power; as Jean Paul again says, "The dream is an involuntary art of poetry." The value of the products of our imagination depends of course on the number, accuracy, and clearness of our impressions, on our judgment and taste in selecting or rejecting the involuntary combinations, and to a certain extent on our power of voluntarily combining them. As dogs, cats, horses, and probably all the higher animals, even birds have vivid dreams, and this is shown by their movements and the sounds uttered, we must admit that they possess some power of imagination. There must be something special which causes dogs to howl in the night, and especially during moonlight, in that remarkable and melancholy manner called baying. All dogs do not do so; and, according to Houzeau, they do not then look at the moon, but at some fixed point near the horizon. Houzeau thinks that their imaginations are disturbed by the vague outlines of the surrounding objects, and conjure up before them fantastic images; if this be so, their feelings may almost be called superstitions.

Of all the faculties of the human mind, it will, I presume, be admitted that *Reason* stands at the summit. Only a few persons now dispute that animals possess some power of reasoning. Animals may constantly be seen to pause, deliberate, and resolve. It is a significant fact, that the more the habits of any particular animal are studied by a naturalist, the more he attributes to reason and the less to unlearnt instincts. In future chapters we shall see that some animals extremely low in the scale apparently display a certain amount of reason. . . .

We can only judge by the circumstances under which actions are performed, whether they are due to instinct, or to reason, or to the mere association of ideas: this latter principle, however, is intimately connected with reason. A curious case has been given by Prof. Möbius, of a pike, separated by a plate of glass from an adjoining aquarium stocked with fish, and who often dashed himself with such violence against the glass in trying to catch the other fishes, that he was sometimes completely stunned. The pike went on thus for three months, but at last learnt caution, and ceased to do so. The plate of glass was then removed, but the pike would not attack these particular fishes, though he would devour others which were afterwards introduced; so strongly was the idea of a violent shock associated in his feeble mind with the attempt on his former neighbours. If a savage, who had never seen a large plate-glass window, were to dash himself even once against it, he would for a long time afterwards associate a shock with a windowframe; but very differently from the pike, he would probably reflect on the nature of the impediment, and be cautious under analogous circumstances. Now with monkeys, as we shall presently see, a painful or merely a disagreeable impression, from an action once performed, is sometimes sufficient to prevent the animal from repeating it. If we attribute this difference between the monkey and the pike solely to the association of ideas being so much stronger and more persistent in the one than the other, though the pike often received much the more severe injury, can we maintain in the case of man that a similar difference implies the possession of a fundamentally different mind?

ALBERT SCHWEITZER

The Ethic
of Reverence
for Life

Descartes tells us that philosophizing is based on the judgment: "I think, therefore I am." From this meagre and arbitrarily selected beginning it is inevitable that it should wander into the path of the abstract. It does not find the entrance to the ethical realm, and remains held fast in a dead view of the world and of life. True philosophy must commence with the most immediate and comprehensive facts of consciousness. And this may be formulated as follows: "I am life which wills to live, and I exist in the midst of life which wills to live." This is no mere excogitated subtlety. Day after day and hour after hour I proceed on my way invested in it. In every moment of reflection it forces itself on me anew. A living world- and life-view, informing all the facts of life, gushes forth from it continually, as from an eternal spring. A mystically ethical oneness with existence grows forth from it unceasingly.

Just as in my own will-to-live there is a yearning for more life, and for that mysterious exaltation of the will-to-live which is called pleasure, and

Albert Schweitzer (1875–1965), renowned missionary and winner of the Nobel Peace Prize of 1952, was active in philosophy, theology, and music.

From Albert Schweitzer, *Civilization and Ethics* (Part II of *The Philosophy of Civilization*), trans. John Naish. Reprinted by permission of A. & C. Black Ltd. and Macmillan Publishing Co., Inc.

terror in face of annihilation and that injury to the will-to-live which is called pain; so the same obtains in all the will-to-live around me, equally whether it can express itself to my comprehension or whether it remains unvoiced.

Ethics thus consists in this, that I experience the necessity of practising the same reverence for life toward all will-to-live, as toward my own. Therein I have already the needed fundamental principle of morality. It is *good* to maintain and cherish life; it is *evil* to destroy and to check life.

As a matter of fact, everything which in the usual ethical valuation of inter-human relations is looked upon as good can be traced back to the material and spiritual maintenance or enhancement of human life and to the effort to raise it to its highest level of value. And contrariwise everything in human relations which is considered as evil, is in the final analysis found to be material or spiritual destruction or checking of human life and slackening of the effort to raise it to its highest value. Individual concepts of good and evil which are widely divergent and apparently unconnected fit into one another like pieces which belong together, the moment they are comprehended and their essential nature is grasped in this general notion.

The fundamental principle of morality which we seek as a necessity for thought is not, however, a matter only of arranging and deepening current views of good and evil, but also of expanding and extending these. A man is really ethical only when he obeys the constraint laid on him to help all life which he is able to succour, and when he goes out of his way to avoid injuring anything living. He does not ask how far this or that life deserves sympathy as valuable in itself, nor how far it is capable of feeling. To him life as such is sacred. He shatters no ice crystal that sparkles in the sun, tears no leaf from its tree, breaks off no flower, and is careful not to crush any insect as he walks. If he works by lamplight on a summer evening, he prefers to keep the window shut and to breathe stifling air, rather than to see insect after insect fall on his table with singed and sinking wings.

If he goes out into the street after a rainstorm and sees a worm which has strayed there, he reflects that it will certainly dry up in the sunshine, if it does not quickly regain the damp soil into which it can creep, and so he helps it back from the deadly paving stones into the lush grass. Should he pass by an insect which has fallen into a pool, he spares the time to reach it a leaf or stalk on which it may clamber and save itself.

He is not afraid of being laughed at as sentimental. It is indeed the fate of every truth to be an object of ridicule when it is first acclaimed. It was once considered foolish to suppose that coloured men were really human beings and ought to be treated as such. What was once foolishness has now become a recognized truth. Today it is considered as exaggeration to proclaim constant respect for every form of life as being the serious demand of a rational ethic. But the time is coming when people will be amazed that the human race was so long before it recognized thoughtless injury to life as incompatible with real ethics. Ethics is in its unqualified form extended responsibility with regard to everything that has life.

The general idea of ethics as a partaking of the mental atmosphere of reverence for life is not perhaps attractive. But it is the only complete notion possible. Mere sympathy is too narrow a concept to serve as the intellectual expression of the ethical element. It denotes, indeed, only a sharing of the suffering of the will-to-live. But to be ethical is to share the whole experience of all the circumstances and aspirations of the will-to-live, to live with it in its pleasures, in its yearnings, in its struggles toward perfection.

Love is a more inclusive term, since it signifies fellowship in suffering, in joy, and in effort. But it describes the ethical element only as it were by a simile, however natural and profound that simile may be. It places the solidarity created by ethics in analogy to that which nature has caused to come into being in a more or less superficial physical manner, and with a view to the fulfillment of their destiny, between two sexually attracted existences, or between these and their offspring.

Thought must strive to find a formula for the essential nature of the ethical. In so doing it is led to characterize ethics as self-devotion for the sake of life, motivated by reverence for life. Although the phrase "reverence for life" may perhaps sound a trifle unreal, yet that which it denotes is something which never lets go its hold of the man in whose thought it has once found a place. Sympathy, love, and, in general, all enthusiastic feeling of real value are summed up in it. It works with restless vitality on the mental nature in which it has found a footing and flings this into the restless activity of a responsibility which never ceases and stops nowhere. Reverence for life drives a man on as the whirling thrashing screw forces a ship through the water.

The ethic of reverence for life, arising as it does out of an inward necessity, is not dependent on the question as to how far or how little it is capable of development into a satisfactory view of life. It does not need to prove that the action of ethical men, as directed to maintaining, enhancing and exalting life, has any significance for the total course of the world-process. Nor is it disturbed by the consideration that the preservation and enhancement of life which it practises are of almost no account at all beside the mighty destruction of life which takes place every moment as the result of natural forces. Determined as it is to act, it is yet able to ignore all the problems raised as to the result of its action. The fact that in the man who has become ethical a will informed by reverence for life and self-sacrifice for the sake of life exists in the world, is itself significant for the world.

The universal will-to-live experiences itself in my personal will-to-live otherwise than it does in other phenomena. For here it enters on an individualization, which, so far as I am able to gather in trying to view it from the outside, struggles only to live itself out, and not at all to become one with will-to-live external to itself. The world is indeed the grisly drama of will-to-live at variance with itself. One existence survives at the expense of another of which it yet knows nothing. But in me the will-to-live has become cognizant of the existence of other will-to-live. There is in it a yearning for unity with itself, a longing to become universal.

Why is it that the will-to-live has this experience only in myself? Is it a result of my having become capable of reflection about the totality of existence? Whither will the evolution lead which has thus begun in me?

There is no answer to these questions. It remains a painful enigma how I am to live by the rule of reverence for life in a world ruled by creative will which is at the same time destructive will, and by destructive will which is also creative.

I can do no other than hold on to the fact that the will-to-live appears in me as will-to-live which aims at becoming one with other will-to-live. This fact is the light which shines for me in the darkness. My ignorance regarding the real nature of the objective world no longer troubles me. I am set free from the world. I have been cast by my reverence for life into a state of unrest foreign to the world. By this, too, I am placed in a state of beatitude which the world cannot give. If in the happiness induced by our independence of the world I and another afford each other mutual help in understanding and in forgiveness, when otherwise will would harass other will, then the will-to-live is no longer at variance with itself. If I rescue an insect from a pool of water, then life has given itself for life, and again the self-contradiction of the will-to-live has been removed. Whenever my life has given itself out in any way for other life, my eternal will-to-live experiences union with the eternal, since all life is one. I possess a cordial which secures me from dying of thirst in the desert of life.

Therefore I recognize it as the destiny of my existence to be obedient to the higher revelation of the will-to-live which I find in myself. I choose as my activity the removal of the self-contradiction of the will-to-live, as far as the influence of my own existence extends. Knowing as I do the one thing needful, I am content to offer no opinion about the enigma of the objective world and my own being.

Thought becomes religious when it thinks itself out to the end. The ethic of reverence for life is the ethic of Jesus brought to philosophical expression, extended into cosmical form, and conceived as intellectually necessary.

The surmising and longing of all deeply religious personalities is comprehended and contained in the ethic of reverence for life. This, however, does not build up a world-view as a completed system, but resigns itself to leave the cathedral perforce incomplete. It is only able to finish the choir. Yet in this true piety celebrates a living and continuous divine service. . . .

What does reverence for life teach us about the relations of man and the nonhuman animals?

Whenever I injure life of any kind I must be quite clear as to whether this is necessary or not. I ought never to pass the limits of the unavoidable, even in apparently insignificant cases. The countryman who has mowed down a thousand blossoms in his meadow as fodder for his cows should take care that on the way home he does not, in wanton pastime, switch off the head of a single flower growing on the edge of the road, for in so doing he injures life without being forced to do so by necessity.

Those who test operations or drugs on animals, or who inoculate them with diseases so that they may be able to help human beings by means of the results thus obtained, ought never to rest satisfied with the general idea that their dreadful doings are performed in pursuit of a worthy aim. It is their duty to ponder in every separate case whether it is really and truly necessary thus to sacrifice an animal for humanity. They ought to be filled with anxious care to alleviate as much as possible the pain which they cause. How many outrages are committed in this way in scientific institutions where narcotics are often omitted to save time and trouble! How many also when animals are made to suffer agonizing tortures, only in order to demonstrate to students scientific truths which are perfectly well known. The very fact that the animal, as a victim of research, has in his pain rendered such services to suffering men, has itself created a new and unique relation of solidarity between him and ourselves. The result is that a fresh obligation is laid on each of us to do as much good as we possibly can to all creatures in all sorts of circumstances. When I help an insect out of his troubles all that I do is to attempt to remove some of the guilt contracted through these crimes against animals.

Wherever any animal is forced into the service of man, the sufferings which it has to bear on that account are the concern of every one of us. No one ought to permit, in so far as he can prevent it, pain or suffering for which he will not take the responsibility. No one ought to rest at ease in the thought that in so doing he would mix himself up in affairs which are not his business. Let no one shirk the burden of his responsibility. When there is so much maltreatment of animals, when the cries of thirsting creatures go up unnoticed from the railway trucks, when there is so much roughness in our slaughter-houses, when in our kitchens so many animals suffer horrible deaths from unskillful hands, when animals endure unheard-of agonies from heartless men, or are delivered to the dreadful play of children, then we are all guilty and must bear the blame.

We are afraid of shocking or offending by showing too plainly how deeply we are moved by the sufferings which man causes to the nonhuman creatures. We tend to reflect that others are more "rational" than we are, and would consider that which so disturbs us as customary and as a matter of course. And then, suddenly, they let fall some expression which shows us that they, too, are not really satisfied with the situation. Strangers to us hitherto, they are now quite near our own position. The masks, in which we had each concealed ourselves from the other, fall off. We now know that neither of us can cut ourselves free from the horrible necessity which plays ceaselessly around us. What a wonderful thing it is thus to get to know each other!

The ethic of reverence for life forbids any of us to deduce from the silence of our contemporaries that they, or in their case we, have ceased to feel what as thinking men we all cannot but feel. It prompts us to keep a mutual watch in this atmosphere of suffering and endurance, and to speak and act without panic according to the responsibility which we feel. It inspires us to join in a search for opportunities to afford help of some kind or other to the animals, to make up for the great amount of misery which they endure at our hands, and thus to escape for a moment from the inconceivable horrors of existence.

PART TWO
The Nature of Humans and Other Animals

R. G. FREY

Why Animals Lack Beliefs and Desires

Do animals . . . have interests in the . . . sense of having wants which can be satisfied or left unsatisfied? In this sense, of course, it appears that tractors do not have interests; for though being well-oiled may be conducive to tractors being good of their kind, tractors do not *have an interest* in being well-oiled, since they cannot *want* to be well-oiled, cannot, in fact, have any wants whatever. But farmers can have wants, and they certainly have an interest in their tractors being well-oiled.

What, then, about animals? Can they have wants? By "wants," I understand a term that encompasses both needs and desires, and it is these that I shall consider.

If to ask whether animals can have wants is to ask whether they can have needs, then certainly animals have wants. A dog can need water. But *this* cannot be the sense of "want" on which having interests will depend, since it does not exclude things from the class of want-holders. Just as dogs need water in order to function normally, so tractors need oil in order to function normally; and just as dogs will die unless their need for water is

R. G. Frey teaches philosophy at Bowling Green State University. His books include *Interests and Rights: The Case against Animals* (Oxford, 1980).

R. G. Frey, "Rights, Interests, Desires, and Beliefs." *American Philosophical Quarterly*, Vol. 16, July 1979, pp. 233–39.

satisfied, so trees and grass and a wide variety of plants and shrubs will die unless their need for water is satisfied. Though we should not give the fact undue weight, someone who in ordinary discourse says "The tractor wants oiling" certainly means the tractor needs oiling, if it is not to fall away from those standards which make tractors good of their kind. Dogs, too, need water, if they are not to fall away from the standards which make them good of their kind. It is perhaps worth emphasizing, moreover, as the cases of the tractor, trees, grass, etc., show, that needs do not require the presence either of consciousness or of knowledge of the lack which makes up the need. If, in sum, we are to agree that tractors, trees, grass, etc., do not have wants, and, therefore, interests, it cannot be the case that wants are to be construed as needs.

This, then, leaves desires, and the question of whether animals can have wants as desires. I may as well say at once that I do not think animals can have desires. My reasons for thinking this turn largely upon my doubts that animals can have beliefs, and my doubts in this regard turn partially, though in large part, upon the view that having beliefs is not compatible with the absence of language and linguistic ability. I realize that the claim that animals cannot have desires is a controversial one; but I think the case to be made in support of it, complex though it is, is persuasive. . . .

Suppose I am a collector of rare books and desire to own a Gutenberg Bible: my desire to own this volume is *to be traced* to my belief that I do not now own such a work and that my rare book collection is deficient in this regard. By "to be traced" here, what I mean is this: if someone were to ask *how* my belief that my book collection lacks a Gutenberg Bible is connected with my desire to own such a Bible, what better or more direct repy could be given than that, without this belief, I would not have this desire? For if I believed that my rare book collection *did* contain a Gutenberg Bible and so was complete in this sense, then I would not desire a Gutenberg Bible in order to make up what I now believe to be a notable deficiency in my collection. (Of course, I might desire to own more than one such Bible, but this contingency is not what is at issure here.)

Now what is it that I believe? I believe that my collection lacks a Gutenberg Bible; that is, I believe that the sentence "My collection lacks a Gutenberg Bible" is true. In constructions of the form "I believe that . . . ," what follows upon the "that" is a declarative sentence; and *what* I believe is that that sentence is true. The same is the case with constructions of the form "He believes that . . .": what follows upon the "that" is a declarative sentence, and what the "he" in question believes is that that sentence is true. The difficulty in the case of animals should be apparent: if someone were to say, e.g., "The cat believes that the door is locked," then that person is holding, as I see it, that the cat holds the declarative sentence "The door is locked" to be true; and I can see no reason whatever for crediting the cat or any other creature which lacks language, including human infants, with entertaining declarative sentences and holding certain declarative sentences to be true.

Importantly, nothing whatever in this account is affected by changing the example, in order to rid it of sophisticated concepts like "door" and "locked," which in any event may be thought beyond cats, and to put in their place more rudimentary concepts. For the essence of this account is not about the relative sophistication of this or that concept but rather about the relationship between believing something and entertaining and regarding as true certain declarative sentences. If what is believed is that a certain declarative sentence is true, then no creature which lacks language can have beliefs; and without beliefs, a creature cannot have desires. And this is the case with animals, or so I suggest; and if I am right, not even in the sense, then, of wants as desires do animals have interests . . .

But is what is believed that a certain declarative sentence is true? I think there are three arguments of sorts that shore up the claim that this *is* what is believed.

First, I do not see how a creature could have the concept of belief without being able to distinguish between true and false beliefs. When I believe that my collection of rare books lacks a Gutenberg Bible, I believe that it is true that my collection lacks a Gutenberg Bible; put another way, I believe that it is false that my collection contains a Gutenberg Bible. I can distinguish, and do distinguish, between the sentences "My collection lacks a Gutenberg Bible" and "My collection contains a Gutenberg Bible," and it is only the former I hold to be true. According to my view, what I believe in this case is that this sentence is true; and sentences are the sorts of things we regard as or hold to be true. As for the cat, and leaving aside now all questions about the relative sophistication of concepts, I do not see how it could have the belief that the door is locked unless it could distinguish this true belief from the false belief that the door is unlocked. But what is true or false are not states of affairs which correspond to or reflect or pertain to these beliefs; states of affairs are not true or false but either are or are not the case, either do or do not obtain. If, then, one is going to credit cats with beliefs, and cats must be able to distinguish true from false beliefs, and states of affairs are not true or false, then what exactly is it that cats are being credited with distinguishing as true or false? Reflection on this question, I think, forces one to credit cats with language, in order for there to be something that can be true or false in belief; and it is precisely because they lack language that we cannot make this move.

Second, if in order to have the concept of belief a creature must be possessed of the difference between true and false belief, then in order for a creature to be able to distinguish true from false beliefs that creature must—simply must, as I see it—have some awareness of, to put the matter in the most general terms, how language connects with, links up with the world; and I see no reason to credit cats with such an awareness. My belief that my collection lacks a Gutenberg Bible is true if and only if my collection lacks a Gutenberg Bible; that is, the *truth* of this belief cannot be entertained by me without it being the case that I am aware that the truth of the sentence "My collection lacks a Gutenberg Bible" is *at the very least* partially a function of how the world is. However difficult to capture, it is this relationship between language and the world a grasp of which is necessary if a creature is to grasp the difference between true and false belief, a distinction which it must grasp, if it is to possess the concept of belief at all.

Third, I do not see how a creature could have an awareness or grasp of how language connects with, links up with the world, to leave the matter at its most general, unless that creature was itself possessed of language; and cats are not possessed of language. If it were to be suggested, for example, that the sounds that cats make do amount to a language, I should deny it. This matter is far too large and complex to be tackled here; but the general line of argument I should use to support my denial can be sketched in a very few words. Can cats lie? If they cannot, then they cannot assert anything; and if they lack assertion, I do not see how they could possess a language. And I should be strict: I do not suggest that, lacking assertion, cats possess a language in some attenuated or secondary sense; rather, I suggest that. lacking assertion, they do not possess a language *at all*.

BERNARD ROLLIN

Thought without Language

THE CLAIM THAT ANIMALS LACK CONCEPTS

It was sometimes said by scientists and philosophers that animal pain, while perhaps present momentarily, was insignificant. The reasoning behind this claim was as follows: Since animals lack concepts enabling them to anticipate and remember, the kind of suffering engendered in us by worrying about and anticipating going to the dentist, which makes the pain of dental work so much worse, simply does not arise in animals.

It is worth pausing to examine this contention, which, in its own way, has done much to shore up the common sense of science's view of animals. Historically, it is rooted in Descartes's claim that only language, a 'universal instrument' as he called it, can evidence mind and go beyond immediate particularity. The equation of thought with the ability to universalize and generalize and go beyond the particulars given in sensation was made explicit by Kant, who made thought propositional and rooted thinking in the organization of sensory data by concepts.[1] This tradition has assumed that since animals lack language, they must lack concepts, and are therefore trapped forever in the momentary. Only a linguistic being has concepts, and only concepts enable a being to universalize,

Bernard Rollin teaches philosophy at Colorado State University. Among his books is *Animal Rights and Human Morality* (Prometheus Books, 1981).

Rollin, B. (1989), *The Unheeded Cry*. Reprinted by permission of Oxford University Press.

generalize, refer to what is absent, counter-factual, non-existent, past, future, and so forth. Since animals lack language, they must lack concepts; and since they lack concepts, they can live at best only in a world of isolated, fragmented, momentary particulars: William James's 'buzzing blooming confusion'. This claim is pithily captured in a poem by the twentieth-century poet Edwin Muir:

The Animals

They do not live in the world,
Are not in time and space.
From birth to death hurled
No word do they have, not one
To plant a foot upon,
Were never in any place.

For with names the world was called
Out of the empty air,
With names was built and walled,
Line and circle and square,

Dust and emerald;
Snatched from deceiving death
By the articulate breath.

But these have never trod
Twice the familiar track,
Never never turned back
Into the memoried day.
All is new and near
In the unchanging Here
Of the fifth great day of God,
That shall remain the same,
Never shall pass away.

On the sixth day we came.[2]

I would venture to guess that if there is anything like a philosophical orthodoxy in the twentieth century, that is it. Philosophers like Davidson, Bennett, Frey, and innumerable others have constantly rebottled the same wine.[3] Extraordinarily, even Wittgenstein[4], the most anti-Cartesian of all philosophers, shares the Cartesian bias against animal mentation by virtue of the absence of language in animals. His works are peppered with cryptic, sceptical remarks about predicating mentalistic attributes to animals. In one famous passage, he tells us that if a lion could speak, we couldn't understand him; in another he suggests that it is conceptually impossible for an animal to smile. He also suggests that a dog cannot simulate pain or feel remorse, that an animal cannot hope or consciously imitate, and that a dog cannot mean something by wagging its tail and a crocodile cannot think.

Wittgenstein's reasoning is somewhat different from Descartes' of course. For Descartes, language expresses thought and codifies it, but an individual human being in a solipsistic universe logically *could* have thought even in the absence of a public language. This is true for Kant as well; an individual human has an a priori conceptual apparatus that is logically independent of public language. Furthermore, as the *Critique of Pure Reason* implies, this apparatus is and must be the same for all beings who synthesize sensations to create experience and knowledge, and thus Kant never feels the need to address the problem of other minds.[5] For Wittgenstein, on the other hand, thought is constituted by the social system of conventional signs one is brought up in; without such a system there is neither thought nor concepts; there can be no 'private language', for there are no publicly checkable criteria and rules for correct and incorrect application of concepts in a private language, and if there is no way to be incorrect, there is also no way to be correct. Since animals lack a system of conventional signs, they lack the fundamental tools for a mental life. Second, language is a 'form of life', which both expresses and shapes the nature of one's *Umwelt*. The comment about the lion suggests that since animals have such a radically different form of life, we could not become privy to it even if they did have a rule-governed language.

All these arguments contain a great deal of implausibility, and the fact that they have endured virtually unchallenged attests to the power of ideology in philosophy, as in science. I say *virtually* unchallenged because . . . associationists like Hume, at once both the great challenger of common sense and its strongest supporter in practical matters, considered it patently obvious that animals think and feel more or less as we do. This sort of appeal to common sense was echoed by the Scottish common-sense philosophers.

Any argument which equates thought and language and which denies any sort of significant thought in the absence of language, be the argument Cartesian or Wittgensteinean, must be hard pressed to explain how humans ever acquire language in the first place.[6] The acquisition of language entails that experiences and thoughts be processed at some stage without language. Even if one believes, with Chomsky, that the essential skeleton of language is innate, so that linguistic competence is native rather than acquired, it must still be triggered and fleshed out by non-linguistic experiences, which determine the particular version of universal language that the child learns. Further, as Thomas Reid pointed out, understanding of reference and meaning requires some non-linguistic comprehension of the linkage between sign and what is signified (such as ostension) prior to the acquisition of language; otherwise the entire process would never get off the ground.[7] In short, language requires a peg of non-linguistic experience on which to be hung.

Given the logic of the Kantian position equating having a mind with having concepts to organize the particulars given in sensory experience, denying this ability to animals on the grounds that they do not have language to betoken the concepts is self-defeating. For any careful reader of Kant will recall that he is not ever doing psychology. In ethics or epistemology, he believes himself to be doing conceptual analysis. In his ethics, he tells us that nothing he has to say depends upon or uniquely pertains to human nature, for ethics must be true of 'any rational being in general'.[8] Similarly, in his epistemology, Kant clearly asserts that everything he is saying about knowledge and experience is true for any being possessed of an 'ectypal intellect',—that is, an intellect which depends on material received from outside itself for its experience. No one, including Kant, can deny that animals with sense-organs perceive objects; after all, dogs regularly pursue rabbits, fetch bones, avoid cars, and jump on little boys. But if he admits this, he is undone. For the arguments which Kant marshals against an atomistic, associationistic epistemology of the Humean sort regarding human experience would apply equally well against any empiricistic account of animal perception. If animals have perceptions of objects and causal relations, they must be doing something other than merely sensing. For as Kant himself points out, the senses supply only momentary, ever changing fragments. To experience, to perceive, one must tie these particulars together—'synthesize' them, in Kant's terminology. But this in turn means that there must be some internal mechanism for synthesis. The essence of Kant's argument against the atomistic empiricism of Hume was the insight that we cannot possibly be passive dartboards upon which atoms of unrelated sensation fall. While it is surely true, says Kant, that our experience is *composed* of sensory atoms, the end product is not fragmented, but is, rather, the experience of objects which endure and interact, notably causally. Clearly the sensory atoms end up being organized into wholes, showing that the experience is active rather than passive. The principles of synthesis are, for Kant, concepts—a priori concepts by which our sensory atoms are moulded into objects, standing in relationships with one another.

But by parity of reasoning, animals must be in precisely the same situation! As mentioned earlier, they obviously experience objects and causal interaction. By the same token, their access to the world is via sense-organs which are extremely similar to ours, and which, in and of themselves, can provide only fragmented atoms of experience. Therefore, as Kantians, we must conclude that they, too, possess a priori concepts fairly similar to our own. And since they learn from experience, even, as Hume points out, from single experiences—for example, to avoid hot objects after being hurt—they must surely possess a mechanism for generating empirical concepts. After all, an organism with no power of generalization and abstraction, which could experience only particulars, could neither learn nor survive.

As Hume said, all this is no surprise to common sense, which knows quite well that animals possess at least some concepts—dogs, for example, clearly have concepts of food, water, danger, play, stranger, dog (or scent of other dog), and so forth. As to how these concepts, or abilities to pick out common features of the world, are symbolized, that is an open question; but it is plausible to suggest that animals have some mental tokens or images which serve in this capacity.

One can take Kant's logic a bit further. According to Kant, having innate concepts allows one to have a 'transcendental unity of apperception'—that is, a unity of self-awareness. What this means is that in order for a being to have unified experience of objects in relations, it must be the same consciousness which experiences the beginning of an event as the end, or the top of an object and its bottom. In other words, if it were not the same you that viewed the top of a tall building as the bottom and the middle, there could be no experience of 'the tall building'. But this same point must hold true for animals too; they must be able to realize that an event is happening to them in order to learn from it. We are surely licensed, I believe, to assert that animals have a sense of self as distinguished from the world; what we do not know is what form it takes. Once again, common sense assumes that animals know the difference between what happens to them and what doesn't. The efforts of animals to protect themselves certainly supports our claim, and if one is willing to admit that animals feel pain, it follows that pain would not be of much use were it not referred to a self. In a now classic piece of research done earlier this century, the philosopher physiologist Buytendijk showed persuasively that an octopus could distinguish between actively touching something and being passively touched and concluded from this that even octopuses have a mental image, betokening a concept, of self and other.[9] (Incidentally, further research indicates that octopuses and squid can solve problems, learn, and be anaesthetized!)

THE WITTGENSTEIN VERSION

But what of Wittgenstein's point that mental images cannot serve as markers for concepts, since there is no public check for correctness of application? Let us recall that to have a concept, so the argument goes, there must be rules for the use of the concept which can be checked publicly. That means that there must be ways in which one can conceivably *misapply* the concept and be detected and corrected. This is possible only when the vehicles of the concept are public and accessible to others, who can see how one is using a concept and who can correct deviations from proper use. Thus, consider a child learning the concept 'dog'. He may try to group a cow with dogs. But when he calls the cow a 'dog', someone corrects him. In the absence of a public way of expressing a concept and of being corrected, however, what is to stop a person from using it differently each time? What criteria does one have for deciding whether a concept does or doesn't apply to some new case? Such a state, says Wittgenstein, is comparable to a game in which one makes up the rules as one goes along. Without some fixed, externally verifiable rules, the activity is not really a game at all.

This is a strong argument. But does it really count against animals having concepts? Let us see. A person has words for his concepts. These words can be checked against what other people say. This is supposed to be different from the case of animals, who presumably only have some ideas in their heads, or perhaps certain perceptions to use as marks of their concepts. For example, an animal may have only some memory of the appearance of water or the visual appearance of the water itself—for example, its shimmering—to serve as a mark of his concept.[10]

Is there ultimately a difference between the two situations? On the surface, yes. But in a deeper sense, perhaps no. According to the private-language argument the animal must rely on memory and thus has no way of being shown to be wrong. But suppose, as we all know happens, a puppy sees me rattling a martini-shaker and approaches me, thinking that it is about to be fed. I say, 'No, that's not for you,' and don't give it any food. Its initial concept of 'dish rattling—food time' is thereby corrected. I see no relevant difference between this case and the case of the child who calls a cow a 'dog'. Nor does this process of public correction require a human being. Let us return to the shimmering perception which serves as the visual sign of water. An animal may see shimmering on asphalt and believe it to mean water (even as we do), but he is 'publicly' corrected when he reaches the road and finds no water there. In other words, the fact that the animal is an active *agent* can serve as a basis for correction.

If the private-language theorist is persistent, he may say 'But how does the animal know the next time that he is using the sign or idea in anything like the way he did before? The animal has only memory; we at least have other people.' The answer is simple. If we can be sceptical about memory, we can also be sceptical about other people's memory, and ask how we ever really know that they are using a word or concept the way they did before? So public checks don't really help in the face of extreme scepticism.

This discussion has, of course, presupposed that memory without language is possible, and that animals can remember without language. Aside from the fact that behavioural evidence supports this claim, it is obvious that we humans must be able to remember without language; otherwise, as we said, we could never learn language in the first place.

There is an even deeper philosophical response to the private-language argument. The possibility of publicly checking linguistic concepts itself depends on leaving certain linguistic concepts unchecked. For example, let us return to the case of the child who calls a cow a 'dog' and is corrected by a parent who says, 'No, cow.' The presupposition here is that the child's concept of 'No' is correct. How do we check that publicly without presupposing some other concept that we cannot check without presupposing some other concept, and on and on, *ad infinitum*? We do not, of course, worry about this; we take subsequent correct behaviour as evidence that the child has the concept straight. But if that is so, why do we not take an animal's correct behaviour in context as evidence that it, too, has concepts? Its concepts are, as Berkeley said, learned from the language of nature and are certainly not as complex or abstract or variable or (sometimes as) precise as ours, but they still seem to be concepts—that is, some sort of intellectual capability that allows a creature to recognize repeatable features of the world and to synthesize experiences.

It is hugely ironic that Wittgenstein, the philosopher who stressed the sagacity of common sense and ordinary language and wished to protect both from taint by philosophical mischief-makers, should have had such a blind spot *vis-à-vis* animal thought. For if, as he said, 'ordinary language is all right as it is', he should surely have acknowledged that for ordinary language, as for common sense, animals unquestionably do have full mental lives. As we said earlier, ordinary people simply could not discuss animals without using terms like 'bored', 'is hungry', 'wants to play', 'doesn't like the mailman', 'is depressed since the kids left home', and so on. In the same vein, classic research by D. O. Hebb showed that zoo attendants simply could not do their job if they were barred from using mentalistic locutions about animals.[11]

Wittgenstein's second point, that since language separates humans from animals, and since language is a 'form of life' which both shapes and is shaped by one's *Umwelt*, we could not understand a lion if it spoke, seems implausible. I venture to suggest that our forms of life are not all that dissimilar: both the lion and I have interests in eating, sleeping, sex, avoiding encroachments on our environments, and so forth, about which we could doubtless make small talk. He might lose me if he went off on how one anticipates a gazelle's next turn, and I might lose him if I raised questions about animal rights (specifically gazelle's rights), but that sort of thing often happens when I'm talking to fundamentalist ministers or accountants, whose forms of life and language games are also incomprehensible to me. Lloyd Morgan once asserted that about the only human beings he could be sure of understanding were other upper-class educated Englishmen, and that he despaired of comprehending the minds of primitive men.[12] I doubt that most of us could understand the mind of an SS man, even if he spoke English; a lion would be *much* easier.

As to Wittgenstein's claims that an animal can't hope or simulate pain, these are truly perplexing. What else can one say of a dog when it sits at attention while you are eating but that it is hoping you will give it a scrap? As to simulating pain, any pet-owner and any veterinarian can relate cases in which animals simulated pain in order to get attention, avoid punishment, and so on, especially if they have been fussed over in the past when they had an injury.

But let us return to our main discussion of pain. We were examining the claim that since animals lack concepts which would allow them to anticipate and remember, and since a good part of pain is anticipating and remembering, animal pain is momentary and insignificant. We have just seen that there is little reason to deny concepts to animals; that standard philosophical gymnastics, however tortured, simply cannot touch the plain, commonsensical fact, embodied in all cultures of all ages, that animals do anticipate and remember, and that that is how they learn and fear. And if this entails having concepts, as surely it does, then animals have concepts, which should come as no surprise if they are to deal with the world. They certainly behave *as if* they had concepts, and the best explanation for this behaviour is that they do have them, especially since the aforementioned arguments totally fail to show that this is impossible. In general, the most powerful reason for believing in animal mental states is that they constitute the best way of explaining what animals do, how they behave, and how they survive, both philosophically *and* scientifically. The fact that we cannot experience these states directly is of little consequence, of as little consequence as the fact that we cannot directly experience the particles of microphysics or the past is to the explanatory value of postulating particles and a past.

NOTES

1. I. Kant, *Critique of Pure Reason.*
2. E. Muir, *Collected Poems 1921–1958* (London: Faber and Faber, 1963).
3. D. Davidson, "Thought and talk," in S. Guttenplan (ed.), *Mind and Language* (Oxford: Oxford University Press, 1974); J. Bennett, *Rationality* (London: Routledge and Kegan Paul, 1964); R. G. Frey, *Interests and Rights: The Case Against Animals* (Oxford: Oxford University Press, 1980).
4. L. Wittgenstein, *Philosophical Investigations* (Oxford: Blackwell, 1958), pp. 90, 153, 166, 174, 224; *Zettel* (Berkeley: University of California Press, 1970), pp. 70, 91.
5. See B. Rollin, "There is only one categorical imperative," *Kant-Studien*, 67, No. 1 (1976).
6. B. Rollin, *Natural and Conventional Meaning: An Examination of the Distinction* (The Hague: Mouton, 1976).
7. T. Reid, *Inquiry into the Human Mind on the Principles of Common Sense*, Chapter 5. Many editions.
8. I. Kant, *Foundations of the Metaphysics of Morals*, 1785; trans. by L. W. Beck. (Indianapolis: Bobbs-Merrill, 1959), pp. 5–6.
9. F. J. J. Buytendijk, "Toucher et être touche." *Arch. Neerl. Zool.*, 10, suppl. 2 (1953).
10. See H. H. Price, *Thinking and Experience* (Cambridge, Mass.; Harvard University Press, 1953).
11. D. O. Hebb, "Emotion in man and animal," *Psychology Review*, 53 (1946).
12. C. L. Morgan, *An Introduction to Comparative Psychology* (London: Walter Scott, 1894), pp. 41–42.

DONALD R. GRIFFIN

Ethology and Animal Minds

WHAT BEHAVIOR SUGGESTS CONSCIOUS THINKING?

Just what is it about some kinds of behavior that leads us to feel that it is accompanied by conscious thinking? Comparative psychologists and biologists worried about this question extensively around the turn of this century. No clear and generally accepted answers emerged from their thoughtful efforts, and this is one reason why the behavioristic movement came to dominate psychology.

Complexity is often taken as evidence that some behavior is guided by conscious thinking. But complexity is a slippery attribute. One might think that simply running away from a frightening stimulus was a rather simple response, yet if we make a detailed description of every muscle contraction during turning and running away, the behavior becomes extremely complex. But, one might object, this complexity involves the physiology of locomotion; what is simple is the direction in which the animal moves. If we then ask what sensory and central nervous mechanisms cause the animal to move in this direction, the matter again becomes complex. Does the animal continuously listen to the danger signal and push more or less hard with its

Donald R. Griffin is an animal behaviorist at Rockefeller University. His many writings include *The Question of Animal Awareness: Evolutionary Continuity of Mental Experience* (The Rockefeller University Press, 1976).

Reprinted by permission.

right or left legs in order to keep the signal directly behind it? Or does it head directly toward some landmark? If the latter, how does it coordinate vision and locomotion? Again one might say that the direction of motion is simple, and it is irrelevant to worry about the complexities of the physiological mechanisms involved.

But how is this simple direction "away from the danger" represented within the animal's central nervous system? Does the animal employ the concepts of *away from* and *danger*? If so, how are such concepts established? Even though we cannot answer the question in neurophysiological terms, it is clear that running away from something is a far simpler behavior than, say, the construction of a bird's nest. Conversely, even the locomotor motions of a caterpillar that will move toward a light with a machine-like consistency hour after hour are not simple when examined in detail. What is simple is the abstract notion of *toward* or *away*, but the mechanistic interpretation of animal behavior tends to deny that the animal could think in terms of even such a simple abstraction.

One very important attribute of animal behavior that seems intuitively to suggest conscious thinking is its adaptability to changing circumstances. If an animal repeats some action in the same way regardless of the results, we assume that a rigid physiological mechanism is at work, especially if the behavior is ineffective or harmful to the animal. When a moth flies again and again at a bright light or burns itself in an open flame, it is difficult to imagine that the moth is thinking, although one can suppose that it is acting on some thoughtful but misguided scheme. When members of our own species do things that are self-damaging or even suicidal, we do not conclude that their behavior is the result of a mechanical reflex. But to explain the moth flying into the flame as thoughtful but misguided seems far less plausible than the usual interpretation that such insects automatically fly toward a bright light, which leads them to their death in the special situation where the brightest light is an open flame.

Conversely, if an animal manages to obtain food by a complex series of actions that it has never performed before, intentional thinking seems more plausible than rigid automatism. For example, Japanese macaques learned a new way to separate grain from inedible material by throwing the mixture into the water; the kernels of grain would float while the inorganic sand and other particles tended to sink.[1] These new types of food handling were first devised by a few monkeys, then were gradually acquired by other members of their social group through observational learning. . . .

CONNECTED PATTERNS OF BEHAVIOR

Another criterion upon which we tend to rely in inferring conscious thinking is the element of interactive steps in a relatively long sequence of appropriate behavior patterns. Effective and versatile behavior often entails many steps, each one modified according to the results of the previous actions. In such a complex sequence the animal must pay attention not only to the immediate stimuli, but also to information obtained in the past. Psychologists once postulated that complex behavior can be understood as a chain of rigid reflexes, the outcome of one serving as stimulus for the next. Students of insect behavior have generally accepted this explanation for such complex activities as the construction of elaborate shelters or prey-catching devices, ranging from the underwater nets spun by certain caddis-fly larvae to the magnificent webs of spiders. But the steps an animal takes often vary, depending on the results of the previous behavior and on many influences from the near or distant past. The choice of *which* past events to attend to may be facilitated by conscious selection from a broad spectrum of memories.

An outstanding example of such sequences of interactive behaviors is the use of probes by chimpanzees to gather termites from their mounds.[2] The chimpanzee prepares a probe by selecting a suitable branch, pulling off its leaves and side branches, breaking the stick to the right length, carrying it—often for several minutes—to a termite mound, and then probing into the openings used by the termites. If the hole yields nothing, the chimpanzee moves to another one. Even after the tool has been prepared, its use is far from stereotyped. When curious scientists try to imitate the chimpanzees' techniques, they find it rather difficult and seldom gather as many termites. It is especially interesting that the young chimpanzees seem to learn this use of tools by watching their mothers or other members of their social group. Youngsters have been observed making crude and relatively ineffective attempts to prepare and use their own termite probes; the termite "fishing" of chimpanzees gives every evidence of being learned. . . .

ADAPTATIONS TO NOVELTY

One further consideration can help refine the criteria for determining the presence of conscious thought. We can easily change back and forth between thinking consciously about our own behavior and not doing so. When we are learning some new task such as swimming, riding a bicycle, driving an automobile, flying an airplane, operating a vacuum cleaner, caring for our teeth by some new technique recommended by a dentist, or any of the large number of actions we did not formerly know how to do, we think about it in considerable detail. But once the behavior is thoroughly mastered, we give no conscious thought to the details that once required close attention.

This change can also be reversed, as when we make the effort to think consciously about some commonplace and customary activity we have been carrying out for some time. For example, suppose you are asked about the pattern of your breathing, to which you normally give no thought whatsoever. But you can easily take the trouble to keep track of how often you inhale and exhale, how deeply, and what other activities accompany different patterns of breathing. You can find out that it is extremely difficult to speak while inhaling, so talking continuously requires rapid inhalation and slower exhalation. This and other examples that will readily come to mind if one asks the appropriate questions show that we can bring into conscious focus activities that usually go on quite unconsciously.

The fact that our own consciousness can be turned on and off with respect to particular activities tells us that in at least one species it is not true that certain behavior patterns are always carried out consciously while others never are. It is reasonable to guess that this is true also for other species. Well-learned behavior patterns may not require the same degree of conscious attention as those the animal is learning how to perform. This in turn means that conscious awareness is more likely when the activity is novel and challenging; striking and unexpected events are more likely to produce conscious awareness.

Thus it seems likely that a widely applicable, if not all-inclusive, criterion of conscious awareness in animals is *versatile adaptability of behavior to changing circumstances and challenges*. If the animal does much the same things regardless of the state of its environment or the behavior of other animals nearby, we are less inclined to judge that it is thinking about its circumstances or what it is doing. Consciously motivated behavior is more plausibly inferred when an animal behaves appropriately in a novel and perhaps surprising situation that requires specifications not called for under ordinary circumstances. This is a special case of versatility, of course, but the rarity of the challenge combined with the appropriateness and effectiveness of the response are important indicators of thoughtful actions.

For example, Janes observed nesting ravens make an enterprising use of rocks.[3] He had been closely observing ten raven nests in Oregon, eight of which were near the top of rocky cliffs. At one of these nests two ravens flew in and out of a vertical crack that extended from top to bottom of a twenty-meter cliff. Janes and a companion climbed up the crevice and inspected the six nearly fledged nestlings. As they started down, both parents flew at them repeatedly, calling loudly, then landed at the top of the cliff, still calling. One of the ravens then picked up small rocks in its bill and dropped them at the human intruders. Several of the rocks showed markings where they had been partly buried in the soil, so the birds presumably had pried them loose. Only seven rocks were dropped, but the raven seemed to be seeking other loose ones and apparently stopped only because no more suitable rocks were available.

While many birds make vigorous efforts to defend their nests and young from intruders, often flying at people who come too close, regurgitating or defecating on them, and occasionally striking them with their bills, rock throwing is most unusual. Nor do ravens pry out rocks and drop them in other situations. It is difficult to avoid the inference that this quite intelligent and adaptable bird was anxious to chase the human intruders away from its nest and decided that dropping rocks might be effective.

There are limits to the amount of novelty with which a species can cope successfully, and this range of versatility is one of the most significant measures of mental adaptability. This discussion of adaptable versatility as a criterion of consciousness implies that conscious thinking occurs only during learned behavior, but we should be cautious in accepting this belief as a rigid doctrine.

Another aspect of conscious thinking is anticipation and intentional planning of an action with conscious awareness of its likely results. An impressive example is the use of small stones by sea otters to detach and open shellfish.[4] These intelligent aquatic carnivores feed mostly on sea urchins and mollusks. The sea otter must dive to the bottom and pry the mollusk loose with claws or teeth, but some shells, especially abalones, are tightly attached to the rocks and have shells that are too tough to be loosened in this fashion. The otter will search for a suitable stone, which it carries while diving, then uses the stone to hammer the shellfish loose, holding its breath all the while.

The otter usually eats while floating on its back. If it cannot get at the fleshy animal inside the shell, it will hold the stone on its chest with one paw while pounding a shell against it. The otter often tucks a good stone under an armpit as it swims or dives. Although otters do not alter the shapes of the stones, they do select ones of suitable size and weight and often keep them for considerable periods. The otters use tools only in areas where sufficient food cannot be obtained by other methods. In some areas only the young and very old sea otters use stones; vigorous adults can dislodge the shellfish with their unaided claws or teeth. Thus it is far from a simple stereotyped behavior pattern, but one that is used only when it is helpful. Sea otters sometimes use floating beer bottles to hammer open shells. Since the bottles float, they need not be stored under the otter's armpit. . . .

ANIMAL COMMUNICATION

The very fact that intention movements so often evolve into communicative signals may reflect a close linkage between thinking and the intentional communication of thoughts from one conscious animal to another. These considerations lead us directly to a recognition that because communicative behavior, especially among social animals, often seems to convey thoughts and feelings from one animal to another, it can tell us something about animal thinking: it can be an important "window" on the minds of animals. . . .

Vervet monkeys, for example, have at least three different categories of alarm calls, which were described by Struhsaker after extensive periods of observation.[5] He found that when a leopard or other large carnivorous mammal approached, the monkeys gave one type of alarm call; quite a different call was used at the sight of a martial eagle, one of the few flying predators that captures vervet monkeys. A third type of alarm call was given when a large snake approached the group. This degree of differentiation of alarm calls is not unique, although it has been described in only a few kinds of animals. For example, ground squirrels of western North America use different types of calls when frightened by a ground predator or by a predatory bird such as a hawk.[6]

The question is whether the vervet monkey's three types of alarm calls convey to other monkeys information about the type of predator. Such information is important because the animal's defensive tactics are different in the three cases. When a leopard or other large carnivore approaches, the monkeys climb into trees. But leopards are good climbers, so the monkeys can escape them only by climbing out onto the smallest branches, which are too weak to support a leopard. When the monkeys see a martial eagle, they move into thick vegetation close to a tree trunk or at ground level. Thus the tactics that help them escape from a leopard make them highly vulnerable to a martial eagle, and vice versa. In repsonse to the threat of a large snake they stand on their hind legs and look around to locate the snake, then simply move away from it, either along the ground or by climbing into a tree.

To answer this question, Seyfarth, Cheney, and Marler conducted some carefully controlled playback experiments under natural conditions in East Africa.[7] From a concealed loudspeaker, they played tape recordings of vervet alarm calls and found that the playbacks of the three calls did indeed elicit the appropriate responses. The monkeys responded to the leopard alarm call by climbing into the nearest tree; the martial eagle alarm caused them to dive into thick vegetation; and the python alarm produced the typical behavior of standing on the hind legs and looking all around for the nonexistent snake.

Inclusive behaviorists—that is, psychologists interested only in contingencies of reinforcement during an individual's lifetime, and ethologists or behavioral ecologists solely concerned with the effects of natural selection on behavior—insist on limiting themselves to stating that an animal benefits from accurate information about what the other animal will probably do. But within a mutually interdependent social group, an individual can often anticipate a companion's behavior most easily by emphatic appreciation of his mental state. The inclusive behaviorists will object that all we need postulate is behavior appropriately matched to the probabilities of the companions *behaving* in this way or that—all based on contingencies of reinforcement learned from previous situations or transmitted generically.

But empathy may well be a more efficient way to gauge a companion's disposition than elaborate formulas describing the contingencies of reinforcement. All the animal may need to know is that another is aggressive, affectionate, desirous of companionship, or in some other common emotional state. Judging that he is aggressive may suffice to predict, economically and parsimoniously, a wide range of behavior patterns depending on the circumstances. Neo-Skinnerian inclusive behaviorists may be correct in saying that this empathy came about by learning, for example, the signals that mean a companion is aggressive. But our focus is on the animal's possible thoughts and feelings, and for this purpose the immediate situation is just as important as the history of its origin. . . .

THE ADAPTIVE ECONOMY OF CONSCIOUS THINKING

The natural world often presents animals with complex challenges best met by behavior that can be rapidly adapted to changing circumstances. Environmental conditions vary so much that for an animal's brain to have programmed specifications for optimal behavior in all situations would require an impossibly lengthy instruction book. Whether such instructions stem from the animal's DNA or from learning and environmental influences within its own lifetime, providing for all likely contingencies would require a wasteful volume of specific directions. Concepts and generalizations, on the other hand, are compact and efficient. An instructive analogy is provided by the hundreds of pages of official rules for a familiar game such as baseball. Once the general principles of the game are understood, however, quite simple thinking suffices to tell even a small boy approximately what each player should do in most game situations.

Of course, simply thinking about various alternative actions is not enough; successful coping with the challenges of life requires that thinking be relatively rapid and that it lead both to reasonably accurate decisions and to their effective execution. Thinking may be economical without being easy or simple, but consideration of the likely results of doing this or that is far more efficient than blindly trying every alternative. If an animal thinks about what it might do, even in very simple terms, it can choose the actions that promise to have desirable consequences. If it can anticipate probable events, even if only a little way into the future, it can avoid wasted effort. More important still is being able to avoid dangerous mistakes. To paraphrase Popper, [8]a foolish impulse can die in the animal's mind rather than lead it to needless suicide.

I have suggested that conscious thinking is economical, but many contemporary scientists counter that the problems mentioned above can be solved equally well by unconscious information-processing. It is quite true that skilled motor behavior often involves complex, rapid, and efficient reactions. Walking over rough ground or through thick vegetation entails numerous adjustments of the balanced contraction and relaxation of several sets of opposed muscles. Our brains and spinal cords modulate the action of our muscles according to whether the ground is high or low or whether the vegetation resists bending as we clamber over it. Little, if any, of this process involves conscious thought, and yet it is far more complex than a direct reaction to any single stimulus.

We perform innumerable complex actions rapidly, skillfully, and efficiently without conscious thought. From this evidence many have argued that an animal does not need to think consciously to weigh the costs and benefits of various activities. Yet when we acquire a new skill, we have to pay careful conscious attention to details not yet mastered. Insofar as this analogy to our own situation is valid, it seems plausible that when an animal faces new and difficult challenges, and when the stakes are high—often literally a matter of life and death—conscious evaluation may have real advantages.

Inclusive behaviorists often find it more plausible to suppose that an animal's behavior is more efficient if it is automatic and uncomplicated by conscious thinking. It has been argued that the vacillation and uncertainty involved in conscious comparison of alternatives would slow an animal's reactions in a maladaptive fashion. But when the spectrum of possible challenges is broad, with a large number of environmental or social factors to be considered, conscious mental imagery, explicit anticipation of likely outcomes, and simple thoughts about them are likely to achieve better results than thoughtless reaction. Of course, this is one of the many areas where we have no certain guides on which to rely. And yet, as a working hypothesis, it is attractive to suppose that if an animal can consciously anticipate and choose the most promising of various alternatives, it is likely to succeed more often than an animal that cannot or does not think about what it is doing.

REFERENCES

Baker, L. R. 1981. Why computers can't act. *Am. Philos. Q.* 18:157–63.

Boden, M. A., ed. 1977. *Artificial Intelligence and Natural Man.* Basic Books.

Daanje, A. 1951. On the locomotory movements in birds and the intention movements derived from them. *Behaviour* 3:48–98.

NOTES

1. See M. Kawai, "Newly acquired pre-cultural behavior of the natural troop of Japanese monkeys on Koshima Islet." *Primates* 6 (1975), pp. 1–30.

2. See J. van Lawick Goodall, "Behavior of free-living chimpanzees of the Gombe Stream area." *Animal Behavior Monograph* 1 (1968), pp. 165–311; and *In the Shadow of Man* (New York: Houghton Mifflin, 1971).

3. S. W. Janes, "The apparent use of rocks by a raven in nest defense." *Condor* 78 (1976), p. 409.

4. See K. W. Kenyon, *The Sea Otter in the Eastern Pacific Ocean.* North American Fauna, no. 68, 1969. U.S. Bureau of Sport Fisheries and Wildlife.

5. T. T. Struhsaker, *The Red Columbus Monkey* (Chicago: University of Chicago Press, 1967).

6. See D. H. Owings and D. W. Leger, "Chatter vocalizations of California ground squirrels: Predator—and social—role specificity." *Z. Tierpsychol.* 54 (1980), pp. 163–84.

7. R. M. Seyfarth, D. L. Cheney, and P. Marler, "Monkey responses to three different alarm calls: Evidence for predator classification and semantic communication." *Science,* 210 (1980), pp. 801–803; and "Vervet monkey alarm calls: Semantic communication in a free-ranging primate." *Animal Behavior,* 28 (1980), pp. 1070–94.

8. K. R. Popper, *Objective Knowledge* (Oxford: Oxford University Press, 1972).

BERNARD ROLLIN

Animal Pain

PAIN AND THE INTELLECTUAL LIMITATIONS OF ANIMALS

In terms of countering the pernicious moral power of the claim that animals can't anticipate and remember pain and that therefore their pain is insignificant, the most relevant point has little to do with the presence or absence of concepts. It comes rather from the following insight: that If animals are indeed, as the above argument suggests, inexorably locked into what is happening in the here and now, we are all the more obliged to try to relieve their suffering, since they themselves cannot look forward to or anticipate its cessation, or even remember, however dimly, its absence. If they are in pain, their whole universe is pain; there is no horizon; they *are* their pain. So, if this argument is indeed correct, then animal pain is terrible to contemplate, for the dark universe of animals logically cannot tolerate any glimmer of hope within its borders.

In less dramatic and more philosophical terms, Spinoza pointed out that understanding the cause of an unpleasant sensation diminishes its severity, and that, by the same token, not understanding its cause can increase its severity.[1] Common sense readily supports this conjecture—indeed this is something we have all experienced with lumps, bumps, headaches, and, most famously, suspected heart attacks which turn out to be gas pains.

Rollin, B. (1989), *The Unheeded Cry*. Reprinted by permission of Oxford University Press.

Spinoza's conjecture is thus borne out by common experience and by more formal research. But this would be reason to believe that animals, especially laboratory animals, suffer *more* severely than humans, since they have no grasp of the cause of their pain, and thus, even if they *can* anticipate, have no ability to anticipate the cessation of pain experiences outside their normal experience. At least one major pain physiologist, Professor Kitchell supports this conjecture. According to Kitchell, following a suggestion of Melzack, response to pain is divided into a sensory-discriminative dimension and a motivational-affective dimension. The former is concerned with locating and understanding the source of pain, its intensity, and the danger with which it is correlated; the latter with escaping from the painful stimulus. Kitchell speculates that since animals are more limited than humans in the first dimension, since they lack human intellectual abilities, it is plausible to think that the second dimension is correlatively stronger, as a compensatory mechanism. In short, since animals cannot deal intellectually with danger and injury as we do, their motivation to flee must be correlatively stronger than ours—in a word, they probably hurt more.[2]

At the risk of provoking an avalanche of indignation at my 'anthropomorphism', I would like to suggest the following thought experiment. Consider an animal, say a dog, which has spent its life as a pet, experiencing nothing worse than an occasional reprimand or slap on the rump. Let us suppose that the animal is turned in to the pound and ends up as a research subject in a learned helplessness experiment (as permitted in the United States, though not in Britain), wherein he is subjected to *inescapable,* painful electrical shock to see if he develops the helplessness syndrome which is alleged to model human depression. If one is at all willing to admit any consciousness in animals, one must surely affirm that this animal feels pain and fear. Furthermore, and disanalogously to the case of a human being, the animal has no notion whatever of why and how the pain comes. Any human put into such a situation would at least be able to formulate hypotheses—for example, 'I am being tortured for political reasons,' or 'I am being used for research.' But the animal cannot even begin to plug his pain into any of his categories of understanding. His cognitive tools simply don't fit. As a result, there is no possibility of cognitive moderation of the pain and fear. Whereas a person can say, 'Perhaps I can reason with my captors,' or 'Perhaps this is of short duration,' the animal cannot begin to get a purchase on any aspect of the experience. So the pain which is experienced must surely be deepened and rendered more extreme by its total incomprehensibility. As we all know, the unknown is by its very nature terrifying. And given an animal's intellectual limitations, most of what is suffered at our hands in research contexts must be totally incomprehensible. This insight is probably the basis for people's objections to the use of what were formerly pet animals as research animals.

ANTHROPOMORPHISM AND ANIMAL PAIN

In any case, let us turn our attention to what I consider to be the most ironic and perverse argument of all in attempts to justify lack of concern with animal pain in the common sense of science. It is often claimed that worry about animal pain is misplaced anthropomorphism, for in circumstances in which humans would be screaming and writhing, many animals show very few signs of extreme pain. Aside from the point made earlier that stoic behaviour doubtless confers a selective advantage on animals, we can make a more subtle point. It is not the people who impute pain to animals who are anthropomorphic; they have good evolutionary, physiological, and behavioural reasons to do so. It is, rather, those who *deny* pain to animals on the grounds that their behaviour is unlike ours who are anthropomorphic; for who else besides someone guilty of the grossest anthropomorphism would expect expressions of animal feelings to be precisely like ours, would expect a cow in pain, for example, to run about beating its breast and bellowing 'Oy Vay'? (Gentiles don't even do this.) Animals do show unique pain behaviour. It just doesn't happen to be human pain behaviour. But then why should it be? We would expect its behaviour to be appropriate to its *telos*—the unique, evolutionarily determined, genetically encoded, environmentally shaped set of needs and interests which characterize the animal in question—the 'pigness' of the pig, the 'dogness' of the dog, and so on.[3] People who deal with horses a great deal—and who follow the dictates of experience and common sense—are aware that in some cases mere tightening of the palpebral (eyelid) muscles eloquently bespeaks great agony, but obviously not to the person who is expecting the full range of human pain behaviour from the horse.

In one extraordinary case, a veterinary student working with the department of wildlife in a western state was shocked to learn that some members of the department were routinely doing Caesarean sections on moose which had been rendered immobile by injection of succinylcholine chloride, a curare-like drug which paralyzes all muscles by blocking neurotransmission across the neuro-muscular junction, but has no anaesthetic or analgesic properties. On the contrary, reports from humans on whom it has been used indicate that it heightens pain response, given the extraordinary panic which accompanies total paralysis (including respiratory paralysis), even when one understands *exactly* what is happening and why. In the case of an animal, one can only begin to imagine the utter black terror experienced. In any event, the student's objections fell upon deaf jug ears perched on thick red necks. 'Those animals ain't hurtin',' he was told. 'If they was, they'd be hollerin' '—no mean feat when totally paralyzed.

This is an extreme case, but not all that extreme. Succinylcholine has been routinely used for castration of horses in the American West, and until recently, was the drug of choice for 'chemical restraint' in procedures like stereotaxic (cranial) experimental surgery, which require that the animal be conscious—whatever that means to a behaviourist—yet immobile. Many researchers and veterinarians do not distinguish between anaesthesia and chemical restraint. Amazingly enough, the USDA has used succinyl-choline to 'euthanize' thousands of pigs afflicted with cholera, and has then frantically back-pedalled and funded research to prove that this was really 'humane'. . . .

THE SCIENTIFIC INCOHERENCE OF DENYING
PAIN IN ANIMALS

Let us refocus our discussion. Our concern has been with demonstrating that there is no good reason, philosophical or scientific, to deny pain in animals. The indubitable fact of such denial has to do with the powerful ideology we have been discussing, which saturates scientists with a questionable philosophy while disavowing that it is doing any such thing, and makes a value out of denying a legitimate place in science for value questions. Thus scientists can officially repudiate the legitimacy of talking about animal pain, at the same time as they presuppose it in their research.

We have seen that this ideology is powerful enough to eclipse the value of consistency in science, and to submerge coherence as well. For, as Darwinians recognized, it is arbitrary and incoherent, given the theories and information current in science, to rule out mentation for animals, particularly such a basic, well-observed mental state as pain.

We have already mentioned the tendency of scientists to acknowledge pain in animals only in terms of the machinery, or plumbing, of pain. One can well believe that only by thinking of animal pain in terms of Cartesian, mechanical processes devoid of an experiential, morally relevant dimension, could scientists have done the experimental work which has created the sophisticated neurophysiology we have today. But given that science, the neurophysiological analogies that have been discovered between humans and animals, certainly at least through the vertebrates, are powerful arguments against the Cartesianism which made it possible. In a dialectical irony which would surely have pleased Hegel, Cartesianism has been its own undoing, by demonstrating more and more identical neurophysiological mechanisms in humans and animals, mechanisms which make it highly implausible that animals are merely machines if we are not.[4]

Pain and pleasure centres, like those found in humans, have been reported in the brains of birds, mammals, and fish; and the neural mechanisms responsible for pain behaviour are remarkably similar in all vertebrates. Anaesthetics and analgesics control what appears to be pain in all vertebrates and some invertebrates; and, perhaps most dramatically, the biological feedback mechanisms for controlling pain seem to be remarkably similar in all vertebrates, involving serotonin, endorphins and enkephalins, and substance P. (Endorphins have been found even in earthworms.) The very existence of endogenous opiates in animals is powerful evidence that they feel pain. Animals would hardly have neurochemicals and pain-inhibiting systems identical to ours and would hardly show the same diminution of pain signs as we do if their experiential pain was not being controlled by these mechanisms in the same way that ours is. In certain shock experiments, large doses of naloxone have been given to traumatized animals, reversing the effect of endogenous opiates, and it has been shown that animals so treated die as a direct result of uncontrolled pain.[5] In 1987, it was shown that bradykinin antagonists control pain in both humans and animals.

Denial of pain consciousness in animals is incompatible not only with neurophysiology, but with what can be extrapolated from evolutionary theory as well. There is reason to believe that evolution preserves and perpetuates successful biological systems. Given that the mechanisms of pain in vertebrates are the same, it strains credibility to suggest that the experience of pain suddenly emerges at the level of humans. Granted, it is growing increasingly popular, following theorists like Gould and Lewontin, to assume the existence of quantum leaps in evolution, rather than assume that all evolution proceeds incrementally by minute changes. But surely such a hypothesis is most applicable where there is evidence of a morphological trait which seems to suddenly appear in the fossil record. With regard to mental traits, this hypothesis might conceivably apply to the appearance of language in humans, if Chomsky and others are correct in their argument that human language differs in kind, as well as degree, from communication systems in other species. But in other areas of mentation—most areas other than the most sophisticated intellectual abilities—and surely with regard to basic mental survival equipment like that connected with pain, such a hypothesis is both *ad hoc* and implausible. Human pain machinery is virtually the same as that in animals, and we know from experience with humans that the ability to *feel* pain is essential to survival; that people with a congenital or acquired inability to feel pain or with afflictions such as Hansen's disease (leprosy), which affects the ability to feel pain, are unlikely to do well or even survive without extraordinary, heroic attention. Of course, the same is true of animals—witness the recent case of Taub's deafferented monkeys [animals in whom the sensory nerves serving the limbs had been severed], who mutilated themselves horribly in the absence of the ability to feel. *Feeling* pain and the motivational influence of feeling it are essential to the survival of the system, and to suggest that the system is purely mechanical in animals but not in man is therefore highly implausible. If pain had worked well as a purely mechanical system in animals without a subjective dimension, why would it suddenly appear in man *with* such a dimension? (Unless, of course, one invokes some such theological notion as original sin and pain as divine punishment—hardly a legitimate scientific move!) And obviously, a similar argument would hold for discomfort associated with hunger, thirst, and other so-called drives, as well as with pleasures such as that of sexual congress.

So not only does much scientific activity presuppose animal pain, as we have seen *vis-à-vis* pain research and psychological research, it fits better with neurophysiology and evolutionary theory to believe that animals have mental experiences than to deny it. Outside positivistic-behaviouristic ideology, there seems little reason to deny pain (or fear, anxiety, boredom—in short, all rudimentary forms of mentation) to animals on either factual or conceptual grounds. (Indeed, research indicates that all vertebrates have receptor sites for benzodiazepine, which, in turn, suggests that the physiological basis of anxiety exists in all vertebrates.[6]) One may cavil at attributing higher forms of reason to animals, as Lloyd Morgan did, but that is ultimately a debatable, and in large part empirically decidable, question.

NOTES

1. B. Spinoza, *Ethics*, Parts III, IV, V.
2. R. L. Kitchell, personal communication.
3. B. Rollin, *Animal Rights and Human Morality* (Buffalo, NY: Prometheus Books, 1981), p. 38 ff.
4. Stephen Walker's recent book *Animal Thought* (London: Routledge and Kegan Paul, 1983) elegantly documents the neurophysiological similarity between humans and animals.
5. M. Fettman *et al.*, "Naloxone therapy in awake endotoxemic Yucatan minipigs," *Journal of Surgical Research* 37 (1984).
6. J. A. Gray, *The Neuropsychology of Anxiety* (Oxford: Oxford University Press, 1982).

ERIK ECKHOLM

Language Acquisition
in Nonhuman Primates

A 4-year-old pygmy chimpanzee at a research center near Atlanta has demonstrated what scientists say are the most humanlike linguistic skills ever documented in another animal.

The researchers say that the pygmy chimpanzee, Kanzi, has learned to communicate, using geometric symbols representing words, without the arduous training required by the famous "talking apes" of earlier studies, and that he is the first ape to show, in rigorous scientific tests, an extensive understanding of spoken English words.

Chimpanzees and other apes are not physically capable of speech. Some have been trained to use sign language or other symbols.

The scientists believe that Kanzi's linguistic achievements reflect a higher intellectual capacity in pygmy chimpanzees than in gorillas, orang-utans, and common chimpanzees, the three other species of great apes. They expect that this discovery and ensuing work with the species will aid in exploring how children learn to talk and how human language first evolved.

Erik Eckholm has been active in the areas of environmental protection and economic development. Among his books is *Losing Ground: Environmental Stress and Food Prospects* (Norton, 1976).

Copyright © 1985 by The New York Times Company. Reprinted by permission.

As Kanzi roams the 55 wooded acres of the Language Research Center, human companions and computers record his every request to play tag, to hike to the treehouse for a banana or to watch a videotape of Jane Goodall amid chimpanzees in Africa.

Punching geometric symbols on a keyboard to express himself, Kanzi is opening a new chapter in a history of ape studies marked by harsh disagreement over research methods and over the definition of language itself.

"I was astounded when the evidence began to appear that Kanzi was acquiring symbols spontaneously, and that he was comprehending spoken English," said E. Sue Savage-Rumbaugh, who directs research on ape language at the institute, which is jointly administered by Georgia State University and the Yerkes Primate Center of Emory University.

"I've worked with chimps virtually 12 to 15 hours a day since 1971," she said, "and these things just had not occurred." Her earlier work had been with common chimpanzees.

Herbert S. Terrace, a psychologist at Columbia University who has been a strong critic of many ape language studies, praised the Atlanta researchers for their step-by-step dissection of word usage and for their rigorous testing procedures. He and other scientists who have recently visited the Atlanta facility have come away impressed by Kanzi's precociousness.

NATURE OF LANGUAGE

"The extent of his learning through observation, without repeated training and prompting, is unique," said Dr. Carolyn Ristau of the Rockefeller University.

But whether the communications of Kanzi or any other trained apes can be called conscious language remains hotly disputed.

A crucial first step toward language is the ability to use words in the abstract way humans do: as names that stand for something rather than as learned ways to trigger rewards. Determining whether apes can use even a single word abstractly has proved to be awesomely complex.

Pygmy chimpanzees have been less studied than the other great apes. Like common chimpanzees, they have been determined in genetic studies to be closely related to humans.

Based on observations of the behavior of other pygmy chimpanzees, the Atlanta researchers believe Kanzi's achievements indicate a higher intellect on the part of the species in general, not that he is an isolated case.

Pygmy chimpanzees have already developed a reputation as the most humanlike animals. Their faces look less apelike, and they walk upright more often than other apes do. Alone among nonhuman primates, pygmy chimpanzee females are receptive to sex throughout their menstrual cycles; partners often mate face to face, gazing into each other's eyes.

PHYSICAL BARRIER TO SPEECH

Scientists believe that apes cannot duplicate human speech because they are physically unable to pronounce consonants. The symbols with which Kanzi and his teachers communicate are geometric symbols on a keyboard, each standing for a word.

The system, often connected to a computer for instant recording of each statement, was developed in the 1970's by Duane M. Rumbaugh, director of the Language Research Center and chairman of psychology at Georgia State University.

As an infant Kanzi had played in the laboratory while researchers were teaching word symbols to his mother. To the amazement of researchers, at the age of 2½ Kanzi spontaneously began using several of the symbols correctly, apparently having mastered them by watching others.

Since then he has been introduced to new symbols as they became relevant to his daily life. By the age of 3 he showed communication skills that two common chimpanzees in the same laboratory had not attained until the age of 7 after years of training, constantly reinforced with food rewards.

Public and scientific interest in the question of apes' ability to use language first soared some 15 years ago when Washoe, a chimpanzee raised like a human child by R. Allen Gardner and Beatrice Gardner of the University of Nevada, learned to make hand signs for many words and even seemed to be making short sentences.

Since then researchers have taught many chimpanzees and a few gorillas and orangutans to "talk" using the sign language of deaf humans, plastic chips or, like Kanzi, keyboard symbols. Washoe, Sarah, a chimpanzee trained by David Premack of the University of Pennsylvania, and Koko, a gorilla trained by the psychologist Francine Patterson, became media stars.

The ability to use language, to manipulate abstract concepts, has often been seen as the divide between humans and other animals. The assertion in 1978 by Dr. Patterson that "language is no longer the exclusive domain of man" presented a philosophical challenge to the definition of humanity and generated much debate.

SIMPLE CURIOSITY

Pervading all the studies and public reactions has been simple curiosity about the minds of other species. If apes could learn to talk, what might they tell us about their world and ours?

Studying the way apes learn language has also yielded practical benefits, illuminating how human children acquire language. Findings from chimpanzee experiments have yielded new approaches for helping severely retarded people communicate, which is one reason the research on apes at the Atlanta center has been financed by the National Institute of Child Health and Human Development.

In the 1970's, as apes enlarged their sign-language vocabularies, enthusiastic observers wondered what they would say next. But Dr. Terrace, the Columbia University researcher, dashed cold water on the enterprise in 1979.

Scrutinizing videotapes of sign-language conversations with Nim Chimpsky, a chimpanzee he had previously said was creating rudimentary sentences, Dr. Terrace reversed himself. He concluded that most of Nim's signing was prompted by his teacher's gestures or was imitative of his teacher's previous words. He argued that apes were incapable of grammar, unable to reliably combine symbols "in order to create new meanings."

MORE BASIC QUESTIONS

The field was thrown into turmoil. Other scientists criticized the training methods used with Nim and charged that Dr. Terrace's negative conclusions were too sweeping. But Dr. Terrace's well-publicized turnabout dampened public enthusiasm about talking apes and caused many researchers to rethink their methods and goals.

"The field has turned back to more basic questions: What is a word? What is meaning?" said Dr. Ristau.

In the view of Dr. Terrace, satisfactory evidence has not yet been marshaled that any ape does in fact know what he is saying. "My question is this: Is it anything more than a sophisticated way of asking for things?" Dr. Terry said. "Dogs can make symbols to ask to go outside. But that is different from what a child does when it names something." Infants, he noted, learn that they can use words simply to indicate to a parent that they have noticed an object.

But Dr. Ristau, reflecting the views of other experts, argued that several researchers had provided "converging evidence that some apes have learned to use words referentially," as abstract names rather than as memorized associations with rewards.

Allison Jolly, author of "The Evolution of Primate Behavior," said that some studies "show unequivocally, in the minds of most experts," that apes have used symbols abstractly.

UNDERSTANDING WORDS

In earlier work with the chimpanzees Sherman and Austin, Dr. Savage-Rumbaugh found that learning a word is a surprisingly intricate act involving several subskills. The animals showed real understanding of words only after being trained in each of the subskills individually.

For example, their learned ability to punch the symbol or key for an apple did not translate into an ability to pick that object out of a group when the human punched the symbol.

"It was hard to believe they couldn't reverse themselves," recalled Dr. Savage-Rumbaugh. "If they could name it, why couldn't they give it to me?" Specific training for these and other more elaborate actions, including cooperative use of tools by the two animals, led eventually to what in her view was a true understanding that the words stood for the objects. But the path to that point was "long and arduous."

Dr. Savage-Rumbaugh cites evidence that human infants pass through similar stages of word comprehension. But most humans develop abstract word skills so readily and rapidly that the complexity of the achievement is not easily perceived.

KANZI'S MASTERY OF WORDS

In stark contrast to Sherman and Austin, Kanzi has demonstrated the ability to manipulate words without specific training in each subskill. He identifies objects by name, comments on his actions, describes actions he intends to carry out and responds accurately to the symbols used by others.

While the Atlanta researchers do not say that Kanzi creates grammatical sentences, they have documented that his two-and three-word statements are often made without prompting, systematically add useful new information and represent his own creative responses to novel situations.

For example, when the chimpanzee Austin was moved out of the compound for a period, Kanzi seemed to miss his customary bedtime visit with his friend. After several lonely nights he solved the problem by typing the symbols "Austin" and "TV."

"When a videotape was played of Austin," the researchers noted, "Kanzi vocalized happily and loudly and then settled into his nest for the night."

Even more unusual, Kanzi often makes statements about actions by others. He does not merely ask a companion to tickle him or to chase him, a commonplace ape request. He also enjoys, as a visitor soon discovers, asking one person to tickle another while he watches. And then he asks the second to tickle the first.

"I think it's the beginning of some sort of grammar," Dr. Savage-Rumbaugh said.

SPOKEN WORDS UNDERSTOOD

Perhaps the most profound difference between Kanzi and common chimpanzees is his extensive understanding of spoken English words in controlled tests.

Many casual observers of trained apes, and some scientists, avow that the animals understand a great deal of what they hear. Chimpanzees like Sherman and Austin can give that impression. "Anyone who watched us would swear up and down that the chimps understood spoken words," said Dr. Savage-Rumbaugh. "I thought so myself. If you're cooking, and you ask them to bring you a spoon, they'll do it."

Other researchers have trained apes to produce the proper hand signs when certain familiar words were spoken. But in repeated experiments where contextual information and the influence of the speaker's gestures were eliminated, Sherman and Austin proved unable to comprehend words they had mastered on the keyboard and that they had been hearing constantly for years.

In a typical test the teacher placed a blanket over her head to assure experimental "blindness" and asked the animal to pick out one of three shuffled pictures of familiar objects. When asked on the keyboard, the chimpanzees performed almost perfectly. But when asked orally, they picked the right picture little more often than chance would dictate. But Kanzi was nearly perfect in both the oral and the keyboard trials.

The researchers say that Kanzi often understands somewhat complex spoken sentences. If asked, without gestures, "Will you go get a diaper for your sister Mulika?" or, "Do you want to get out the hose and play in your swimming pool?" he will take a diaper to his sister, or head for the hose.

The scientists are now looking for ways to test his comprehension of sentences. "We don't have unequivocal proof, and the skeptics will come up with any number of ways to discredit this," noted Dr. Savage-Rumbaugh. "It's just something unexpected that we are seeing."

Even in ape terms, Kanzi is still a child. His linguistic skills "continue to improve," Dr. Savage-Rumbaugh reported, "but at a much slower rate" than in human children. His current abilities, she believes, are comparable to those of a child of 1 to 2 years old, and this despite the handicap of having to speak with symbols.

Gorillas and orangutans have not been studied as thoroughly as chimpanzees and could also turn out to have greater linguistic abilities than many scientists now believe, said Dr. Rumbaugh, the Atlanta center's director.

The signing gorilla Koko, who, according to his trainer, has even discussed the idea of death, "is obviously an impressive animal," Dr. Rumbaugh said. "But we don't know how much is science and how much is fantasy. Data have not been presented in a way that scientists can analyze."

KANZI'S SKILLS POSE QUESTIONS

If the pygmy chimpanzee's language skills are indeed unique among the apes, then scientists are presented with both a mystery and an opportunity.

"From an evolutionary perspective, there's no explanation for the cognitive differences we're seeing in this species," said Dr. Savage-Rumbaugh. "Why would evolution operate this way, giving an animal an ability to understand human speech when it would never use that in its own world?"

What this could mean, she said, is that human ancestors may have somehow developed an ability to comprehend speech before they had the ability to speak.

Other scientists have already suggested, from genetic and behavioral evidence, that pygmy chimpanzees may be the closest living approximation of the ancient hominid primates that were the precursors of humans.

Scientists such as Randall L. Susman of the State University of New York at Stony Brook, who is observing pygmy chimpanzees in their natural home in the rain forests of Zaire, believe study of the species will improve understanding of how human intelligence and communications evolved.

'IT WOULD ONLY TAKE ONE'

"If the capacity to understand speech is there, waiting to be tapped into, it would only take one animal who developed an innovative way to produce sounds to change the behavior of the group in drastic ways," the Atlanta researchers write in a forthcoming paper.

At some unknown time, in one of the most momentous advances of human evolution, ancient hominids began to use sounds to refer to events or objects out of view, to create words and then sentences. The advantages of this skill for hominids, vulnerable animals struggling to find food and avoid predators, are not hard to imagine.

Over the millennia, under the competitive pressures of natural selection, the capacity for manipulating concepts improved to the point where Homo sapiens, able to debate metaphysics and build nuclear bombs, was produced.

Some scientists testing the linguistic limits of nonhuman primates believe they are, in a sense, retracing the first halting steps by which human ancestors entered the liberating new realm of abstract communication.

PART THREE
Equal Consideration
for Animals

PETER SINGER

All Animals
Are Equal

In recent years a number of oppressed groups have campaigned vigorously for equality. The classic instance is the Black Liberation movement, which demands an end to the prejudice and discrimination that has made blacks second-class citizens. The immediate appeal of the black liberation movement and its initial, if limited, success made it a model for other oppressed groups to follow. We became familiar with liberation movements for Spanish-Americans, gay people, and a variety of other minorities. When a majority group—women—began their campaign, some thought we had come to the end of the road. Discrimination on the basis of sex, it has been said, is the last universally accepted form of discrimination, practiced without secrecy or pretense even in those liberal circles that have long prided themselves on their freedom from prejudice against racial minorities.

One should always be wary of talking of "the last remaining form of discrimination." If we have learnt anything from the liberation move-

Peter Singer is Director of the Center for Human Bioethics at Monash University, Australia. His many writings in ethics include *Practical Ethics* (Cambridge University Press, 1979) and, as editor, *In Defense of Animals* (Blackwell, 1986).

From *Philosophic Exchange,* vol. 1, no. 5 (Summer 1974). Parts of this article appeared in a review of *Animals, Men and Morals,* Godlovitch and Harris (eds.), in *The New York Review of Books,* April 5, 1973.

ments, we should have learnt how difficult it is to be aware of latent prejudice in our attitudes to particular groups until this prejudice is forcefully pointed out.

A liberation movement demands an expansion of our moral horizons and an extension or reinterpretation of the basic moral principle of equality. Practices that were previously regarded as natural and inevitable come to be seen as the result of an unjustifiable prejudice. Who can say with confidence that all his or her attitudes and practices are beyond criticism? If we wish to avoid being numbered amongst the oppressors, we must be prepared to re-think even our most fundamental attitudes. We need to consider them from the point of view of those most disadvantaged by our attitudes, and the practices that follow from these attitudes. If we can make this unaccustomed mental switch we may discover a pattern in our attitudes and practices that consistently operates so as to benefit one group—usually the one to which we ourselves belong—at the expense of another. In this way we may come to see that there is a case for a new liberation movement. My aim is to advocate that we make this mental switch in respect of our attitudes and practices towards a very large group of beings: members of species other than our own—or, as we popularly though misleadingly call them, animals. In other words, I am urging that we extend to other species the basic principle of equality that most of us recognize should be extended to all members of our own species.

All this may sound a little far-fetched, more like a parody of other liberation movements than a serious objective. In fact, in the past the idea of "The Rights of Animals" really has been used to parody the case for women's rights. When Mary Wollstonecraft, a forerunner of later feminists, published her *Vindication of the Rights of Women* in 1792, her ideas were widely regarded as absurd, and they were satirized in an anonymous publication entitled *A Vindication of the Rights of Brutes.* The author of this satire (actually Thomas Taylor, a distinguished Cambridge philosopher) tried to refute Wollstonecraft's reasonings by showing that they could be carried one stage further. If sound when applied to women, why should the arguments not be applied to dogs, cats, and horses? They seemed to hold equally well for these "brutes"; yet to hold that brutes had rights was manifestly absurd; therefore the reasoning by which this conclusion had been reached must be unsound, and if unsound when applied to brutes, it must also be unsound when applied to women, since the very same arguments had been used in each case.

One way in which we might reply to this argument is by saying that the case for equality between men and women cannot validly be extended to nonhuman animals. Women have a right to vote, for instance, because they are just as capable of making rational decisions as men are; dogs, on the other hand, are incapable of understanding the significance of voting, so they cannot have the right to vote. There are many other obvious ways in which men and women resemble each other closely, while humans and other animals differ greatly. So, it might be said, men and women are similar beings and should have equal rights, while humans and nonhumans are different and should not have equal rights.

The thought behind this reply to Taylor's analogy is correct up to a point, but it does not go far enough. There *are* important differences between humans and other animals, and these differences must give rise to *some* differences in the rights that each have. Recognizing this obvious fact, however, is no barrier to the case for extending the basic principle of equality to nonhuman animals. The differences that exist between men and women are equally undeniable, and the supporters of Women's Liberation are aware that these differences may give rise to different rights. Many feminists hold that women have the right to an abortion on request. It does not follow that since these same people are campaigning for equality between men and women they must support the right of men to have abortions too. Since a man cannot have an abortion, it is meaningless to talk of his right to have one. Since a pig can't vote, it is meaningless to talk of its right to vote. There is no reason why either Women's Liberation or Animal Liberation should get involved in such nonsense. The extension of the basic principle of equality from one group to another does not imply that we must treat both groups in exactly the same way, or grant exactly the same rights to both groups. Whether we should do so will depend on the nature of the members of the two groups. The basic principle of equality, I shall argue, is equality of consideration; and equal consideration for different beings may lead to different treatment and different rights.

So there is a different way of replying to Taylor's attempt to parody Wollstonecraft's arguments, a way which does not deny the differences between humans and nonhumans, but goes more deeply into the question of equality and concludes by finding nothing absurd in the idea that the basic principle of equality applies to so-called "brutes." I believe that we reach this conclusion if we examine the basis on which our opposition to discrimination on grounds of race or sex ultimately rests. We will then see that we would be on shaky ground if we were to demand equality for blacks, women, and other groups of oppressed humans while denying equal consideration to nonhumans.

When we say that all human beings, whatever their race, creed, or sex, are equal, what is it that we are asserting? Those who wish to defend a hierarchical, inegalitarian society have often pointed out that by whatever test we choose, it simply is not true that all humans are equal. Like it or not, we must face the fact that humans come in different shapes and sizes; they come with differing moral capacities, differing intellectual abilities, differing amounts of benevolent feeling and sensitivity to the needs of others, differing abilities to communicate effectively, and differing capacities to experience pleasure and pain. In short, if the demand for equality were based on the actual equality of all human beings, we would have to stop demanding equality. It would be an unjustifiable demand.

Still, one might cling to the view that the demand for equality among human beings is based on the actual equality of the different races and sexes. Although humans differ as individuals in various ways, there are no differences between the races and sexes *as such*. From the mere fact that a person is black, or a woman, we cannot infer anything else about that person. This, it may be said, is what is wrong with racism and sexism. The white racist claims that whites are superior to blacks, but this is false—although there are differences between individuals, some blacks are superior to some whites in all of the capacities and abilities that could conceivably be relevant. The opponent of sexism would say the same: a person's sex is no guide to his or her abilities, and this is why it is unjustifiable to discriminate on the basis of sex.

This is a possible line of objection to racial and sexual discrimination. It is not, however, the way that someone really concerned about equality would choose, because taking this line could, in some circumstances, force one to accept a most inegalitarian society. The fact that humans differ as individuals, rather than as races or sexes, is a valid reply to someone who defends a hierarchical society like, say, South Africa, in which all whites are superior in status to all blacks. The existence of individual variations that cut across the lines of race or sex, however, provides us with no defence at all against a more sophisticated opponent of equality, one who proposes that, say, the interests of those with I.Q. ratings above 100 be preferred to the interests of those with I.Q.s below 100. Would a hierarchical society of this sort really be so much better than one based on race or sex? I think not. But if we tie the moral principle of equality to the factual equality of the different races or sexes, taken as a whole, our opposition to racism and sexism does not provide us with any basis for objecting to this kind of inegalitarianism.

There is a second important reason why we ought not to base our opposition to racism and sexism on any kind of factual equality, even the limited kind which asserts that variations in capacities and abilities are spread evenly between the different races and sexes: we can have no absolute guarantee that these abilities and capacities really are distributed evenly, without regard to race or sex, among human beings. So far as actual abilities are concerned, there do seem to be certain measurable differences between both races and sexes. These differences do not, of course, appear in each case, but only when averages are taken. More important still, we do not yet know how much of these differences is really due to the different genetic endowments of the various races and sexes, and how much is due to environmental differences that are the result of past and continuing discrimination. Perhaps all of the important differences will eventually prove to be environmental rather than genetic. Anyone opposed to racism and sexism will certainly hope that this will be so, for it will make the task of ending discrimination a lot easier; nevertheless it would be dangerous to rest the case against racism and sexism on the belief that all significant differences are environmental in origin. The opponent of, say, racism who takes this line will be unable to avoid conceding that if differences in ability did after all prove to have some genetic connection with race, racism would in some way be defensible.

It would be folly for the opponent of racism to stake his whole case on a dogmatic commitment to one particular outcome of a difficult scientific issue which is still a long way from being settled. While attempts to prove that differences in certain selected abilities between races and sexes are primarily genetic in origin have certainly not been conclusive, the same must be said of attempts to prove that these differences are largely the result of environment. At this stage of the investigation we cannot be certain which view is correct, however much we may hope it is the latter.

Fortunately, there is no need to pin the case for equality to one particular outcome of this scientific investigation. The appropraite response to those who claim to have found evidence of genetically-based differences in ability between the races or sexes is not to stick to the belief that the genetic explanation must be wrong, whatever evidence to the contrary may turn up: instead we should make it quite clear that the claim to equality does not depend on intelligence, moral capacity, physical strength, or similar matters of fact. Equality is a moral ideal, not a simple assertion of fact. There is no logically compelling reason for assuming that a factual difference in ability between two people justifies any difference in the amount of consideration we give to satisfying their needs and interests. The principle of the equality of human beings is not a description of an alleged actual equality among humans: it is a prescription of how we should treat animals.

Jeremy Bentham incorporated the essential basis of moral equality into his utilitarian system of ethics in the formula: "Each to count for one and none for more than one." In other words, the interests of every being affected by an action are to be taken into account and given the same weight as the like interests of any other being. A later utilitarian, Henry Sidgwick, put the point in this way: "The good of any one individual is of no more importance, from the point of view (if I may say so) of the Universe, than the good of any other."[1] More recently, the leading figures in contemporary moral philosophy have shown a great deal of agreement in specifying as a fundamental presupposition of their moral theories some similar requirement which operates so as to give everyone's interests equal consideration—although they cannot agree on how this requirement is best formulated.[2]

It is an implication of this principle of equality that our concern for others ought not to depend on what they are like, or what abilities they possess—although precisely what this concern requires us to do may vary according to the characteristics of those affected by what we do. It is on this basis that the case against racism and the case against sexism must both ultimately rest; and it is in accordance with this principle that speciesism is also to be condemned. If possessing a higher degree of intelligence does not entitle one human to use another for his own ends, how can it entitle humans to exploit nonhumans?

Many philosophers have proposed the principle of equal consideration of interests, in some form or other, as a basic moral principle; but, as we shall see in more detail shortly, not many of them have recognised that this principle applies to members of other species as well as to our own. Bentham was one of the few who did realize this. In a forward-looking passage, written at a time when black slaves in the British dominions were still being treated much as we now treat nonhuman animals, Bentham wrote:

> The day *may* come when the rest of the animal creation may acquire those rights which never could have been witholden from them but by the hand of tyranny. The French have already discovered that the blackness of the skin is no reason why a human being should be abandoned without redress to the caprice of a tormentor. It may one day come to be recognized that the number of the legs, the villosity of the skin, or the termination of the *os sacrum,* are reasons equally insufficient for abandoning a sensitive being to the same fate. What else is it that should trace the insuperable line? Is it the faculty of reason, or perhaps the faculty of discourse? But a full-grown horse or dog is beyond comparison a more rational, as well as a more conversable animal, than an infant of a day, or a week, or even a month, old. But suppose they were otherwise, what would it avail? The question is not, Can they reason? nor Can they *talk?* but, *Can they suffer?*[3]

In this passage Bentham points to the capacity for suffering as the vital characteristic that gives a being the right to equal consideration. The capacity for suffering—or more strictly, for suffering and/or enjoyment or happiness—is not just another characteristic like the capacity for language, or for higher mathematics. Bentham is not saying that those who try to mark "the insuperable line" that determines whether the interests of a being should be considered happen to have selected the wrong characteristic. The capacity for suffering and enjoying things is a prerequisite for having interests at all, a condition that must be satisfied before we can speak of interests in any meaningful way. It would be nonsense to say that it was not in the interests of a stone to be kicked along the road by a schoolboy. A stone does not have interests because it cannot suffer. Nothing that we can do to it could possibly make any difference to its welfare. A mouse, on the other hand, does have an interest in not being tormented, because it will suffer if it is.

If a being suffers, there can be no moral justification for refusing to take that suffering into consideration. No matter what the nature of the being, the principle of equality requires that its suffering be counted equally with the like suffering—in so far as rough comparisons can be made—of any other being. If a being is not capable of suffering, or of experiencing enjoyment or happiness, there is nothing to be taken into account. This is why the limit of sentience (using the term as a convenient, if not strictly accurate, shorthand for the capacity to suffer or experience enjoyment or happiness) is the only defensible boundary of concern for the interests of others. To mark this boundary by some characteristic like intelligence or rationality would be to mark it in an arbitrary way. Why not choose some other characteristic, like skin color?

The racist violates the principle of equality by giving greater weight to the interests of members of his own race, when there is a clash between their interests and the interests of those of another race. Similarly the speciesist allows the interests of his own species to override the greater interests of members of other species.[4] The pattern is the same in each case. Most human beings are speciesists. I shall now very briefly describe some of the practices that show this.

For the great majority of human beings, especially in urban, industrialized societies, the most direct form of contact with members of other species is at mealtimes: we eat them. In doing so we treat them purely as means to our ends. We regard their life and well-being as subordinate to our taste for a particular kind of dish. I say "taste" deliberately—this is purely a matter of pleasing our palate. There can be no defence of eating flesh in terms of satisfying nutritional needs, since it has been established beyond doubt that we could satisfy our need for protein and other essential nutrients far more efficiently with a diet that replaced animal flesh by soy beans, or products derived from soy beans, and other high-protein vegetable products.[5]

It is not merely the act of killing that indicates what we are ready to do to other species in order to gratify our tastes. The suffering we inflict on the animals while they are alive is perhaps an even clearer indication of our speciesism than the fact that we are prepared to kill them.[6] In order to have meat on the table at a price that people can afford, our society tolerates methods of meat production that confine sentient animals in cramped, unsuitable conditions for the entire durations of their lives. Animals are treated like machines that convert fodder into flesh, and any innovation that results in a higher "conversion ratio" is liable to be adopted. As one authority on the subject has said, "cruelty is acknowledged only when profitability ceases."[7] . . .

Since, as I have said, none of these practices cater for anything more than our pleasures of taste, our practice of rearing and killing other animals in order to eat them is a clear instance of the sacrifice of the most important interests of other beings in order to satisfy trivial interests of our own. To avoid speciesism we must stop this practice, and each of us has a moral obligation to cease supporting the practice. Our custom is all the support that the meat-industry needs. The decision to cease giving it that support may be difficult, but it is no more difficult than it would have been for a white Southerner to go against the traditions of his society and free his slaves: if we do not change our dietary habits, how can we censure those slaveholders who would not change their own way of living?

The same form of discrimination may be observed in the widespread practice of experimenting on other species in order to see if certain substances are safe for human beings, or to test some psychological theory about the effect of severe punishment on learning, or to try out various new compounds just in case something turns up. . . .

In the past, argument about vivisection has often missed the point, because it has been put in absolutist terms: Would the abolitionist be prepared to let thousands die if they could be saved by experimenting on a single animal? The way to reply to this purely hypothetical question is to pose another: Would the experimenter be prepared to perform his experiment on an orphaned human infant, if that were the only way to save many lives? (I say "orphan" to avoid the complication of parental feelings, although in doing so I am being overfair to the experimenter, since the nonhuman subjects of experiments are not orphans.) If the experimenter is not prepared to use an orphaned human infant, then his readiness to use nonhumans is simple discrimination, since adult apes, cats, mice, and other mammals are more aware of what is happening to them, more self-directing and, so far as we can tell, at least as sensitive to pain, as any human infant. There seems to be no relevant characteristic that human infants possess that adult mammals do not have to the same or a higher degree. (Someone might try to argue that what makes it wrong to experiment on a human infant is that the infant will, in time and if left alone, develop into more than the nonhuman, but one would then, to be consistent, have to oppose abortion, since the fetus has the same potential as the infant—indeed, even contraception and abstinence might be wrong on this ground, since the egg and sperm, considered jointly, also have the same potential. In any case, this argument still gives us no reason for selecting a nonhuman, rather than a human with severe and irreversible brain damage, as the subject for our experiments).

The experimenter, then, shows a bias in favor of his own species whenever he carries out an experiment on a nonhuman for a purpose that he would not think justified him in using a human being at an equal or lower level of sentience, awareness, ability to be self-directing, etc. No one familiar with the kind of results yielded by most experiments on animals can have the slightest doubt that if this bias were eliminated the number of experiments performed would be a minute fraction of the number performed today.

Experimenting on animals, and eating their flesh, are perhaps the two major forms of speciesism in our society. By comparison, the third and last form of speciesism is so minor as to be insignificant, but it is perhaps of some special interest to those for whom this article was written. I am referring to speciesism in contemporary philosophy.

Philosophy ought to question the basic assumptions of the age. Thinking through, critically and carefully, what most people take for granted is, I believe, the chief task of philosophy, and it is this task that makes philosophy a worthwhile activity. Regrettably, philosophy does not always live up to its historic role. Philosophers are human beings, and they are subject to all the preconceptions of the society to which they belong. Sometimes they succeed in breaking free of the prevailing ideology: more often they become its most sophisticated defenders. So, in this case, philosophy as practiced in the universities today does not challenge anyone's preconceptions about our relations with other species. By their writings, those philosophers who tackle problems that touch upon the issue reveal that they make the same unquestioned assumptions as most other humans, and what they say tends to confirm the reader in his or her comfortable speciesist habits.

I could illustrate this claim by referring to the writings of philosophers in various fields—for instance, the attempts that have been made by those interested in rights to draw the boundary of the sphere of rights so that it runs parallel to the biological boundaries of the species *homo sapiens,* including infants and even mental defectives, but excluding those other beings of equal or greater capacity who are so useful to us at mealtimes and in our laboratories. I think it would be a more appropriate conclusion to this article, however, if I concentrated on the problem with which we have been centrally concerned, the problem of equality.

It is significant that the problem of equality, in moral and political philosophy, is invariably formulated in terms of human equality. The effect of this is that the question of the equality of other animals does not confront the philosopher, or student, as an issue itself—and this is already an indication of the failure of philosophy to challenge accepted beliefs. Still, philosophers have found it difficult to discuss the issue of human equality without raising, in a paragraph or two, the question of the status of other animals. The reason for this, which should be apparent from what I have said already, is that if humans are to be regarded as equal to one another, we need some sense of "equal" that does not require any actual, descriptive equality of capacities, talents or other qualities. If equality is to be related to any actual characteristics of humans, these characteristics must be some lowest common denominator, pitched so low that no human lacks them—but then the philosopher comes up against the catch that any such set of characteristics which covers *all* humans will not be possessed *only by humans.* In other words, it turns out that in the only sense in which we can truly say, as an assertion of fact, that all humans are equal, at least some members of other species are also equal—equal, that is, to each other and to humans. If, on the other hand, we regard the statement "All humans are equal" in some non-factual way, perhaps as a prescription, then, as I have already argued, it is even more difficult to exclude non-humans from the sphere of equality.

This result is not what the egalitarian philosopher originally intended to assert. Instead of accepting the radical outcome to which their own reasonings naturally point, however, most philosophers try to reconcile their beliefs in human equality and animal inequality by arguments that can only be described as devious.

As a first example, I take William Frankena's well-known article "The Concept of Social Justice." Frankena opposes the idea of basing justice on merit, because he sees that this could lead to highly inegalitarian results. Instead he proposes the principle that

> all men are to be treated as equals, not because they are equal, in any respect, but simply because they are human. They are human because they have emotions and desires, and are able to think, and hence are capable of enjoying a good life in a sense in which other animals are not.[8]

But what is this capacity to enjoy the good life which all humans have, but no other animals? Other animals have emotions and desires and appear to be capable of enjoying a good life. We may doubt that they can think—although the behavior of some apes, dolphins, and even dogs suggests that some of them can—but what is the relevance of thinking? Frankena goes on to admit that by "the good life" he means "not so much the morally good life as the happy or satisfactory life," so thought would appear to be unnecessary for enjoying the good life; in fact to emphasise the need for thought would make difficulties for the egalitarian since only some people are capable of leading intellectually satisfying lives, or morally good lives. This makes it difficult to see what Frankena's principle of equality has to do with simply being *human*. Surely every sentient being is capable of leading a life that is happier or less miserable than some alternative life, and hence has a claim to be taken into account. In this respect the distinction between humans and nonhumans is not a sharp division, but rather a continuum along which we move gradually, and with overlaps between the species, from simple capacities for enjoyment and satisfaction, or pain and suffering, to more complex ones.

Faced with a situation in which they see a need for some basis for the moral gulf that is commonly thought to separate humans and animals, but can find no concrete difference that will do the job without undermining the equality of humans, philosophers tend to waffle. They resort to high-sounding phrases like "the intrinsic dignity of the human individual";[9]

they talk of the "intrinsic worth of all men" as if men (humans?) had some worth that other beings did not,[10] or they say that humans, and only humans, are "ends in themselves," while "everything other than a person can only have value for a person."[11]

This idea of a distinctive human dignity and worth has a long history; it can be traced back directly to the Renaissance humanists, for instance to Pico della Mirandola's *Oration on the Dignity of Man*. Pico and other humanists based their estimate of human dignity on the idea that man possessed the central, pivotal position in the "Great Chain of Being" that led from the lowliest forms of matter to God himself; this view of the universe, in turn, goes back to both classical and Judeo-Christian doctrines. Contemporary philosophers have cast off these metaphysical and religious shackles and freely invoke the dignity of mankind without needing to justify the idea at all. Why should we not attribute "intrinsic dignity" or "intrinsic worth" to ourselves? Fellow-humans are unlikely to reject the accolades we so generously bestow on them, and those to whom we deny the honor are unable to object. Indeed, when one thinks only of humans, it can be very liberal, very progressive, to talk of the dignity of all human beings. In so doing, we implicitly condemn slavery, racism, and other violations of human rights. We admit that we ourselves are in some fundamental sense on a par with the poorest, most ignorant members of our own species. It is only when we think of humans as no more than a small sub-group of all the beings that inhabit our planet that we may realize that in elevating our own species we are at the same time lowering the relative status of all other species.

The truth is that the appeal to the intrinsic dignity of human beings appears to solve the egalitarian's problems only as long as it goes unchallenged. Once we ask *why* it should be that all humans—including infants, mental defectives, psychopaths, Hitler, Stalin, and the rest—have some kind of dignity or worth that no elephant, pig, or chimpanzee can ever achieve, we see that this question is as difficult to answer as our original request for some relevant fact that justifies the inequality of humans and other animals. In fact, these two questions are really one: talk of intrinsic dignity or moral worth only takes the problem back one step, because any satisfactory defence of the claim that all and only humans have intrinsic dignity would need to refer to some relevant capacities or characteristics that all and only humans possess. Philosophers frequently introduce ideas of dignity, respect, and worth at the point at which other reasons appear to be lacking, but this is hardly good enough. Fine phrases are the last resource of those who have run out of arguments.

In case there are those who still think it may be possible to find some relevant characteristic that distinguishes all humans from all members of other species, I shall refer again, before I conclude, to the existence of some humans who quite clearly are below the level of awareness, self-consciousness, intelligence, and sentience, of many non-humans. I am thinking of humans with severe and irreparable brain damage, and also of infant humans. To avoid the complication of the relevance of a being's potential, however, I shall henceforth concentrate on permanently re-tarded humans.

Philosophers who set out to find a characteristic that will distinguish humans from other animals rarely take the course of abandoning these groups of humans by lumping them in with the other animals. It is easy to see why they do not. To take this line without re-thinking our attitudes to other animals would entail that we have the right to perform painful experiments on retarded humans for trivial reasons; similarly it would follow that we had the right to rear and kill these humans for food. To most philosophers these consequences are as unacceptable as the view that we should stop treating nonhumans in this way.

Of course, when discussing the problem of equality it is possible to ignore the problem of mental defectives, or brush it aside as if somehow insignificant.[12] This is the easiest way out. What else remains? My final example of speciesism in contemporary philosophy has been selected to show what happens when a writer is prepared to face the question of human equality and animal inequality without ignoring the existence of mental defectives, and without resorting to obscurantist mumbo-jumbo. Stanley Benn's clear and honest article "Egalitarianism and Equal Consid-eration of Interests"[13] fits this description.

Benn, after noting the usual "evident human inequalities" argues, correctly I think, for equality of consideration as the only possible basis for egalitarianism. Yet Benn, like other writers, is thinking only of "equal consideration of human interests." Benn is quite open in his defence of this restriction of equal consideration:

> . . . not to possess human shape *is* a disqualifying condition. However faithful or intelligent a dog may be, it would be a monstrous sentimentality to at-tribute to him interests that could be weighed in an equal balance with those of human beings . . . if, for instance, one had to decide between feeding a hungry baby or a hungry dog, anyone who chose the dog would generally be reckoned morally defective, unable to recognize a fundamental inequality of claims.
>
> This is what distinguishes our attitude to animals from our attitude to imbeciles. It would be odd to say that we ought to respect equally the dignity or personality of the imbecile and of the rational man . . . but there is nothing odd about saying that we should respect their interests equally, that is, that we should give to the interests of each the same serious consideration as claims to considerations necessary for some standard of well-being that we can recog-nize and endorse.

Benn's statement of the basis of the consideration we should have for imbeciles seems to me correct, but why should there be any fundamental inequality of claims between a dog and a human imbecile? Benn sees that if equal consideration depended on rationality, no reason could be given against using imbeciles for research purposes, as we now use dogs and guinea pigs. This will not do: "But of course we do distinguish imbeciles from animals in this regard," he says. That the common distinction is justifiable is something Benn does not question; his problem is how it is to be justified. The answer he gives is this:

> ... we respect the interests of men and give them priority over dogs not *insofar* as they are rational, but because rationality is the human norm. We say it is *unfair* to exploit the deficiencies of the imbecile who falls short of the norm, just as it would be unfair, and not just ordinarily dishonest, to steal from a blind man. If we do not think in this way about dogs, it is because we do not see the irrationality of the dog as a deficiency or a handicap, but as normal for the species. The characteristics, therefore, that distinguish the normal man from the normal dog make it intelligible for us to talk of other men having interests and capacities, and therefore claims, of precisely the same kind as we make on our own behalf. But although these characteristics may provide the point of the distinction between men and other species, they are not in fact the qualifying conditions for membership, or the distinguishing criteria of the class of morally considerable persons; and this is precisely because a man does not become a member of a different species, with its own standards of normality, by reason of not possessing these characteristics.

The final sentence of this passage gives the argument away. An imbecile, Benn concedes, may have no characteristics superior to those of a dog; nevertheless this does not make the imbecile a member of "a different species" as the dog is. *Therefore* it would be "unfair" to use the imbecile for medical research as we use the dog. But why? That the imbecile is not rational is just the way things have worked out, and the same is true of the dog—neither is any more responsible for their mental level. If it is unfair to take advantage of an isolated defect, why is it fair to take advantage of a more general limitation? I find it hard to see anything in this argument except a defence of preferring the interests of members of our own species because they are members of our own species. To those who think there might be more to it, I suggest the following mental exercise. Assume that it has been proven that there is a difference in the average, or normal, intelligence quotient for two different races, say whites and blacks. Then substitute the term "white" for every occurrence of "men" and "black" for every occurrence of "dog" in the passage quoted; and substitute "high I.Q." for "rationality" and when Benn talks of "imbeciles" replace this term by "dumb whites"—that is, whites who fall well below the normal white I.Q. score. Finally, change "species" to "race." Now re-read the passage. It has become a defence of a rigid, no-exceptions division between whites and blacks, based on I.Q. scores, *not withstanding an admitted overlap* between whites and blacks in this respect. The revised passage is, of course, outrageous, and this is not only because we have made fictitious assumptions in our substitutions. The point is that in the original passage Benn was defending a rigid division in the amount of consideration due to members of different species, despite admitted cases of overlap. If the original did not, at first reading strike us as being as outrageous as the revised version does, this is largely because although we are not racists ourselves, most of us are speciesists. Like the other articles, Benn's stands as a warning of the ease with which the best minds can fall victim to a prevailing ideology.

NOTES

1. *The Methods of Ethics* (7th Ed.), p. 382.
2. For example, R. M. Hare, *Freedom and Reason* (Oxford, 1963) and J. Rawls, *A Theory of Justice* (Harvard, 1972); for a brief account of the essential agreement on this issue between these and other positions, see R. M. Hare, "Rules of War and Moral Reasoning," *Philosophy and Public Affairs*, vol. I, no. 2 (1972).
3. *Introduction to the Principles of Morals and Legislation*, ch. XVII.
4. I owe the term *speciesism* to Richard Ryder.
5. In order to produce 1 lb. of protein in the form of beef or veal, we must feed 21 lbs. of protein to the animal. Other forms of livestock are slightly less inefficient, but the average ratio in the United States is still 1:8. It has been estimated that the amount of protein lost to humans in this way is equivalent to 90 percent of the annual world protein deficit. For a brief account, see Frances Moore Lappé, *Diet for a Small Planet* (Friends of The Earth/Ballantine, New York 1971), pp. 4–11.
6. Although one might think that killing a being is obviously the ultimate wrong one can do to it, I think that the infliction of suffering is a clearer indication of speciesism because it might be argued that at least part of what is wrong with killing a human is that most humans are conscious of their existence over time and have desires and purposes that extend into the future—see, for instance, M. Tooley, "Abortion and Infanticide," *Philosophy and Public Affairs*, vol. 2, no. 1 (1972). Of course, if one took this view one would have to hold—as Tooley does—that killing a human infant or mental defective is not in itself wrong and is less serious than killing certain higher mammals that probably do have a sense of their own existence over time.
7. Ruth Harrison, *Animal Machines* (Stuart, London, 1964). For an account of farming conditions, see my *Animal Liberation* (New York Review Company, 1975) from which "Down on the Factory Farm," is reprinted in this volume.
8. In R. Brandt (ed.), *Social Justice* (Prentice Hall, Englewood Cliffs, 1962), p. 19.
9. Frankena, *op. cit.*, p. 23.
10. H. A. Bedau, "Egalitarianism and the Idea of Equality," in *Nomos IX: Equality*, ed. J. R. Pennock and J. W. Chapman, New York, 1967.
11. G. Vlastos, "Justice and Equality," in Brandt, *Social Justice*, p. 48.
12. For example, Bernard Williams, "The Idea of Equality," in *Philosophy, Politics, and Society* (second series), ed. P. Laslett and W. Runciman (Blackwell, Oxford, 1962), p. 118; J. Rawls, *A Theory of Justice*, pp. 509–10.
13. *Nomos IX: Equality;* the passages quoted are on p. 62ff.

LAWRENCE C. BECKER

The Priority
of Human Interests

My purpose here is to put forward an argument in defense of the moral priority, for humans, of human interests over comparable ones in animals.[1]

In outline, the argument is simply this: There are certain traits of character that people ought to have—traits constitutive of moral excellence or virtue. Some of these traits order preferences by "social distance"—that is, give priority to the interests of those "closer" to us in social relationships over the interests of those farther away. Animals are typically "farther away" from us than human beings. Thus, to hold that people ought to have the traits constitutive of virtue is to hold, as a consequence, that people ought (typically) to give priority to the interests of members of their own species.

That is the outline, and it will require a great deal of filling in to make it convincing. But I want to make it clear from the outset that no amount of filling in will turn this argument into a defense of the proposition that humans are morally superior to animals (whatever that might mean). Nor will the argument deny consideration to the interests of animals in the

Lawrence Becker teaches philosophy at Hollins College. In addition to his writings in moral philosophy, he is the General Editor of the Encyclopedia of Ethics Project.

Reprinted from Lawrence C. Becker, "The Priority of Human Interests," pp. 225–235 in H. Miller and W. Williams, *Ethics and Animals*. Clifton, NJ: Humana Press, 1983.

making of moral decisions, or deny that those interests can often override human ones. My argument is not a defense of the cruelty to animals found in factory farming and much scientific experimentation. (But as far as I can tell, the argument is indeterminate with regard to using some sorts of animals for food and for some experiments.) . . .

ASSUMPTIONS ABOUT VIRTUE

I begin with some assumptions about moral virtue. The assumptions are as uncontroversial as I can make them—which does not mean, of course, that I think they can always be used without analysis and justificatory argument. But for present purposes they seem to be unproblematic.

The first is that moral virtue is, at bottom, a matter of character traits. It is defined by a complex of propensities and dispositions to feel, to imagine, to deliberate, to choose, and to act. Being a good person is not just acting on principle, or doing the right thing, for the right reasons, most of the time. To be a good person is to be someone for whom right conduct is "in character." The good person is, in part, one whose responses, impulses, inclinations, and initiatives—*prior* to a reasoned assessment of the alternatives—are typically toward morally good feelings, deliberations, choices, and conduct.

The second assumption about moral virtue, or moral character, is that it sometimes produces spontaneous, uncalculated conduct. Utility theory itself requires that we develop habits of thought, expectations, rules of thumb, reflexive responses, and so on. The alternative is a ludicrous form of paralysis that is self-defeating on rigorously act-utilitarian principles alone. I take it that the other standard types of moral theory come to the same conclusion: that the good person is one who *sometimes* acts without weighing the consequences, or canvassing peoples' rights and duties, or in any other way deliberating about what to do. Sometimes, *as a necessary consequence of being morally virtuous,* a good person just has, and acts on, uncalculated feelings, beliefs, expectations, and preferences.

The third assumption I make about moral excellence is that the character traits that define it form a coherent system constrained both by welfare needs and by obligations. Coherence is assumed to avoid the problems raised by conflicts among traits: Unconditional truth-telling may conflict with tact; but I am assuming that as these things enter into the dispositions that define virtue, a rough balance is struck that in principle permits both tactful and truthful behavior. Constraints imposed by welfare needs and by obligations are assumed to avoid the problems raised by fanaticism. Loyalty may be an element of virtue, but not when it is blind to the consequences for welfare, or to the violation of rights and duties, or to the requirements of justice generally.

The fourth assumption is that the ability to develop and sustain friendships is a necessary part of moral excellence. (I mean to restrict this assumption to situations in which people can meet their survival needs without extreme difficulty, and in which they are dealing with people of good will. Further, as I use the term friendship, it includes intimate and intense love relationships as well as those characterized by mutual respect, admiration, and affection.)

Finally, I assume that the traits that define moral excellence produce "open" but stable and unambivalent feelings, beliefs, expectations, and preferences. The feelings, beliefs, and so on must be open to change in the sense that the moral person must be *persuadable*. Fixed attitudes, as opposed to stable ones, are not part of moral excellence. But the person who lives in an agony of uncertainty about every act, every feeling, every preference, or who is thrown into confusion by every *suggestion* of error, does not exemplify moral excellence either. That is why the traits that make up moral character must be stable and the beliefs, attitudes, and so forth that the traits produce must be unambivalent.

With these few assumptions about moral excellence in the background, then, I want to argue for some favoritism toward members of our own species.

SOCIAL DISTANCE AND PREFERENCES

When hard choices have to be made, I am ordinarily expected to rank the interests of my family above those of my friends, friends' above neighbors', neighbors' above acquaintances', and acquaintances' above strangers', and so on. In general, the expected preference ordering follows typical differences in the intimacy, interdependency, and reciprocity in human relationships. Such differences are constitutive of what may be called "social distance"—an imprecise amalgam of relevant facts about tolerable spatial arrangements, the frequency and nature of permissible social interactions, and roles in social structures.[2]

There are exceptions to these expected preferences, of course, along several dimensions. One is obligations: I may have made agreements with strangers that override ordinary commitments to family. Another is proportionality: the trivial interests of a friend do not outweigh the survival needs of an acquaintance, for example. And still another dimension of exceptions has to do with deviations from the typical pattern of relationships: if my family has abused me and cast me out, whereas some friends have taken me in, I may be expected to reverse the usual preference order. (People sometimes explain this by saying: These friends are my *real* family.)

In addition to the exceptions, there are the well-known conceptual problems raised by any such ordering of preferences. Who is my neighbor?

Is it mostly a matter of geography or of social organization? Is a family a biological unit or a sociological one? Where are the lines between friendship and mere acquaintance, and between acquaintance and lack of it?

Finally, the operation of such preference ordering is constrained by principles of justice: Similar cases must still be treated similarly; decisions should be non-arbitrary; and in some highly regularized cases, we require that the decision process not be covert, or manipulative, or involve ex post facto legislation or self-interested adjudication.

I do not mean to minimize the importance of all these matters. But I am concerned here with two other issues: the moral justification, if there is one, that can be given for any preference ordering by social distance; and the consequences of that for our treatment of animals. . . .

Virtue and Social Distance

What I want to explore is the notion that some traits of character that are constitutive of moral excellence entail social distance preferences. The traits I have in mind are reciprocity (i.e., the disposition to make a proportional return of good for good), and empathic identification with others. (There are no doubt other traits for which the same argument could be made. I do not propose my list as exhaustive.)

Reciprocity.   Reciprocity is a pervasive social phenomenon—and one that appears not only as a mere practice, but as a norm for conduct in virtually every society of record.[3] Returning good in proportion to good received—at least in many common social exchanges—is prescribed, as well as predictable, human behavior.[4] It is evident, by inference, that the *disposition* to reciprocate (leaving aside the issue of proper motives) is quite generally regarded as an element of moral virtue.

Further, it seems clear that one can justify the inclusion of such a disposition in an account of moral virtue. It has obvious social utility that its absence or opposite would lack. It is, for example, necessary for sustaining conviviality, friendships, and certain sorts of cooperative endeavors. For those reasons, and perhaps others, it is also plausible to think that rational contractors would choose a world in which people had such dispositions over one that differed only in lacking them. Rights theory insists on the mutual respect, balanced exchanges, and so on that are characteristic of reciprocity. And reciprocity is obviously embedded in Aristotelian accounts of moral character. In short, if any traits of character can be given a reasoned justification as necessary parts of moral virtue, reciprocity is among them.

Empathic Identification.   A similar case can be made for the ability and the propensity to see situations from other points of view, to understand

and indeed to share others' experience empathetically. (I include here also the ability to identify with characters in narrative art and to have vicarious experience through such identification.) Aside from its utility in settling conflicts, empathy is a prerequisite for applying the utility calculus. How else can we estimate utilities for others?

I assume that other standard moral theories would also list empathy as an element of virtue. Rational contractors would most likely prefer a world in which agents had this trait to one in which they did not. Deontological theory cannot work without the means for deciding what counts as a violation—an injury—to another. And that seems to require in moral agents the ability and propensity to understand the suffering of others. (I assume that right conduct, in deontological terms, is more than a mere mechanical performance of tasks—that it requires proper motives as well.)

Relation to Social Distance. It is easily seen, I think, that both the disposition to reciprocate and the disposition to empathize ordinarily result in *distributions* ordered by social distance. Given limited resources with which to reciprocate, and limited energy, time, and imaginative ability for empathic identification, those closest to us will inevitably get a disproportionate share—both of the goods we distribute and the attention we pay to them. But do we prefer satisfying the interests of those closer to us? That is, supposing we have the dispositions to reciprocate and empathize, do we, as a consequence of that fact, order *preferences* (as well as actual distributions) by social distance? I think so, for the following reasons.

Take reciprocity first.

(1) The smaller the social distance between people, the more intricate and pervasive are the exchanges between them. Consequently, the difficulty of deciding who is in debt to whom, or when equilibrium has been achieved in a relationship, varies inversely with the distance. Such calculations are virtually impossible within a nuclear family, and extremely difficult even for close friends. In such relationships, it would nearly always be reasonable for everyone involved to feel either in debt or cheated no matter what choices were made—at least, that would be possible if people tried to keep a strict accounting of who owed what to whom. The potential for continuous ill-feeling—and the consequent breakdown of close relationships— is obvious. With good reason, therefore, we do not cultivate "reciprocity accounting" *at all* in close relationships—as long as the relationships remain stable and roughly balanced.

(2) This seems an eminently justifiable position to take with regard to moral excellence. If it is a part of moral excellence to be able to develop and sustain friendships, and if the parts of moral excellence must form a coherent whole (both of which I am assuming here), then the disposition to reciprocate must be compatible with the ability to develop and sustain

friendships. Thus the disposition to avoid strict accounting—at least in close friendships—is required.

(3) The required disposition changes as social distance increases, however, partly because the potential for reasonable disagreement over credits and debits decreases. Many exchanges with strangers are discrete and of assessable value. And many of the benefits we receive from strangers are so indirect that reciprocity for these can be equally indirect (e.g., by our being law-abiding, productive citizens). So the stability of relatively distant relationships is not threatened by a more calculative approach.

(4) Finally, we are, typically, *always* more "in debt" to family than to friends, to friends than to acquaintances—if for no other reason than the sheer frequency of exchanges. The more transactions there are in a relationship, the more likely it is that there will be "loose ends." When all of this is put together—the fact that the closer the relationship, the more likely we are to be "in debt," and the fact that the closer the relationship, the less exact is our knowledge of debts—it follows that it is always reasonable for virtuous people to think that anything they have to give is more likely "owed" to those closer than those farther away. Distributional preferences, given the disposition to reciprocate, will therefore be ordered in terms of social distance.

Something similar may be said of empathy. We identify most fully with those closest to us. That is, their interests are "real" to us in a way that the interests of more distant people are not. Empathic identification with the suffering (or pleasure) of people whose very existence we know about only indirectly (through the descriptions of others) cannot help but have an imaginative, dilute, and dubitable quality. In contrast, the interests of those close to us—the interests communicated to us directly—have a vividness, immediacy, and *in*dubitability that imaginatively constructed empathy can never match. It is certainly plausible to support that, insofar as empathic identification produces conduct "for" the interests of others, it will produce preferences for those with whom our empathy is strong over those with whom our empathy is weak. The consequence is preferences ordered by social distance.

SOCIAL DISTANCE ACROSS SPECIES LINES

My argument so far has been that the virtuous person—as a consequence of certain traits constitutive of virtue—orders preferences by social distance. I want to argue now that, certain exceptions aside, the social distance from us to members of other species is greater than to members of our own species. The consequence—for virtuous people—is a systematic preference for the interests of humans over the interests of other animals. The argument is fairly straightforward.

First Step

Social distance decreases as the quantity and "immediacy" of social inter-action increases. This is just definitional. When I interact *directly* with someone—without intermediaries—and when I do so frequently, the social distance between us (other things being equal) is less than it would be if the interactions were indirect and infrequent.[5] That is part of what is meant by "social distance." (I say "part" because there are other ways in which social distance can increase or decrease.)

Second Step

Dependence, when it is recognized as such by one or more of the parties, is a feature of relationships that typically reduces social distance—by in-creasing both the quantity and immediacy of interactions. The dependent one struggles to stay "close"; the one depended upon must continually deal with the demands of the other—even if only by rejecting them. Thus, the more dependent a being is on another, the smaller the social distance between the two tends to be.[6]

It is again definitional, at least when the notion of a "relationship" is suitably restricted. *Social* distance concerns interactions in which beings may be said to be acting *toward, with, for,* or *against* each other. It is only those sorts of interactions that I refer to as "relationships." Thus the causal relation (of interdependence) that we have with certain symbiotic micro-organisms is not a relation*ship* in this sense. (Or, put another way, it is one in which the social distance between the parties is infinite.) Similarly, our dependence on oxygen is not to be analyzed in terms of social distance, nor as the causal relations between ourselves and vegetables. But we *can* have relationships in the requisite sense with many sorts of animals, and with virtually all human beings. In these relationships, our recognition of the truth about dependence is one of the factors that determines social dis-tance. And the more the dependence, the less the social distance.

Third Step

Animals are typically much less dependent on us, in our relationships with them, than are those humans (infants and so on) to whom the animals are comparable (in terms of their interests, intelligence and so forth). Romulus and Remus aside, helpless humans are dependent on other humans for survival, health, and happiness to a degree that the comparable animals are not. The social distance from human adults to human infants is thus typically smaller than the distance to comparable animals.

Final Step

Consequently, given the ordering of preferences by social distance entailed by moral excellence, we will typically prefer the humans. (I say "typically" because in special cases—such as pets, wounded or crippled animals, and those who suffer directly from human actions—the same kind of dependence can exist.)

A much richer account of the increases in social distance across species lines can probably by constructed from social-psychological findings—for example, about the propensity for and limitations of empathic identification. But such complications are not necessary to the argument already made. Similarly, it would be possible to enrich the argument greatly by developing an account of the greater intricacy and potency of reciprocal relationships among normal adult humans compared to that between humans and animals. But that would take the argument well beyond its present purpose. . . .

NOTES

1. I shall usually follow the convention of excluding humans from the class denoted by "animals."
2. The concept of social distance is a slippery one. As it has been used in social psychology, it mostly has to do with tolerable levels of social "relatedness": Would you marry a——? Would you accept a——as a close relative by marriage? As a roommate? As a neighbor? As a member of your club? The answers to such questions are thought to establish a social distance scale—particularly with respect to race, nationality, social class, and religion. See C. W. Sherif, *Orientation in Social Psychology* (New York: Harper & Row, 1976), for an overview of this material. Her references to the work of H. C. and L. M. Triandis are especially worth pursuing. The relation of spatial arrangements to social distance has also been explored. See the discussion and references in K. G. Shaver, *Principles of Social Psychology* (Cambridge, MA: Winthrop, 1977), pp. 108–111. But I have not been able to find—either in texts or in primary sources—a careful analysis of the *concept* of social distance. And the empirical work so far done in the area has ignored the feature that is of most concern to me here—namely, preferences in the distribution of scarce goods. Would you give the last available food to——over——? is a sort of question that has not been asked in these studies. As a result, I shall have to proceed in terms of what seem to me to be plausible assumptions. Cultural anthropology seems to promise more, but it too (at least to the untrained eye) operates without a detailed analysis of the concept of social distance. See, for example, the interesting material in L. Bonaman and P. Bonaman, *The Tiv of Central Nigeria* (London: International African Institute, 1953), pp. 25–30 and J. Middleton, *The Lugbara of Uganda* (New York: Holt, Rinehart and Winston, 1965), Ch. 4.
3. See, for example, A. Gouldner, "The norm of reciprocity: A preliminary statement," *American Sociological Review* 25 (1960), pp. 161–78.
4. The return of bad for bad is a much more complex matter.
5. The "other things being equal" clause is crucial here. After all, the interactions in hand-to-hand combat are direct and immediate. And though there is sometimes a bond between enemies that could conceivably be described as "closeness," its relation to social distance as I am using the term is certainly not an easy one to explicate.
6. It is worth noting that *affection* between the parties is not necessarily involved at all. Affection is one sort of "closeness" in relationships, but not the only sort. See, for example, H. M. Hacker, "Women as a minority group," *Social Forces* 30 (1951), pp. 60–69.

JAMES RACHELS

Darwin, Species, and Morality

The idea that Darwinism undermines religion is, of course, familiar, even though it is by no means obvious how it does so. I will not discuss the relation between Darwinism and religion. Instead I will focus on the other, less well-explored idea: that Darwinism also undermines some aspects of traditional morality. Traditional morality depends, at crucial points, on the assumption that there is something morally special about being human—the fact that a being is human, rather than, say, canine or bovine, makes a big difference, according to traditional morality, in how it may be treated. My thesis is that "the gradual illumination of men's minds," of the sort provided by Darwin's theory, must lead inevitably to the conclusion that this assumption is false. . . .

Is the fact that a being is a member of a certain species, in and of itself, a morally good reason for treating it in a certain way? Is the fact that a being is *human* a reason for treating it with greater consideration than is given members of other species? There are (at least) three possible answers.

1. *Unqualified Speciesism.* First it might be held that mere species alone is morally important. On this view, the bare fact that an individual is

James Rachels teaches philosophy at the University of Alabama at Birmingham. His most recent book is *The Elements of Moral Philosophy* (Random House, 1987).

a member of a certain species, unsupplemented by any other consideration, is enough to make a difference in how that individual should be treated.

This is not a very plausible way of understanding the relation between species and morality, and generally it is not accepted even by those who are sympathetic to what I am calling "traditional morality." Consider, for example, the old science-fiction story "The Teacher from Mars" by Eando Binder.[1] The main character is a Martian who has come to earth to teach in a school for boys. Because he is "different"—seven feet tall, thin, with tentacles and leathery skin—he is taunted and abused by the students until he is almost driven out. Then, however, an act of heroism makes the boys realize they have been wrong, and the story ends happily with the ringleader of the bullies vowing to mend his ways.

Written in 1941, the story is a not-so-thinly-disguised morality tale about racism. But the explicit point concerns species, not race.[2] The teacher from Mars is portrayed as being, psychologically, exactly like a human: he is equally as intelligent and equally as sensitive, with just the same cares and interests as anyone else. The only difference is that he has a different kind of body. And surely *that* does not justify treating him with less respect. Having appreciated this point, the reader is then expected to draw the obvious conclusion: the fact that there are physical differences between whites and blacks—skin color, for example—should make no moral difference either.

However, it has been suggested by some philosophers that species alone *can* make a difference in our moral duties toward a being. In his review of Tom Regan's *The Case for Animal Rights*,[3] Robert Nozick speculates that, in a satisfactory moral scheme,

> . . . perhaps it will turn out that the bare species characteristic of simply being human . . . will command special respect only from other humans—this is an instance of the general principle that the members of any species may legitimately give their fellows more weight than they give members of other species (or at least more weight than a neutral view would grant them). Lions, too, if they were moral agents, could not then be criticized for putting other lions first.[4]

Nozick illustrates the point with his own science-fiction example: "denizens of Alpha Centauri" would be justified in giving greater weight to the interests of other such Alpha Centaurians than they give to our interests, he says, even if we were like them in all other relevant respects. But this isn't at all obvious—in fact, it seems wrong on its face. If we substitute an Alpha Centaurian for a Martian in Binder's story, it makes no difference. Treating him less well because he is "different" (in this case, a member of a different species) still seems like unjustified discrimination.

What of the "general principle" Nozick suggests? It seems to be an expanded version of something that most people find plausible—namely, that one is justified in giving special weight to the interests of one's family or neighbors. If it is permissible to have special regard for family or neighbors, why not one's fellow species-members? The problem with this way of thinking is that there are lots of groups to which one naturally belongs, and these group-memberships are not always (if they are ever) morally significant. The progression from family to neighbor to species passes through other boundaries on the way—through the boundary of race, for example. Suppose it were suggested that we are justified in giving the interests of our own race greater weight than the interests of other races? (Blacks, too, it might be said, could not then be criticized for putting other blacks first.) This would rightly be resisted, but the case for distinguishing by species alone is little better. As Binder's story suggests, unqualified speciesism and racism are twin doctrines.

2. *Qualified Speciesism.* But there is a more sophisticated view of the relation between morality and species, and it is this view that defenders of traditional morality most often adopt. On this view, species alone is not regarded as morally significant. However, species-membership is correlated with *other* differences that *are* significant. Humans, it might be said, are in a special moral category because they are rational, autonomous agents. (Other special human qualities are sometimes mentioned, but, at least since Kant, this one has been most popular.) It is this fact, rather than the "mere" fact that they are human, that qualifies them for special consideration. This is why their interests are more important, morally speaking, than the interests of other species, although, presumably, if the members of any other species were rational, autonomous agents, they would also go into the special moral category and would qualify for the favored treatment. However, defenders of traditional morality insist that, as a matter of fact, no other species has this characteristic. So humans alone are entitled to full moral consideration.

Darwin . . . resisted the idea that humans have characteristics that are not shared by other animals. Instead he emphasized the continuities between species: if humans are more rational than the apes, it is only a matter of degree, not of kind. But let us set this point aside, and grant for the purpose of argument that humans are the only fully rational, autonomous agents. What would follow from this assumption? I want to make two comments.

(a) The first comment has to do with the logical structure of qualified speciesism. It is important to see *exactly* what function the reference to man's rationality is supposed to serve. The reference to rationality comes at a certain point in the discussion of morality and species and has a certain purpose. Let us see what that purpose is.

The discussion begins with the observation that we use nonhuman animals in a variety of ways: to name a few, we raise and eat them as food;

we use them in laboratories, not only for medical and psychological experiments, but to test products such as soap and cosmetics; we dissect them in classrooms for educational purposes; we use their skins as clothing, rugs, and wall decoration; we make them objects of our amusement in zoos, circuses, and rodeos; we use them as work animals on farms; we keep them as pets; and we have a popular sport that consists of tracking them down and killing them for the pleasure of it.

Next, it is noted that we would think it deeply immoral if *humans* were used in any of these ways. But this leads to a problem. Ever since Aristotle it has been recognized as a fundamental rule of moral reasoning that:

> When individuals are treated differently, we need to be able to point to a difference between them that justifies the difference in treatment.

Thus we have to face this question: what is the difference between humans and nonhumans that justifies us in treating nonhumans so differently?

That is where the reference to rationality comes in. Qualified speciesism attempts to answer this question by pointing to the fact that humans are rational, autonomous agents, while the other animals are not—*that* is what is supposed to justify treating nonhumans differently.

But now notice this crucial point: we treat nonhumans in a *variety* of ways in which we think it would be wrong to treat humans. In the attempt to justify this, qualified speciesism mentions *one* difference between humans and nonhumans. Will this work? Is the fact that humans are rational, while other animals are not, relevant to *all* the differences in treatment?

As a general rule, relevant differences vary with the different kinds of treatment. A difference between individuals that justifies *one* sort of difference in treatment might be completely irrelevant to justifying *another* difference in treatment. Suppose, for example, the admissions committee of a law school accepts one applicant but rejects another. Asked to justify this, they might explain that the first applicant had excellent college grades and test scores, while the second applicant had a miserable record. Or, to take a different sort of example, suppose a doctor treats two patients differently: he gives one a shot of penicillin, and puts the other's arm in a plaster cast. Again, this can be justified by pointing to a relevant difference between them: the first patient had an infection while the second had a broken arm.

Now, suppose we switch things around. Suppose the law school admissions committee is asked to justify admitting A while rejecting B and replies that A had an infection but B had a broken arm. Or suppose the doctor is asked to justify giving A a shot of penicillin while putting B's arm in a cast and replies that A had better college grades and test scores. Both replies are, of course, silly, for it is clear that what is relevant in the one context is irrelevant in the other.

We might express this point in a general principle:

Whether a difference between individuals justifies a difference in treatment depends on the kind of treatment that is in question. A difference that justifies one kind of difference in treatment need not justify another.

Once this is made explicit, this principle seems obvious and indisputable. But once it is accepted, qualified speciesism is seen to be untenable.

Does the fact that someone is a rational, autonomous agent make a difference in how he should be treated? Certainly it may. For such a being, the self-direction of his own life is a great good, valued not only for its instrumental worth but for its own sake. Thus paternalistic interference may be seen as an evil. To take a simple example: a woman might have a certain conception of how she wants to live her life. This conception might involve taking risks that we think are foolish. We might therefore try to change her mind; we might call attention to the risks and argue that they are not worth it. But suppose she does not accept our arguments: are we then justified in forcibly preventing her from living her life as she chooses? It may be argued that we are not justified, for she is, after all, a rational, autonomous agent. But suppose we contrast this with how we may treat someone who is *not* a rational being—a small child, for example. Then we feel perfectly justified in interfering with his conduct, to prevent him from taking foolish risks. The fact that the child is not (yet, anyway) a fully rational agent justifies us in treating him differently from the way we would treat someone who is a fully rational agent.

The same would be true if the comparison were between a (normal adult) human being and a nonhuman animal. If we forcibly intervened to protect the animal from danger but did not do so for the human, we might justify this by pointing to the fact that the human is a rational, autonomous being, who knew what she was doing and who had the right to make her own choice, while this was not true of the animal. But this difference is not relevant to justifying just *any* kind of difference in treatment. Suppose what is in question is not paternalistic interference, but putting chemicals in rabbits' eyes to test the "safety" of a new shampoo. Why, it might be asked, is it all right to treat rabbits in this way, when we would not treat humans similarly? To reply that humans are rational agents, while rabbits are not, is comparable to noting that the rejected law-school applicant had a broken arm rather than an infection.

Therefore, the observation that humans are rational agents cannot justify the whole range of differences between our treatment of humans and our treatment of nonhumans. It can (at best) justify *some* differences in treatment, but not others. So, as a justification of our general practice of treating nonhumans "differently," qualified speciesism fails.

It might be thought that qualified speciesism could be saved by mentioning a bigger set of differences between humans and nonhumans. Rickaby, for example, points out that "Man alone speaks, man alone worships, man alone hopes to contemplate for ever," and so on.[5] Couldn't a *combination* of such unique characteristics justify placing humans in a special moral category? The logical problem, however, would remain: we would have to ask, for each kind of treatment, whether human's ability to speak, to worship, or to hope for eternal contemplation is really relevant. What do these things have to do with putting chemicals in a rabbit's eyes? Just as there is no one difference between the species that can justify all the differences in treatment, there is no reason to think that a list of such differences could do the job, either.

(b) A different sort of problem is raised by those people who lack the characteristics that supposedly place humans in a privileged moral position. Qualified speciesism says that the interests of humans count for more because they are rational agents. But some humans, perhaps because they have suffered brain damage, are not rational agents. Granting this, the natural conclusion would be that their status is the status of mere animals and that they may be used as nonhuman animals are used (perhaps as laboratory subjects, or as food?).

Of course, traditional moralists do not accept any such conclusion. The interests of humans are regarded as important no matter what their "handicaps" might be. The traditional view is, apparently, that moral status is determined by what is normal for the species. Therefore, because rationality is the norm, even nonrational humans are to be treated with the respect due to the members of a rational species.

This idea—that how individuals should be treated is determined by what is normal for their species—has a certain appeal, because it does seem to express our moral intuition about defective humans. "We should not treat a person worse merely because he has been so unfortunate," we might say about someone who has suffered brain damage. But the idea will not bear close inspection. Suppose (what is probably impossible) that a chimpanzee learned to read and speak English. And suppose he eventually was able to converse about science, literature, and morals. Finally he wants to attend university classes. Now there might be various arguments about whether to permit this, but suppose someone argued as follows: "Only humans should be allowed to attend these classes. Humans can read, talk, and understand science. Chimps cannot." But this chimp *can* do those things. "Yes, but *normal* chimps cannot, and that is what matters." Is this a good argument? Regardless of what other arguments might be persuasive, *this* one is weak. It assumes that we should determine how an individual is to be treated, not on the basis of *its* qualities, but on the basis of *other* individuals' qualities. This chimp is not permitted to do something that requires reading, despite the fact that he can read, because other chimps cannot. That seems not only unfair, but irrational.

3. Moral Individualism. All this argues for a quite different approach, one that abandons the whole project of trying to justify a "separate moral category" for humans. On this approach, how an individual may be treated is determined not by considering his group memberships but by considering his own particular characteristics. If A is to be treated differently from B, the justification must be in terms of A's individual characteristics and B's individual characteristics. Treating them differently cannot be justified by pointing out that one or the other is a member of some preferred group.

Where does this leave the relation between species and morality? What of the important differences between humans and other animals? Are they now to be considered irrelevant? The picture that emerges is more complex, but also more true to the facts, than traditional morality. The fact is that human beings are not simply "different" from other animals. In reality, there is a complex pattern of similarities and differences. The matching moral idea is that insofar as a human and a member of another species are similar, they should be treated similarly, while to the extent that they are different, they should be treated differently. This will allow the human to assert a right to better treatment whenever there is some difference between him and other animals (or other humans!) that justifies treating him better. But it will *not* permit him to claim greater rights simply because he is human, or because humans in general have some quality that he lacks, or because he has some characteristic that is irrelevant to the particular type of treatment in question.

There is a striking parallel between this moral individualism and Darwin's view about the nature of species. Before Darwin, when species were thought to be immutable, naturalists believed that membership in a species was determined by whether the organism possessed the qualities that defined the *essence* of the species. This essence was something real and determinate, fixed by nature itself, and the systems of classification devised by biologists were viewed as accurate or inaccurate depending on how well they corresponded to this fixed order of nature. Evolutionary biology implies a very different view. Darwin argued that there are no fixed essences; there is only a multitude of organisms that resemble one another in some ways but differ in others. The only reality is the individual.[6] How those individuals are grouped—into species, varieties, and so on—is more or less arbitrary. In *The Origin of Species* he wrote:

> I look at the term species, as one arbitrarily given for the sake of convenience to a set of individuals closely resembling each other, and that it does not essentially differ from the term variety, which is given to less distinct and more fluctuating forms. The term variety, again, in comparison with mere individual differences, is also applied arbitrarily, and for mere convenience sake.[7]

Thus Darwinian biology substitutes individual organisms, with their profusion of similarities and differences, for the old idea of determinate species; while moral individualism substitutes the view that our treatment of those organisms must be sensitive to those similarities and differences, for the old view that what matters is the species to which the organism belongs.

How does "the gradual illumination of men's minds," of the sort provided by Darwin's theory, lead to the rejection of speciesism? We might think of it as a historical process that has four stages.

In the first stage, traditional morality is comfortably accepted because it is supported by a world-view in which everyone (or, so nearly everyone as makes no difference) has confidence. The moral view is simple. Human beings, as Kant put it, have "an intrinsic worth, i.e., *dignity*," which makes them valuable "above all price"; while other animals "are there merely as means to an end. That end is man."[8] The world-view that supported this ethical doctrine had several familiar elements: the universe, with the earth at its center, was seen as created by God primarily to provide a home for humans, who were made in his image. The other animals were created by God for their use. Humans, therefore, are set apart from other animals and have a radically different *nature*. This justifies their special moral standing.

In the second stage, the world-view begins to break up. This had begun to happen, of course, long before Darwin—it was already known, for example, that the earth is not the center of the cosmos and, indeed, that considered as a celestial body it seems to be nothing special. But Darwin completed the job, by showing that humans, far from being set apart from the other animals, are part of the same natural order and, indeed, are actually kin to them. By the time Darwin was done, the old world-view was virtually demolished.

This did not mean, however, that the associated moral view would be immediately abandoned. Firmly established moral doctrines do not lose their grip overnight, sometimes not even overcentury. As Peter Singer observed, "If the foundations of an ideological position are knocked out from under it, new foundations will be found, or else the ideological position will just hang there, defying the logical equivalent of the law of gravity."[9]

We are now in the third stage, which comes when people realize that, having lost its foundation, the old moral view needs to be reexamined. In his review of Regan's book Nozick remarked that "Nothing much should be inferred from our not presently having a theory of the moral importance of species membership that no one has spent much time trying to formulate because the issue hasn't seemed pressing."[10] The issue hasn't seemed pressing because philosophers have not yet fully assimilated the implications of the collapse of the old world view.

It still might turn out that traditional morality is defensible, if new support can be found for it. Nozick, and a host of others, think this is likely. Philosophers such as Singer and Regan take a different view: "the gradual illumination of men's minds" must lead to a new ethic, in which species membership is seen as relatively unimportant. For the reasons given above, I think that on this broad issue the revisionists are right. The most defensible view seems to be some form of moral individualism, according to which what matters is the individual characteristics of organisms and not the classes to which they are assigned. Whatever the outcome of the debate, the issue can no longer be avoided. What has made it pressing is not simply a faddish interest taken by some philosophers in animal welfare; rather, it is an issue pressed upon us by the disintegration of the pre-Darwinian way of understanding nature. The fourth and final stage of the historical process will be reached if and when a new equilibrium is found in which our morality can once again comfortably co-exist with our understanding of the world and our place in it.

NOTES

1. The story is included in *My Best Science Fiction Story,* edited by Leo Marguiles and Oscar J. Friend (New York: Pocket Books, 1954).
2. It's an interesting twist: today, writers such as Singer take it for granted that racism is wrong, and argue by analogy that speciesism is wrong also; whereas in 1941 Binder took it as obvious that speciesism was wrong, and expected his readers to get the point that racism was wrong. See Peter Singer, *Animal Liberation* (New York: New York Review Books, 1975), ch. 1.
3. Tom Regan, *The Case for Animal Rights* (Berkeley: University of California Press, 1983).
4. Robert Nozick, "About Mammals and People," *The New York Times Book Review,* November 27, 1983, p. 29. For a fuller discussion of Nozick's arguments, see my *The End of Life: Euthanasia and Morality* (Oxford: Oxford University Press, 1986), ch. 4.
5. Father Joseph Rickaby, S. J., *Moral Philosophy* (1901), "Ethics and Natural Law."
6. For the pre-Darwinian naturalist, variations were of little interest, except as curiosities. It was, after all, the "standard" specimen that best represented the eternal essence of the species, which the naturalist was trying to learn about. But for the evolutionary biologist, variation is the very stuff of nature—it is what makes natural selection possible.
7. *The Origin of Species* (London: John Murray, 1859), p. 53. For a recent defense of the idea that there are several equally valid ways species might be identified, each serving a different legitimate need of biologists, see Philip Kitcher, "Species," *Philosophy of Science,* vol. 51 (1984), pp. 308–333.
8. Immanuel Kant, *Foundations of the Metaphysics of Morals,* translated by Lewis White Beck (Indianapolis: Bobbs-Merrill, 1959), p. 47; and *Lectures on Ethics,* translated by Louis Infield (New York: Harper and Row, 1963), pp. 239–240.
9. Peter Singer, *Animal Liberation* op. cit., p. 231.
10. Robert Nozick, op. cit., p. 29.

PART FOUR
Animal Rights

TOM REGAN

The Case
for Animal Rights

How to proceed? We begin by asking how the moral status of animals has been understood by thinkers who deny that animals have rights. Then we test the mettle of their ideas by seeing how well they stand up under the heat of fair criticism. If we start our thinking in this way, we soon find that some people believe that we have no duties directly to animals, that we owe nothing to them, that we can do nothing that wrongs them. Rather, we can do wrong acts that involve animals, and so we have duties regarding them, though none to them. Such views may be called *indirect duty views*. By way of illustration: suppose your neighbor kicks your dog. Then your neighbor has done something wrong. But not to your dog. The wrong that has been done is a wrong to you. After all, it is wrong to upset people, and your neighbor's kicking your dog upsets you. So you are the one who is wronged, not your dog. Or again: by kicking your dog your neighbor damages your

Tom Regan teaches philosophy at North Carolina State University. Among his most recent books are (with Andrew Linzey) *Animals and Christianity: A Book of Readings* (Crossroads, 1988) and *Bloomsbury's Prophet; G. E. Moore and the Development of His Moral Philosophy* (Temple University Press, 1986).

Reprinted by permission from *In Defense of Animals*, Basil Blackwell, Oxford, England. Paper presented at the national conference, "Animals and Humans: Ethical Perspectives," Moorhead State University, Moorhead, MN, April 21–23, 1986.

property. And since it is wrong to damage another person's property, your neighbor has done something wrong—to you, of course, not to your dog. Your neighbor no more wrongs your dog than your car would be wronged if the windshield were smashed. Your neighbor's duties involving your dog are indirect duties to you. More generally, all of our duties regarding animals are indirect duties to one another—to humanity.

How could someone try to justify such a view? Someone might say that your dog doesn't feel anything and so isn't hurt by your neighbor's kick, doesn't care about the pain since none is felt, is as unaware of anything as is your windshield. Someone might say this, but no rational person will, since, among other considerations, such a view will commit anyone who holds it to the position that no human beings feel pain either—that human beings also don't care about what happens to them. A second possibility is that though both humans and your dog are hurt when kicked, it is only human pain that matters. But, again, no rational person can believe this. Pain is pain wherever it occurs. If your neighbor's causing you pain is wrong because of the pain that is caused, we cannot rationally ignore or dismiss the moral relevance of the pain that your dog feels.

Philosophers who hold indirect duty views—and many still do—have come to understand that they must avoid the two defects just noted: that is, both the view that animals don't feel anything as well as the idea that only human pain can be morally relevant. Among such thinkers the sort of view now favored is one or another form of what is called *contractarianism*.

Here, very crudely, is the root idea: morality consists of a set of rules that individuals voluntarily agree to abide by, as we do when we sign a contract (hence the name contractarianism). Those who understand and accept the terms of the contract are covered directly; they have rights created and recognized by, and protected in, the contract. And these contractors can also have protection spelled out for others who, though they lack the ability to understand morality and so cannot sign the contract themselves, are loved or cherished by those who can. Thus young children, for example, are unable to sign contracts and lack rights. But they are protected by the contract nonetheless because of the sentimental interests of others, most notably their parents. So we have, then, duties involving these children, duties regarding them, but no duties to them. Our duties in their case are indirect duties to other human beings, usually their parents.

As for animals, since they cannot understand contracts, they obviously cannot sign; and since they cannot sign, they have no rights. Like children, however, some animals are the object of the sentimental interest of others. You, for example, love your dog or cat. So those animals that enough people care about (companion animals, whales, baby seals, the American bald eagle), though they lack rights themselves, will be protected because of the sentimental interests of people. I have, then, according to contractarianism, no duty directly to your dog or any other animal, not even the duty not to cause them pain or suffering; my duty not to hurt them is a duty I have to those people who care about what happens to them. As for other animals, where no or little sentimental interest is present—in the case of farm animals, for example, or laboratory rats—what duties we have grow weaker and weaker, perhaps to the vanishing point. The pain and death they endure, though real, are not wrong if no one cares about them.

When it comes to the moral status of animals, contractarianism could be a hard view to refute if it were an adequate theoretical approach to the moral status of human beings. It is not adequate in this latter respect, however, which makes the question of its adequacy in the former case, regarding animals, utterly moot. For consider: morality, according to the (crude) contractarian position before us, consists of rules that people agree to abide by. What people? Well, enough to make a difference—enough, that is, *collectively* to have the power to enforce the rules that are drawn up in the contract. That is very well and good for the signatories but not so good for anyone who is not asked to sign. And there is nothing in contractarianism of the sort we are discussing that guarantees or requires that everyone will have a chance to participate equally in framing rules of morality. The result is that this approach to ethics could sanction the most blatant forms of social, economic, moral, and political injustice, ranging from a repressive caste system to systematic racial or sexual discrimination. Might, according to this theory, does make right. Let those who are the victims of injustice suffer as they will. It matters not so long as no one else—no contractor, or too few of them—cares about it. Such a theory takes one's moral breath away . . . as if, for example, there would be nothing wrong with apartheid in South Africa if few white South Africans were upset by it. A theory with so little to recommend it at the level of the ethics of our treatment of our fellow humans cannot have anything more to recommend it when it comes to the ethics of how we treat our fellow animals.

The version of contractarianism just examined is, as I have noted, a crude variety, and in fairness to those of a contractarian persuasion, it must be noted that much more refined, subtle, and ingenious varieties are possible. For example, John Rawls, in his *A Theory of Justice*, sets forth a version of contractarianism that forces contractors to ignore the accidental features of being a human being—for example, whether one is white or black, male or female, a genius or of modest intellect. Only by ignoring such features, Rawls believes, can we ensure that the principles of justice that contractors would agree upon are not based on bias or prejudice. Despite the improvement a view such as Rawls's represents over the cruder forms of contractarianism, it remains deficient: it systematically denies that we have direct duties to those human beings who do not have a sense of justice—young children, for instance, and many mentally retarded humans. And yet it seems reasonably certain that, were we to torture a young child or a retarded elder, we would be doing something that wronged him or her, not something that would be wrong if (and only if) other humans with a sense of justice were upset. And since this is true in the case of these humans, we cannot rationally deny the same in the case of animals.

Indirect duty views, then, including the best among them, fail to command our rational assent. Whatever ethical theory we should accept rationally, therefore, it must at least recognize that we have some duties directly to animals, just as we have some duties directly to each other. The next two theories I'll sketch attempt to meet this requirement.

The first I call the cruelty-kindness view. Simply stated, this says that we have a direct duty to be kind to animals and a direct duty not to be cruel to them. Despite the familiar, reassuring ring of these ideas, I do not believe that this view offers an adequate theory. To make this clearer, consider kindness. A kind person acts from a certain type of motive —compassion or concern, for example. And that is a virtue. But there is no guarantee that a kind act is a right act. If I am a generous racist, for example, I will be inclined to act kindly towards members of my own race, favoring their interests above those of others. My kindness would be real and, so far as it goes, good. But I trust it is too obvious to require argument that my kind acts may not be above moral reproach—may, in fact, be positively wrong because rooted in injustice. So kindness, notwithstanding its status as a virtue to be encouraged, simply will not carry the weight of a theory of right action.

Cruelty fares no better. People or their acts are cruel if they display either a lack of sympathy for or, worse, the presence of enjoyment in another's suffering. Cruelty in all its guises is a bad thing, a tragic human failing. But just as a person's being motivated by kindness does not guarantee that he or she does what is right, so the absence of cruelty does not ensure that he or she avoids doing what is wrong. Many people who perform abortions, for example, are not cruel, sadistic people. But that fact alone does not settle the terribly difficult question of the morality of abortion. The case is no different when we examine the ethics of our treatment of animals. So, yes, let us be for kindness and against cruelty. But let us not suppose that being for the one and against the other answers questions about moral right and wrong.

Some people think that the theory we are looking for is *utilitarianism.* A utilitarian accepts two moral principles. The first is that of equality: everyone's interests count, and similar interests must be counted as having similar weight or importance. White or black, American or Iranian, human or animal—everyone's pain or frustration matters, and matters just as much as the equivalent pain or frustration of anyone else. The second principle a utilitarian accepts is that of utility: do the act that will bring about the best balance between satisfaction and frustration for everyone affected by the outcome.

As a utilitarian, then, here is how I am to approach the task of deciding what I morally ought to do: I must ask who will be affected if I choose to do one thing rather than another, how much each individual will be affected, and where the best results are most likely to lie—which option, in other words, is most likely to bring about the best results, the best balance between satisfaction and frustration. That option, whatever it may be, is the one I ought to choose. That is where my moral duty lies.

The great appeal of utilitarianism rests with its uncompromising *egalitarianism:* everyone's interests count and count as much as the like interests of everyone else. The kind of odious discrimination that some forms of contractarianism can justify—discrimination based on race or sex, for example—seems disallowed in principle by utilitarianism, as is speciesism, systematic discrimination based on species membership.

The equality we find in utilitarianism, however, is not the sort an advocate of animal or human rights should have in mind. Utilitarianism has no room for the equal rights of different individuals because it has no room for their equal inherent value or worth. What has value for the utilitarian is the satisfaction of an individual's interests, not the individual whose interests they are. A universe in which you satisfy your desire for water, food, and warmth is, other things being equal, better than a universe in which these desires are frustrated. And the same is true in the case of an animal with similar desires. But neither you nor the animal have any value in your own right. Only your feelings do.

Here is an analogy to help make the philosophical point clearer: a cup contains different liquids, sometimes sweet, sometimes bitter, sometimes a mixture of the two. What has value are the liquids: the sweeter the better, the bitterer the worse. The cup, the container, has no value. It is what goes into it, not what they go into, that has value. For the utilitarian, you and I are like the cup; we have no value as individuals and thus no equal value. What has value is what goes into us, what we serve as receptacles for; our feelings of satisfaction have positive value, our feelings of frustration negative value.

Serious problems arise for utilitarianism when we remind ourselves that it enjoins us to bring about the best consequences. What does this mean? It doesn't mean the best consequences for me alone, or for my family or friends, or any other person taken individually. No, what we must do is, roughly, as follows: we must add up (somehow!) the separate satisfactions and frustrations of everyone likely to be affected by our choice, the satisfactions in one column, the frustrations in the other. We must total each column for each of the options before us. That is what it means to say the theory is aggregative. And then we must choose that option which is most likely to bring about the best balance of totalled satisfactions over totalled frustrations. Whatever act would lead to this outcome is the one we ought morally to perform—it is where our moral duty lies. And that act quite clearly might not be the same one that would bring about the best results for me personally, or for my family or friends, or for a lab animal. The best aggregated consequences for everyone concerned are not necessarily the best for each individual.

That utilitarianism is an aggregative theory—different individuals' satisfactions or frustrations are added, or summed, or totalled—is the key objection to this theory. My Aunt Bea is old, inactive, a cranky, sour person, though not physically ill. She prefers to go on living. She is also rather rich, I could make a fortune if I could get my hands on her money, money she intends to give me in any event, after she dies, but which she refuses to give me now. In order to avoid a huge tax bite, I plan to donate a handsome sum of my profits to a local children's hospital. Many, many children will benefit from my generosity, and much joy will be brought to their parents, relatives, and friends. If I don't get the money rather soon, all these ambitions will come to naught. The once-in-a-lifetime opportunity to make a real killing will be gone. Why, then, not kill my Aunt Bea? Oh, of course I *might* get caught. But I'm no fool and, besides, her doctor can be counted on to cooperate (he has an eye for the same investment and I happen to know a good deal about his shady past). The deed can be done . . . professionally, shall we say. There is *very* little chance of getting caught. And as for my conscience being guiltridden, I am a resourceful sort of fellow and will take more than sufficient comfort—as I lie on the beach at Acapulco—in contemplating the joy and health I have brought to so many others.

Suppose Aunt Bea is killed and the rest of the story comes out as told. Would I have done anything wrong? Anything immoral? One would have thought that I had. Not according to utilitarianism. Since what I have done has brought about the best balance between totalled satisfaction and frustration for all those affected by the outcome, my action is not wrong. Indeed, in killing Aunt Bea the physician and I did what duty required.

This same kind of argument can be repeated in all sorts of cases, illustrating, time after time, how the utilitarian's position leads to results that impartial people find morally callous. It *is* wrong to kill my Aunt Bea in the name of bringing about the best results for others. A good end does not justify an evil means. Any adequate moral theory will have to explain why this is so. Utilitarianism fails in this respect and so cannot be the theory we seek.

What to do? Where to begin anew? The place to begin, I think, is with the utilitarian's view of the value of the individual—or, rather, the lack of value. In its place, suppose we consider that you and I, for example, do have value as individuals—what we'll call *inherent value*. To say we have such value is to say that we are something more than, something different from, mere receptacles. Moreover, to ensure that we do not pave the way for such injustices as slavery or sexual discrimination, we must believe that all who have inherent value have it equally, regardless of their sex, race, religion, birthplace, and so on. Similarly to be discarded as irrelevant are one's talents or skills, intelligence and wealth, personality or pathology, whether one is loved and admired or despised and loathed. The genius and the retarded child, the prince and the pauper, the brain surgeon and the fruit vendor, Mother Teresa and the most unscrupulous used-car salesman—all have inherent value, all possess it equally, and all have an equal right to be treated with respect, to be treated in ways that do not reduce them to the status of things, as if they existed as resources for others. My value as an individual is independent of my usefulness to you. Yours is not dependent on your usefulness to me. For either of us to treat the other in ways that fail to show respect for the other's independent value is to act immorally, to violate the individual's rights.

Some of the rational virtues of this view—what I call the *rights view*—should be evident. Unlike (crude) contractarianism, for example, the rights view in *principle* denies the moral tolerability of any and all forms of racial, sexual, or social discrimination; and unlike utilitarianism, the view in *principle* denies that we can justify good results by using evil means that violate an individual's rights—denies, for example, that it could be moral to kill my Aunt Bea to harvest beneficial consequences for others. That would be to sanction the disrespectful treatment of the individual in the name of the social good, something the rights view will not—categorically will not—ever allow.

The rights view, I believe, is rationally the most satisfactory moral theory. It surpasses all other theories in the degree to which it illuminates and explains the foundation of our duties to one another—the domain of human morality. On this score it has the best reasons, the best arguments, on its side. Of course, if it were possible to show that only human beings are included within its scope, then a person like myself, who believes in animal rights, would be obliged to look elsewhere.

But attempts to limit its scope to humans only can be shown to be rationally defective. Animals, it is true, lack many of the abilities humans possess. The can't read, do higher mathematics, build a bookcase, or make *baba ghanoush*. Neither can many human beings, however, and yet we don't (and shouldn't) say that they (these humans) therefore have less inherent value, less of a right to be treated with respect, than do others. It is the *similarities* between those human beings who most clearly, most noncontroversially have such value (the people reading this, for example), not our differences, that matter most. And the really crucial, the basic similarity is simply this: we are each of us the experiencing subject of a life, a conscious creature having an individual welfare that has importance to us whatever our usefulness to others. We want and prefer things, believe and feel things, recall and expect things. And all these dimensions of our life, including our pleasure and pain, our enjoyment and suffering, our satisfaction and frustration, our continued existence or our untimely death—all make a difference to the quality of our life as lived, as experienced, by us as individuals. As the same is true of those animals that concern us (the ones that are eaten and trapped, for example), they too must be viewed as the experiencing subjects of a life, with inherent value of their own.

Some there are who resist the idea that animals have inherent value. "Only humans have such value," they profess. How might this narrow view be defended? Shall we say that only humans have the requisite intelligence, or autonomy, or reason? But there are many, many humans who fail to meet these standards and yet are reasonably viewed as having value above and beyond their usefulness to others. Shall we claim that only humans belong to the right species, the species *Homo sapiens?* But this is blatant speciesism. Will it be said, then, that all—and only—humans have immortal souls? Then our opponents have their work cut out for them. I am myself not ill-disposed to the proposition that there are immortal souls. Personally, I profoundly hope I have one. But I would not want to rest my position on a controversial ethical issue on the even more controversial question about who or what has an immortal soul. That is to dig one's hole deeper, not to climb out. Rationally, it is better to resolve moral issues without making more controversial assumptions than are needed. The question of who has inherent value is such a question, one that is resolved more rationally without the introduction of the idea of immortal souls than by its use.

Well, perhaps some will say that animals have some inherent value, only less than we have. Once again, however, attempts to defend this view can be shown to lack rational justification. What could be the basis of our having more inherent value than animals? Their lack of reason, or autonomy, or intellect? Only if we are willing to make the same judgment in the case of humans who are similarly deficient. But it is not true that such humans—the retarded child, for example, or the mentally deranged—have less inherent value than you or I. Neither, then, can we rationally sustain the view that animals like them in being the experiencing subjects of a life have less inherent value. *All* who have inherent value have it *equally*, whether they be human animals or not.

Inherent value, then, belongs equally to those who are the experiencing subjects of a life. Whether it belongs to others—to rocks and rivers, trees and glaciers, for example—we do not know and may never know. But neither do we need to know, if we are to make the case for animal rights. We do not need to know, for example, how many people are eligible to vote in the next presidential election before we can know whether I am. Similarly, we do not need to know how many individuals have inherent value before we can know that some do. When it comes to the case for animal rights, then, what we need to know is whether the animals that, in our culture, are routinely eaten, hunted, and used in our laboratories, for example, are like us in being subjects of a life. And we do know this. We do know that many—literally, billions and billions—of these animals are the subjects of a life in the sense explained and so have inherent value if we do. And since, in order to arrive at the best theory of our duties to one another, we must recognize our equal inherent value as individuals, reason—not sentiment, not emotion—reason compels us to recognize the equal inherent value of these animals and, with this, their equal right to be treated with respect.

That, *very* roughly, is the shape and feel of the case for animal rights. Most of the details of the supporting argument are missing. They are to be found in the book that bears the same title as this essay.[1] Here, the details go begging, and I must, in closing, limit myself to two final points.

The first is how the theory that underlies the case for animal rights shows that the animal rights movement is a part of, not antagonistic to, the human rights movement. The theory that rationally grounds the rights of animals also grounds the rights of humans. Thus those involved in the animal rights movement are partners in the struggle to secure respect for human rights—the rights of women, for example, or minorities, or workers. The animal rights movement is cut from the same moral cloth as these.

Second, having set out the broad outlines of the rights view, I can now say why its implications for farming and science, among other fields, are both clear and uncompromising. In the case of the use of animals in science, the rights view is categorically abolitionist. Lab animals are not our tasters; we are not their kings. Because these animals are treated routinely, systematically as if their value were reducible to their usefulness to others, they are routinely, systematically treated with a lack of respect, and thus are their rights routinely, systematically violated. This is just as true when they are used in trivial, duplicative, unnecessary or unwise research as it is when they are used in studies that hold out real promise of human benefits. We can't justify harming or killing a human being (my Aunt Bea, for example) just for these sorts of reason. Neither can we do so even in the case of so lowly a creature as a laboratory rat. It is not just refinement or reduction that is called for, not just larger, cleaner cages, not just more generous use of anesthesia or the elimination of multiple surgery, not just tidying up the system. It is complete replacement. The best we can do when it comes to using animals in science is—not to use them. That is where our duty lies, according to the rights view.

As for commercial animal agriculture, the rights view takes a similar abolitionist position. The fundamental moral wrong here is not that animals are kept in stressful close confinement or in isolation, or that their pain and suffering, their needs and preferences are ignored or discounted. All these *are* wrong, of course, but they are not the fundamental wrong. They are symptoms and effects of the deeper, systematic wrong that allows these animals to be viewed and treated as lacking independent value, as resources for us—as, indeed, a renewable resource. Giving farm animals more space, more natural environments, more companions does not right the fundamental wrong, any more than giving lab animals more anesthesia or bigger, cleaner cages would right the fundamental wrong in their case. Nothing less than the total dissolution of commercial animal agriculture will do this, just as, for similar reasons I won't develop at length here, morality requires nothing less than the total elimination of hunting and trapping for commercial and sporting ends. The rights view's implications, then, as I have said, are clear and uncompromising.

NOTES

1. *The Case for Animal Rights* (Berkeley: University of California Press, 1983).

R. G. FREY

The Case
against Animal Rights

Regan is convinced that animals have *rights*. Of his rights view, he says
that 'of course, if it were possible to show that only human beings are
included within its scope, then a person like myself, who believes in
animal rights, would be obliged to look elsewhere'.[1] Presumably, Regan
so believes in animal *rights* that any theory whatever that failed to accord
them *rights* would, even if it condemned all the practices he condemned
and found wrong the maltreatment of animals, be unsatisfactory. It is
difficult to know, therefore, how arguments stand that try to weaken his
faith in the *rights* of animals. Are they as it were, bound to go awry, *a
priori?* I am unsure exactly how Regan would respond to such questions;
that is, I do not know what counts as, indeed, whether anything at all
counts as, a challenge to his intuitions on this score. In any event, nothing that follows turns upon Regan's intuition that animals have *rights*,
that they are rights-holders; *this* intuition, though I do not share it, is not
here at issue.

What *is* at issue is Regan's reliance upon variants of the argument
from marginal cases to *support* his claims. In each case, I do not believe
these variants do support his claims, do not believe, that is, that appeal to
the cases of defective humans does the work on behalf of animals that
Regan supposes it does.

First, then, there is Regan's claim of the equal inherent worth of human and animal life:

> Well, perhaps some will say that animals have some inherent value, only less than we have. Once again, however, attempts to defend this view can be shown to lack rational justification. What could be the basis of our having more inherent value than animals? Their lack of reason, or autonomy, or intellect? Only if we are willing to make the same judgment in the case of humans who are similarly deficient. But it is not true that such humans—the retarded child, for example, or the mentally deranged—have less inherent value than you or I.[2]

This affirmation turns entirely upon our agreeing that all human life, however deficient, has the same value; and I, as the reader will know, do not agree. For me, the value of life is a function of its quality, its quality a function of its richness, and its richness a function of its scope or potentiality for enrichment; and the fact is that many humans lead lives of a very much lower quality than ordinary normal lives, lives which lack enrichment and where the potentialities for enrichment are severely truncated or absent. If, then, we confront the fact that not all human life has, not merely the same enrichment, but also the same scope for enrichment, then it follows that not all human life has the same value. (Anyone who thinks that we do not use this argument in order to trade off lives of very low quality would do well to read some of the contributions by health care professionals to many of the contemporary debates in medical ethics over death and dying.) If not all human life has the same value, then Regan's claim of the equal inherent worth of animals collapses; for we do judge some human lives of less value than others.

Second, there is Regan's claim, not of equal inherent worth, but of inherent worth in the first place:

> Some there are who resist the idea that animals have inherent value. "Only humans have such value", they profess. How might this narrow view be defended? Shall we say that only humans have the requisite intelligence, or autonomy, or reason? But there are many, many humans who fail to meet these standards and yet are reasonably viewed as having value above and beyond their usefulness to others.[3]

Again, the case of deficient humans is being appealed to, this time to cede animal life inherent value at all. But I do not regard all human life as of equal value; I do not accept that a very severely mentally-enfeebled human or an elderly human fully in the grip of senile dementia or an infant born with only half a brain has a life whose value is equal to that of normal, adult humans. The quality of human life can plummet, to a point where we would not wish *that* life on even our worst enemies; and I see no reason to pretend that a life I would not wish upon even my worst enemies is nevertheless as valuable as the life of any normal, adult human. As the quality of human life falls, trade-offs between it and other things we value become possible; and if this is what one is going to mean by the phrase 'usefulness to others', then I see no reason to deny that that label can be applied to me and my views. (But so, too, can it be applied to countless other people. Regan's book is littered with warnings against utilitarianism; but any of the numerous textbooks on medical ethics now on offer will show in, e.g., their sections on death and dying that all kinds of people, utilitarians and non-utilitarians alike, are no longer prepared to concede all human life, irrespective of quality, equal value.) Accordingly, Regan's claim of the inherent worth of animals is compromised; for there are good reasons not to judge deficient human life either of equal value to normal, adult human life or, in extreme cases, even of much value at all.

By lives of not much value at all, I have in mind lives whose quality is so low that they are no longer worth living. I concede the difficulty of determining in many cases when a life is no longer worth living; but in other cases, including cases quite apart from those involving the irreversibly comatose, the matter seems far less problematic. Work recently done in Oxford by Ronald Dworkin on some of the policy implications of the prevalence of Altzheimer's disease leaves me in little doubt that a life wholly and irreversibly in the grip of senile dementia is a life not worth living; and the case of infants born without any brain whatever seems an even clearer instance.

Third, there is Regan's claim that attempts to limit the scope of his rights view to humans come unstuck:

> Animals, it is true, lack many of the abilities humans possess. They can't read, do higher mathematics, build a bookcase or make *baba ghanoush*. Neither can many human beings, however, and yet we don't (and shouldn't) say that they (these humans) therefore have less inherent value, less of a right to be treated with respect, than do others.[4]

Perhaps Regan is right, that a human who cannot build a bookcase does not *per se* have a less valuable life than other humans; but what about very severely mentally-enfeebled humans or elderly people fully in the grip of senile dementia or infants born without a brain? I think *these* lives have less value than ordinary human life. What is the difference between these cases and the bookcase example? It is that the inability to build a bookcase is unlikely, bizarre circumstances apart, drastically to affect the quality of one's life, whereas severe mental-enfeebledness, senile dementia, and the absence of a brain quite obviously have a seriously negative effect on the quality of life. But one need not go so far afield to find such negative effects: some of the patients in the final stages of AIDS come to the view, I gather, that life is no longer worth living, as first one illness and then another ravages their bodies.

A word on Regan's point about treating deficient humans with respect is necessary. He ties talk of respect in the passage above to some right to respect, without explaining what justifies this linkage; but the real problem is that the use of some right to respect in the present context begs the question. A doctor friend recently described to me the case of a very severely handicapped child who managed to be kept alive to the age of four through a series of eleven operations; the doctor's wife described the case as one of 'keeping the child alive long enough for nature to kill it', which nature duly did. How exactly does one show respect to this child? By yet another operation, to extend its life a few weeks longer? It is all well and good to advocate treating deficient humans with respect; in the absence of some statement in a particular case about what constitutes respect, however, such talk does not come to much. How, for example, does one show respect for an individual with AIDS, who has thought long and hard about suicide and decided to kill himself? By intervening and stopping him? Or by not intervening and permitting him to carry on?

NOTES

1. Tom Regan, "The Case for Animal Rights," in P. Singer (ed.), *In Defence of Animal Rights* (Oxford: Blackwell, 1985), p. 22.
2. *Ibid.*, p. 23.
3. *Ibid.*, p. 22.
4. *Ibid.*, p. 22; italics in original.

ALAN WHITE

Why Animals Cannot Have Rights

Most discussions about the kinds of things which can possess rights centre on the kinds of capacities either necessary or sufficient for their possible possession, whether it be interests, rationality, sentience, the ability to claim, etc. Advocates of the various capabilities are usually torn between making them so strong, for example rationality or the ability to sue, that they exclude subjects to which they wish to allow rights, whether they be children, the feeble-minded, unborn generations, etc., and making them so weak that they include almost anything, whether they be inanimate objects, artefacts, abstract conceptions etc.

I have tried to show that no criterion couched in terms of substantive characteristics is logically either sufficient or necessary in itself for the possible—or, indeed, the actual—possession of a right. What I would suggest is that such characteristics are at most a mark of a certain type of subject of which the question is whether that type of subject is logically capable of having a right. And the answer to that question depends on whether it is the sort of subject of which it makes sense to use what may be called "the full language of rights."

Alan White is Ferens Professor of Philosophy in the University of Hull. Among his books are *Truth* (Macmillan, 1970) and *Modal Thinking* (Blackwells, 1975).

White, A. (1984), *Rights*. Reprinted by permission of Oxford University Press.

A right is something which can be said to be exercised, earned, enjoyed, or given, which can be claimed,[1] demanded, asserted, insisted on, secured, waived, or surrendered; there can be a right to do so and so or have such and such done for one, to be in a certain state, to have a certain feeling or adopt a certain attitude. A right is related to and contrasted with a duty, an obligation, a privilege, a power, a liability. A possible possessor of a right is, therefore, whatever can properly be spoken of in such language; that is, whatever can intelligibly, whether truly or falsely, be said to exercise, earn, etc. a right, to have a right to such logically varied things, to have duties, privileges, etc. Furthermore, . . . a necessary condition of something's being capable of having a right to V is that it should be something which logically can V.

In the full language of "a right" only a *person* can logically have a right because only a person can be the subject of such predications. Rights are not the sorts of things of which non-persons can be the subjects, however right it may be to treat them in certain ways. Nor does this, as some contend, exclude infants, children, the feeble-minded, the comatose, the dead, or generations yet unborn.[2] Any of these may be for various reasons empirically unable to fulfil the full role of a right-holder. But so long as they are persons—and it is significant that we think and speak of them as young, feeble-minded, incapacitated, dead, unborn *persons*—they are logically possible subjects of rights to whom the full language of rights can significantly, however falsely, be used. It is a misfortune, not a tautology, that these persons cannot exercise or enjoy, claim, or waive, their rights or do their duty or fulfil their obligations. The law has always linked together the notions of a person and of the bearer of rights, duties, privileges, powers, liberties, liabilities, immunities, etc., so that a change in application of one notion has accompanied a parallel change in application of the other.[3] Thus, at various times in the law, gods, idols, unborn and dead human beings, animals, inanimate things, corporations, and governments, have been treated as persons because they were conceived as possible subjects of such jural relations as rights, duties, etc. who can commit or be the victims of torts and crimes. In Roman law slaves were things, not persons, and, hence, had no rights. The attitudes of various legal systems to the possible rights of an unborn child depend on how far they are regarded as legal persons.[4]

What this legal practice brings out is the importance of using a set of concepts, for example rights, duties, privileges, obligations, etc. together and not isolating one of them, for example rights, so that, as Wittgenstein might put it, the lone concept is only "idling." The concept of a right can, of course, be stretched—as when Trollope, for example talks of a house with certain grandiose features as having "the right" to be called a castle—and debates about the rights of foetuses, animals, works of art, or of nature can become merely terminological. What is important is to ask what job, if any, is being done in such contexts by the notion of "a right" as contrasted with that of "right" when it is isolated from such normal companions as the notions of duty, obligation, power, etc.

Something capable only of sentience or of suffering would not necessarily be capable of exercising, owning, or enjoying a right, much less of claiming, asserting, insisting on, or fighting for its rights or of waiving or relinquishing them. Nor of having obligations, duties, privileges, etc. And though it would be capable of having something done for it or of being in a certain state, it would not necessarily be capable of performing tasks, assuming attitudes, or having emotions. Hence, its possible rights, if any, would be confined to the right to have something done for it, such as to be well treated or protected, or to be in a certain state, such as to be happy or free or to remain alive. Moreover, though sentience or capacity to suffer would be necessary for the possible possession of a right to anything relevant to these, such as a right to protection from suffering—because a right to V implies being logically able to V—they would not be sufficient. The fact that an animal can suffer from growing pains or a man suffer from doubt does not in itself prove that it or he is capable of a right to protection from these.

It is a misunderstanding to object to this distinction between the kinds of things which can have rights and those which cannot on the ground that it constitutes a sort of speciesism.[5] For it is not being argued that it is right to treat one species less considerately than another, but only that one species, that is, a person, can sensibly be said to exercise or waive a right, be under an obligation, have a duty, etc., whereas another cannot, however unable particular members of the former species may be to do so.

NOTES

1. The fact that a right can be claimed is no evidence for the mistaken thesis (e.g., Joel Feinberg, "Duties, rights and claims." *American Philosophical Quarterly* 64 [1966], pp. 137–44) that a right is a claim.
2. E.g., W. D. Lamont, *The Principles of Moral Judgement* (Oxford, 1946), pp. 83–85.
3. R. Pound, *Jurisprudence* (St. Paul, MN, 1959), IV. ch. 25 and references on p. 191, n. 1.
4. P.D. Lasok, "The rights of the unborn" in *Fundamental Rights*, ed. J. W. Bridge, D. Lasok, *et al.* (London, 1973), pp. 18–30; and D. W. Louisell, "Abortion, the practice of medicine and the due process of law." *U.C.L.A. Law Review* 16 (1969), 233–54. M. Tooley goes too far in making "is a person" and "has a moral right to life" synonymous. See his "Abortion and infanticide." *Philosophy and Public Affairs* 2 (1972), pp. 37–65.
5. E.g., Peter Singer, "All animals are equal," in this volume.

JAMES RACHELS

Why Animals Have a Right to Liberty

Philosophers used to talk about "natural" rights, but now we don't hear so much about that subject. Instead, books and articles are written about "human" rights. The change in terminology is thought to be a great improvement; first, because talk about human rights does not bring with it the ontological worries that often attended discussions of natural rights, and second, because the new terminology focuses more precisely on what we are trying to understand: the rights that all human beings have in common. One of my motives in arguing for the position expressed is to cast doubt on the importance of human rights. I will maintain that human rights are not nearly so interesting or important as philosophers and politicians have thought.

As Richard Wasserstrom puts it, "If any right is a *human* right, . . . it must be possessed by all human beings, as well as only by human beings."[1] What is usually emphasized is that such rights are possessed by *all* humans; thus the doctrine of human rights has been a formidable weapon against slavery, racism, sexism, and the like. But, as Wasserstrom correctly notes, if any right is a distinctively human right, it is also necessary that it be possessed *only* by humans.[2] It is this side of the doctrine that I want to

This essay appeared for the first time in the first edition of this book.

emphasize. If it can be made plausible that members of other species also have the rights that are most important to humans—such as the right to liberty—then the whole subject of *human* rights will come to have much less interest than before; and it will be seen that the differences between humans and other animals are not nearly so important, from a moral point of view, as we have usually assumed.

Some philosophers believe that nonhuman animals (I will sometimes follow the common practice and call them simply "animals," leaving off the qualifier) have no rights at all, because they are not the sorts of beings that *can* have rights. On their view, it is not logically possible for animals to have rights. Two things need to be done: first, their arguments must be refuted, and second, positive arguments must be advanced to show that animals *do* have specific rights. I by-pass the first task on this occasion and, instead, concentrate on the second, more positive one.[3]

In arguing that animals do have rights—and in particular that they have a right to liberty—we may use the following method. First we select for discussion a right which we are confident that humans do have. Then we ask whether there is a relevant difference between humans and animals which would justify us in denying that right to animals while at the same time granting it to humans. If not, then the right in question is a right possessed by animals as well as by humans.

This method has a number of virtues. First, it has a clear rationale in the familiar principle of justice that we must treat like cases alike; or, to be more precise, that our moral judgments are unacceptably arbitrary if we judge one way in one case and differently in another case, without there being a relevant difference between the two cases which justifies the difference in our assessments. This principle has been used with great effect in arguing against racism. The assumption there has been that a person's race is not in itself a morally relevant consideration in determining how he or she is to be treated. Therefore, racist discrimination is unjustified unless some further differences between blacks and whites can be found which would be relevant to justifying the different modes of treatment. But, because there are no such further differences, such discrimination is unjustified. I am going to make the similar assumption that a mere difference in species is not enough, in itself, to justify any difference in how beings are treated.[4] Thus if we want to grant a right to humans but deny it to members of other species, we must be able to point to some relevant difference between them other than the mere fact that the animals are members of another species. A second advantage of the method is that if we follow it closely we will avoid the trap of lumping all nonhuman animals together, as though what we say about one species we must say about all. For it may turn out that, with respect to some particular right, there is no relevant difference between humans and one species of animal, but there are differences between humans and other species. Finally, I should mention one limitation of this method. The use of this method does not guarantee that we will identify all the rights which animals have, for it is at least logically possible that they have some rights not possessed by humans. If so, then these rights could not be uncovered by my method. However, this is of no concern to me here, for I have no intention of trying to compile a complete list of animal rights.

Now let me give some illustrations of the kinds of results which may be obtained by this method. Article 5 of The United Nations Universal Declaration of Human Rights says that all men have a right not be subjected to torture. But is this, in fact, a distinctively *human* right? If members of other species—say, rabbits or pigs or monkeys—are tortured, they also suffer. Of course, there are many impressive differences between men and these animals, but are they relevant here? A man can learn mathematics, and a rabbit can't; but what does that have to do with the business of being tortured? A man has an interest in not being tortured because he has the capacity to suffer pain, and not because he can do mathematics or anything of that sort. But rabbits, pigs, and monkeys also have the capacity to experience pain, and so they have the same basic interest in not being tortured. The right not to be tortured, then, is shared by all animals that suffer pain; it is not a distinctively human right at all. On the other hand, Article 18 of the same Declaration says that all men have the right to worship as they please. This, I think, *is* a right belonging only to humans, because only humans have religous beliefs and a capacity for worship.

The right not to be tortured and to freedom of worship are relatively clear and unproblematic. But what happens when we consider a more puzzling right, such as the right to property? Here we may proceed by asking why it is thought that men have this right—what is the basis of it?—and then, whether the same case can be made in behalf of animals. Let us consider, for example, Locke's treatment of the right to property. Locke contends that a man has a natural right to his own labor and whatever he produces by it:

> The labor of his body and the work of his hands, we may say, are properly his. Whatsoever then he removes out of the state that nature has provided and left it in, he has mixed his labor with, and joined to it something that is his own, and thereby makes it his property.[5]

Locke then illustrates his view with this example:

> He that is nourished by the acorns he picked up under an oak, or the apples he gathered from the trees in the wood, has certainly appropriated them to himself. Nobody can deny but the nourishment is his. I ask, then, when did they begin to be his? When he digested or when he ate or when he boiled or when he brought them home? Or when he picked them up? And it is plain, if the first gathering made them not his, nothing else could. That labor put a

distinction between them and common; that added something to them more than nature, the common mother of all, had done; and so they became his private right.

If Locke is right, then it follows that animals such as squirrels also have a right to property; for squirrels labor to gather nuts for their own nourishment in exactly the way Locke pictures the man laboring. There is no relevant difference between the man and the squirrel: they both pick up the nuts, take them home, store them away, and then eat them. Therefore there is no justification for saying that the man has a right to the nuts he gathers, but that the squirrel does not.

Now I turn to the right to liberty. The right to liberty has been counted among the most fundamental human rights in all the great liberal manifestos of modern history—the Declaration of Independence of the United States (1776), the French Declaration of the Rights of Man (1789), and the United Nations Universal Declaration of Human Rights (1948), to name three of the most important. Virtually every philosopher who has discussed the subject has followed suit; I have not been able to find any treatment of "human rights" which did not include liberty as a prime example. Considering this, and remembering that some philosophers doubt whether mere animals can have any rights at all, it may not be surprising to find liberty (or freedom, which for present purposes comes to the same thing) being *defined* by some in such a way that only humans could possibly *be* free. According to J. R. Lucas, for example,

> The central sense of Freedom is that in which a rational agent is free when he is able to act as seems best to him without being subject to external constraints on his actions.[6]

If we start off by conceiving freedom in this way, then the question of whether animals have a right to be free will not even arise, since the notion of a "rational agent" who deliberates about which actions are best is so obviously formulated with only humans in mind. But, just as obviously, this definition won't do as a general definition of freedom, for that concept applies to animals as well as to men. A lion left alone in his natural habitat is free; a lion in a zoo is not. A chicken in a small wire cage is less free than one allowed to roam about a barnyard. And a bird who is released from a cage and allowed to fly away is "set free" in a perfectly plain sense. So, rewriting the definition to eliminate the prejuduce in favor of humans, we get:

> The central sense of Freedom is that in which a being is free when he or she is able to do as he or she pleases without being subject to external constraints on his or her actions.

This expresses well enough the concept of liberty with which I shall be concerned. As before, we may proceed by asking why it is thought that humans have this right—what is the basis of it?—and then, whether the same or a very similar case can be made on behalf of members of other species.

One possibility is to take liberty to be, simply and without need of any further justification, good in itself.[7] If we take this approach, then we might argue that men have a right to liberty simply because they have a right not to be deprived of any intrinsic goods which they are capable of enjoying. (And here the usual qualifications will be added, to the effect that the right will be only as extensive as is compatible with others having a similar right, that the right may be forfeited or overridden in certain circumstances, etc.) But this line of reasoning will apply equally well to other species of animals. It is parallel to the right not to be tortured, mentioned above. Any animal that has the capacity for suffering pain has a right not to be tortured; and the reason for this is connected with the fact that suffering pain is intrinsically bad. Similarly, if we grant to humans a right to liberty simply because we regard liberty as something good in itself which they are capable of enjoying, then we must also grant a right to liberty to any other animal that is capable of desiring to act one way rather than another.

However, not many philosophers would be happy with this approach, because most believe it is possible to provide a rationale for the right to liberty that does not simply stop with calling it an intrinsic good. For example, it may be said that humans have a right to liberty because they have various *other* interests that will suffer if their freedom is unduly restricted. The right to liberty—the right to be free of external constraints on one's actions—may then be seen as derived from a more basic right not to have one's interests needlessly harmed.

But the interests of many other species are also harmed by a loss of freedom. It is a familiar fact that many wild animals do not fare at all well in captivity: taken from their natural habitats and put in zoos, they are at first frantic and frustrated because they cannot carry on their normal activities; then they become listless and inactive, shadows of their former selves. Some become vicious and destructive. They often will not reproduce in captivity, and when they do, their young often cannot survive; and finally, members of many species will die sooner in captivity than they would in their natural homes.

Dr. Herbert Ratcliffe, a pathologist, conducted a study of the animals in a Philadelphia zoo. He found that the animals were suffering from sharply increased rates of heart disease, cancer, and ulcers. The metabolism of some white-tailed deer had changed to such an extent that their horns became deformed. The zoo's breeding colony of nutria—small, beaverlike animals—had dwindled because the young animals were born dwarfed, failed to breed, and died early. Dr. Ratcliffe attributes all of this to the effects of the artificial, confined environment of the zoo.[8]

Another example is taken from a widely used psychology textbook, which tells the story of a baboon colony in the London zoo. Investigators

> observed many instances of bloody fighting, brutality, and apparently sense-less violence. Some of the females were torn to pieces, and no infant survived to maturity. From these observations, it was concluded that such violence was typical of the "wild" baboons. . . . But later, when baboons were studied under natural conditions in Africa, in the "wild," it was discovered that they lived in well-organized, peaceful groups, in which the only aggressive behavior was directed at predators and intruders.[9]

Once it has been learned that animals can be made to suffer in a certain way, a new field is opened for scientific research. Experiments may then be performed to discover how they will behave when tormented, and exactly what forms their suffering will take. Numerous studies have been made of the effects of confinement on animals. One such series of experiments was reported in 1972.[10] One of the experimenters, Dr. Harry F. Harlow of the University of Wisconsin, is said to have "created" a vertical chamber, which "is basically a stainless steel trough with sides that slope inward to form a rounded bottom." The whole thing measures about four feet by one foot by a few inches. The idea behind the chamber is explained this way:

> Depression in humans has been characterized as embodying a state of "help-lessness and hopelessness, sunken in a well of despair," and the device was designed on an intuitive basis to reproduce such a well both physically and psychologically for monkey subjects.

Rhesus monkeys were used for the experiments. These animals are often used in such experiments because they are intelligent, sociable creatures that resemble humans in a great many ways. The experiments were conducted by putting six-week-old monkeys into the "well of despair" for a period of *forty-five days*. The purpose of doing this was said to be to "investigate the chamber's effectiveness in production of psychopathology."

The chamber turned out to be very effective. While confined, the "subjects" were said to "typically spend most of their time huddled in a corner of the chamber." "Huddling" is defined as a "self-enclosed, fetal-like position incorporating any or all patterns of self-clasp, self-embrace, or lowered head." A nine-month period of observation following the confinement indicates that the effects on the animals are permanent:

> The results indicated that a 45-day period of vertical chamber confinement early in life produced severe and persistent psychopathological behavior of a

depressive nature in the experimental subjects. These monkeys failed to show appreciable changes in home-cage behavioral levels during the 9-month period following removal from the vertical chamber. In comparison to control groups of cage- and peer-reared monkeys, the chambered subjects exhibited abnormally high levels of self-clasp and huddle and abnormally low levels of locomotion and environmental exploration in both the home-cage and playroom situations. Most striking was the virtual absence of social activity among chambered subjects throughout the 8 months of playroom testing.

This new knowledge was obtained with financial assistance from the United States Public Health Service, the National Institutes of Health, and the National Institute of Mental Health.

Any creature that has interests has at least a *prima facie* right not to have those interests needlessly harmed. Animals that suffer in captivity have an interest in being free, and so at least a *prima facie* right to liberty. Lucas, immediately after giving the definition of "freedom" (restricted to "rational agents") quoted above, says that "not to be free is to be frustrated, impotent, futile." He is obviously thinking only of humans; but the description applies equally well to animals in zoos, and certainly to the monkeys trapped in the well of despair.

Animals raised for food also suffer in confinement. Before being slaughtered cows spend their lives crowded into "feedlots" where they are deprived of any sort of herd life or even adequate exercise. Veal calves are kept in pens so small they cannot even turn around. Peter Singer points out that even the lowly chicken suffers from confinement in the sort of cages used by poultry-farmers:

> . . . hens are crowded four or five to a cage with a floor area of twenty inches by eighteen inches, or around the size of a single page of the *New York Times*. The cages have wire floors, since this reduces cleaning costs, though wire is unsuitable for the hens' feet; the floors slope, since this makes the eggs roll down for easy collection, although this makes it difficult for the hens to rest comfortably. In these conditions all the birds' natural instincts are thwarted; they cannot stretch their wings fully, walk freely, dust-bathe, scratch the ground, or build a nest. Although they have never known other conditions, observers have noticed that the birds vainly try to perform these actions. Frustrated at their inability to do so, they often develop what farmers call "vices," and peck each other to death. To prevent this, the beaks of young birds are often cut off.[11]

Some of these cruelties have to do with the *type* of confinement rather than with the bare fact that the birds are confined. So, if the cages had flat, solid floors, and perches for the hens, some of the grounds for complaint would be eliminated. But so long as the hens are confined to small cages, their natural desire to scratch the dirt, stretch their wings, build a nest, and so forth, will be frustrated. This is not to say that the interests of chickens can be satisfied only in a state of *total* freedom: I can see no harm that would be done to their interests if they were kept captive while being allowed freedom to roam a large area, where they could do the things just mentioned. Thus many vegetarians who refuse to buy eggs produced under the conditions described by Singer nevertheless will buy eggs laid by "free-ranging" hens.

So, we need to distinguish two things: first, we need to distinguish the *kinds* of animals whose interests are harmed by the denial of freedom; and second, we need to distinguish the *degree* of freedom that is required if the animals' interests are not to be harmed. Lions, but not chickens, may need to be set completely free in their natural habitats in order to thrive; whereas the needs of most insects may be so limited that they have no interest in freedom at all.

At this point the business about man's superior rationality must be re-introduced. For, even if it is a mistake to *define* freedom in such a way that only rational agents can be free, it may still be said that freedom has a special kind of importance for rational agents which it cannot have for nonrational beings. In one form or another this thought is found in the writings of almost all the philosophers who discuss the "human right" to liberty. I want to make two preliminary remarks about this. The first has only to do with a certain sentiment that I have—so you may want to discount it as an argument—but I will mention it anyway. It is that there is something very *sad* about a grand animal such as a lion or an elephant being put on exhibit in a zoo, and being reduced to nothing more than a spectacle for people's enjoyment. The reason I mention this here is that, in the past, humans who lacked "rationality" have suffered the same fate. Salt notes that

> Two or three generations ago, pauper-lunatics used to be caged where passers-by—nurses perhaps with children in their charge—could see them as they passed, and the spectacle was sometimes enjoyed. (I remember hearing from my mother that such was the case at Shrewsbury. The nurse would say, "Where shall we go to-day, children?" and the cry would be, "Oh, to see the madmen, please!")[12]

Most of us recoil at this, and many reasons may be given why such practices are barbarous: perhaps because they teach children callous attitudes. But of course making a similar spectacle of animals may also have that effect. However, it is hard to believe that our initial reaction has much to do with such considerations. It has to do rather with the sadness and indignity of the spectacle. And the fact that the being on exhibit is not *rational* hardly matters, either in the case of the lunatic or the lion. The second comment is to express a general doubt about the relevance of rationality to the value of freedom. It may be true, as philosophers have often stressed, that liberty is necessary if we humans are to develop and exercise our powers as rational agents and to have the kinds of lives we want. But it is also true that liberty is necessary for many nonhuman animals if they are to live the sorts of lives, and thrive, in ways that are natural to them; or, to put things more plainly, if the interests they have, in virtue of the kinds of creatures *they* are, are to be realized. . . .

The sum of all this is that, whatever rationale is provided for granting humans a right to liberty, it seems that a relevantly similar one is available in the case of at least some other species of animals. The right to liberty, then, is not a "human" right.

As I said at the outset, my motive in arguing the point is to cast doubt on the importance of the concept of human rights. It is not that I think there are no human rights. On the contrary, I think that there are. But they are *not* rights that we have *simply in virtue of being members of a certain species.* Rather, they are rights that we have in virtue of possessing other characteristics, which members of other species happen not to have: for example, the right to worship seems to be a distinctively human right, because only humans, among all the animals we know, have any interest in or capacity for worship. But once the reason for this is understood, and once it is seen that such important rights as the right to liberty are *not* distinctively human, then most of the interest of the notion of "human" rights is, I think, gone. It would be much better to talk about natural rights, or simply *rights,* and remain alert to the fact that we humans are not the only beings that have them.

NOTES

1. Richard Wasserstrom, "Rights, Human Rights, and Racial Discrimination," *The Journal of Philosophy,* vol. 61 (1964), p. 631.

2. Joel Feinberg defines human rights as those belonging to all humans, but specifically denies that they must be possessed only by humans, "so that a human right held by animals is not excluded by definition." (*Social Philosophy,* Englewood Cliffs, N.J.: Prentice-Hall, 1973, p. 85). I prefer Wasserstrom's definition because, if a right is shared by dogs and cows, there seems little reason to call it human rather than canine or bovine. And, by calling such rights "human," we are directing attention away from the fact that other beings have them, as though all that matters is whether we humans have them.

3. For my response to the first objection, see the "Appendix" in the version of this essay that appeared in the first edition of this book.

4. This point is brought out very powerfully by Peter Singer in "All Animals Are Equal," *Philosophic Exchange,* vol. 1, no. 5 (Summer 1974), pp. 103–16. [See selection included in this volume.]

5. John Locke, *The Second Treatise of Government* (1690), chap. 5, par. 27. The next quotation is from the same chapter of the same work, par. 28.

6. J. R. Lucas, *The Principles of Politics* (Oxford: Oxford University Press, 1966), p. 144.

7. For an account of this type, see Gregory Vlastos, "Justice and Equality," *Social Justice,* ed. Richard B. Brandt (Englewood Cliffs, N.J.: Prentice-Hall, 1962), p. 51.

8. "The Shame of the Naked Cage," *Life,* November 8, 1968, p. 77.

9. Floyd L. Ruch and Philip G. Zimbado, *Psychology and Life,* 8th ed. (Glenview, Ill.: Scott, Foresman and Company, 1967), p. 539.

10. Stephen J. Suomi and Harry F. Harlow, "Depressive Behavior in Young Monkeys Subjected to Vertical Chamber Confinement," *Journal of Comparative and Physiological Psychology*, vol. 80 (1972), pp. 11–18. The quotations that follow are from pp. 11, 12, 13, and 14. For an account of this and related experiments, see Peter Singer, *Animal Liberation* (New York Review, 1975), chap. II.

11. Singer, "All Animals are Equal" *op. cit.*, p. 108.

12. Henry Salt, *The Creed of Kinship* (New York: Dutton, 1935), pp. 60-61.

A CATHOLIC DICTIONARY

Animals Have No Rights

Since man is master of the animal realm he may use animals for his proper purposes; such purposes certainly include food, service, the advantage of the human race, and, it would seem, entertainment. St. Thomas makes this explicit (*contra Gentiles,* 3:112:7): "Thus is excluded the error of those who make it a sin for man to kill animals. By divine providence in the natural order of things they are meant for man's use, and so he may use them, by killing them or in any other way, without doing wrong."

Some pagan writers encouraged kindness to animals, e.g. Pythagoras, who, accepting the doctrine of *metempsychosis,* thought it likely that human souls were reincarnated in animal bodies. There are traces of this attitude in some Roman legislation, and Cicero (*De Finibus,* 3:20) comments upon the error of attributing human rights to animals. The OT also recommended a proper treatment of animals. Jews were forbidden to muzzle the ox that trod out the corn (Deut 25:4) or to yoke ox with ass (Deut 22:10).

Christian authors rarely treat of this theme, though with the Franciscan movement there was an awakening love of Nature and the sense of close kinship with all God's natural creation. . . . St. Thomas encourages kindness towards animals by insisting that pity arises from the sufferings of

A Catholic Dictionary (A work projected with the approval of the Catholic Hierarchy of England and Wales) Vol. I (London and New York: Thomas Nelson and Sons Limited, 1962) pp. 97–8.

others and, since animals may feel pain, men may therefore feel pity for them (1–2ae:102:6:@8). Referring in *contra Gentiles,* 2:112 to prohibitions of the OT favouring animals he states that they were issued, "lest anyone by exercising cruelty towards animals, might become cruel also towards men" or because an injury to animals involved its owner in loss. The human reference is clear throughout. Proper treatment of animals is thought of as a training ground for the proper attitude towards human beings. Cruelty to animals was reprobated largely because of its evil effect upon man.

This had led critics to accuse Catholic teaching of an insensitiveness, a callousness even, towards animals. The charge is more usually levelled in Anglo-Saxon countries where, in the matter of domesticated animals, sensibility has far outrun sense, and where, as in Britain today, animals are sometimes better protected against ill-treatment than are children. The question is made more nebulous by an appeal to the "rights" of animals. If that term be used correctly, animals have no "rights," for these can belong only to persons, endowed with reason and responsibility. Cruelty to animals is certainly wrong: not because it outrages animal "rights" which are non-existent, but because cruelty in a human being is an unworthy and wicked disposition and, objectively, because ill-treatment of animals is an abuse and perversion of God's design. Man has been given dominion over the animal kingdom, and it is to be exercised in conformity with human reason and God's Will.

ANDREW LINZEY

The Theos-Rights
of Animals

For Catholic theology, steeped as it is in scholasticism, animals have no moral status. If we have any duties to them, they are indirect, owing to some human interest involved. Animals are not rational like human beings and therefore cannot possess immortal souls. Even the most hard-boiled scholastic would now probably admit that animals feel *some* pain but, if so, their pain is not regarded as morally relevant or truly analogous to human pain. In consequence, animals have no rights. "Zoophilists often lose sight of the end for which animals, irrational creatures were created by God, viz., the service and use of man," argues the *Dictionary of Moral Theology*. "In fact, Catholic moral doctrine teaches that animals have no rights on the part of man."

It is in this context that we have to understand the present discussion, both philosophical and theological, about animal rights. It is the persistence of scholastic Catholicism which inevitably makes rights the issue it is. When one considers the wealth of positive insight and prescription within the

Andrew Linzey is Director of the Centre for Theology and Ethics at Essex University, England. Among his recent books are *Christianity and the Rights of Animals* (Crossroads, 1987) and, with Tom Regan, *Animals and Christianity: A Book of Readings* (Crossroads, 1988).

Christianity and the Rights of Animals (London: SPCK, 1987), pp. 68–9 and 94–8.
Reprinted by permission of the author.

Christian tradition about animals, it is surely disconcerting that these negative influences should have held, and continue to hold, such prominence. The issue of animal rights is not some concession to secular thinking within theological circles but simply the latest stage of a debate that began hundreds of years ago. John Foster, writing in 1856 (against William Wyndham's opposition to early animal welfare legislation), complains of our being taught "from our very infancy, that the pleasurable and painful sensations of animals are not worth our care; that it is not of the smallest consequence what they are made to suffer, so that they are not rendered less serviceable to us by their suffering . . . that in short they have *no rights* as sentient beings, existing for their own sakes as well as for ours." If today people concerned for animals prefer the term "animal rights" to "animal lovers" or "animal welfare," they are, consciously or unconsciously, linking themselves to a historic debate which is by no means concluded. It is not without significance that the "National Catholic Society for Animal Welfare" in the United States has now become the "International Society for Animal Rights." . . .

The argument that Christians should continue to utilize rights language and extend its use to animals needs to be subject to three qualifications. The first is that Christians should not claim that rights theory is the *only* theory of moral obligation. To the objection that rights theory may in some ways be deficient or inadequate, we have to reply that no one theory can possibly do justice to the complete range of themes and insights from within the Christian tradition. If this sounds like something less than a complete endorsement of rights, then it needs to be considered whether any moral theory, either of divine command or human duty, can claim to be the only possible one from a theological perspective. What we are characterizing in Christian moral theory is nothing less than the will of God. Divine will is undubitably complex, even subtle and possibly developing. When we opt for the language of theos-rights, we do it with necessary reserve and caution, not because this theory is necessarily more difficult than any other, but because *all* moral theory is theologically problematic. Whenever we move from any straightforward identification of God's will with a particular imperative in a specific situation to the work of characterization, that is, to characterizing and systematizing God's will in general terms, then we are faced with the continual danger of over-simplification. Of course God's will can be simple, but it can also be remarkably mysterious. Even Karl Barth, that robust defender of divine commands, accepts that it is not an easy task for Christian ethics to tell us what God's will is. By our intellect and language we are always, through characterization, *approximating* God's will for his creation. Though theos-rights may be the best way of characterizing the divine imperative, it does not follow that we must hold that such theory is in every way adequate or that in God's good time some new form of theo-moral characterization may not better it. Doubtless our own moral reasoning, however inspired, is, like the rest of creaturely life itself, in need of redemption.

The second qualification is that rights language cannot claim to be comprehensive. I mean by this that it cannot exclude other forms of moral language and insight. Talk of generosity, respect, duty, sacrifice and mercy as well as rights is essential. It may be that animal rightists have so stressed the importance of rights as a concept that they have neglected talk of compassion and respect. It may be, but for Christians my hope is that we can take such language for granted. . . . One function of rights language is to provide checks and markers *en route* to living a less exploitative way of life with other creatures. This is surely a valuable function, but by itself does not provide a wholistic or sufficiently positive interpretation of the divine imperative. In other words, Christian ethics is not simply about preventing the worst but promoting the good. For the elaboration, definition and pursuit of the good with animals we require more terms than rights language can provide. It may be in some situations that we should accord animals more than that which rights theory may strictly give them, and err, if we do, on the generous side. For generosity is surely an important notion and rights language must be careful not to limit it even if we cannot persuade ourselves that it has the status of a declared "ought." To those who feel that we should not just respect the rights of say, sparrows, but actually seek loving, caring relationships with them, the rights view offers no obstacle. To those who feel called to especially heroic acts of mercy and self-sacrifice towards particular kinds of animals, the rights view again advances no objection. There will always be people, inspired by the life of Christ and the many saints, who feel moved to morally heroic, sacrificial acts. But, of course, it is not to these people that rights language is normally directed. In short: in fighting for the positive good of animals and humans, Christians will need to utilize a varied vocabulary. All that is claimed here is that rights language should be part of the necessary armoury.

Thirdly, we need to reiterate that the rights of which we speak are properly and solely God's rights. He alone wills that givenness of life which makes them possible; he alone charges man with the stewardship of them; and he alone can in the end properly guarantee them. One conclusion follows from this: as our knowledge of God increases by the power of the Spirit, so may our knowledge of the nature of his will and therefore our understanding of his rights. Some theologians regard rights terminology as far too static a way of describing God's relationship with what is, after all, a dynamic and open creation. But theos-rights are not necessarily as static as may be their secular counterparts. The possibility of change is inherent in the fact that our understanding of God develops, whether for better or worse. It may be that God's Spirit will move us to a new understanding of our place in the universe such as to make previous controversies about individual salvation in the Reformation period appear trivial by comparison. It may be or may not be. In either case it is our responsibility to recognize God's rights in creation and to champion them. . . .

The question may not unreasonably be posed: What then is the overwhelming advantage of rights theory which justifies it in spite of these serious qualifications? The answer may be obvious. Rights language insists that we envisage the claims of animals in analogous terms to those of other, human, beings. This is why [some, perhaps many,] hesitate or reject animal rights: they deny that the claims of other Spirit-filled breathing beings can be in any real sense analogous to human claims. In the issue of animal rights, perhaps more than any other, Christians confront the limitations of their own scholastic history. Scholasticism has for centuries regarded animals as "things." The consequence is unsurprising: animals have been treated as things. For all the intellectual sophistication of the arguments against animal rights, one quite practical consideration is frequently dominant. *To accept that animals have rights must involve accepting that they should be treated differently from the way most of them are treated at present.* Explicitly acknowledging that animals have rights involves accepting that they have a fundamental moral status. If they have no such status, they cannot make claims; and if they have no claims, they can have no rights. Perhaps in the light of their tradition, it is easier for Christians to see the historic significance of the debate about rights than many of their secular contemporaries. Those who deny rights to the non-human do well to ponder the history of what rightlessness has meant for animals; if the opposing arguments do not convince, it is invariably because they do not want to accept that most animals are treated unjustly.

Here is the rub. To grant animal rights is to accept that they can be wronged. According to theos-rights what we do to animals is not simply a matter of taste or convenience or philanthropy. When we speak of animal rights we conceptualize what is objectively owed to animals as a matter of justice by virtue of their Creator's right. Animals can be wronged because their Creator can be wronged in his creation. Some philosophers are still adamant that it is possible to provide a theoretical framework for the better treatment of animals without recourse to the notion of rights. It may be possible in this way to provide for something better, but how much remains historically open. Perhaps through utilitarian calculation it may be possible to prevent some of the worst possible from happening to animals, but will their status be fundamentally changed thereby? Language and history are against those who want the better treatment of animals and who also want to deny the legitimacy of the language of rights. For how can we reverse centuries of scholastic tradition if we still accept the cornerstone of that tradition, namely that all but humans are morally rightless? If the foregoing appears to invoke the dubious need for penitence in formulating ethical theory, it can only be replied that repentance is a cardinal duty for Christians. If calculation of the consequences is to be allowed some say in moral assessments, then we have to accept that Christians have good reason for looking at what their own theology has created and, in the light of this, theologizing afresh.

But apart from this obvious practical need to reverse centuries of neglect, theos-rights makes sense of a whole range of crucial theological insights—three in particular. The first is the sheer giveness of created reality. Unless God is really indifferent to creation, those beings whose lives are filled with his Spirit have special value and therefore require special protection. The second is the need to witness to the electing power of God in his covenant relationship. Man and animals form a moral community, not only because of their common origin, but because God elects them within a special relationship with himself. Catholic scholasticism has denied the possibility of a moral community with brutes. "Nothing irrational can be the object of the Christian virtue of neighbourly love, charity," writes Bernard Häring. "Nothing irrational," he tells us, "is capable of the beautifying friendship with God." What scholasticism here neglects or disputes, theos-rights assumes. Because men and brutes are elected by God, we form one covenanted community of Spirit-filled beings before him. Thirdly, the perspective of theos-rights gives meaning to the long tradition of rating man's God-like powers in creation. According to theos-rights, humans must exercise power, but only towards God's end. The unique significance of man in this respect consists in his capacity to perceive God's will and to actualize it within his own life. Man is "to commit himself to the divine task," argues Edward Carpenter, "of lifting up creation, redeeming those orders of which he forms part, and directing them towards their end."

Those who deny theos-rights to animals need to show how it is that they can give sufficient reality to these insights without participating in the moral neglect of the non-human which still characterizes continuing elements within the Christian tradition.

PART FIVE
Killing and the Value of Life

EDWARD JOHNSON

Life, Death, and Animals

Mill says that it is "better to be a human being dissatisfied than a pig satisfied,"[1] Is it? How does Mill know that? MacIver says this:

> If I tread wantonly on a woodlouse, I do wrong . . . But it is only a very small wrong, and to exaggerate its wrongfulness is sentimentality . . . Little wrongs have to be done, in order that greater wrongs may be avoided. If I kill a Colorado beetle, I do wrong by the beetle; but, if I fail to kill it, I do wrong by all the growers and consumers of potatoes, and their interests are vastly more important.[2]

Are they? How does MacIver know that? Like Mill and MacIver, we all believe, or act as though we believe, that human life is, always or usually, somehow more important than animal life. Indeed, mere pleasure of convenience for humans is commonly supposed to be more important than the lives of nonhuman animals; as Goodrich says, "it seems generally to be held that human life is infinitely more valuable than animal life: there is no

Edward Johnson teaches philosophy at the University of New Orleans. He is a frequent contributor to professional journals in moral, social and political philosophy.

Reprinted from Johnson, Edward, "Life, Death, and Animals," pp. 123–33 in H. Miller and W. Williams (eds.), *Ethics and Animals*. Clifton, NJ: Humana Press, 1983.

number of animals, however great, that is worth the sacrifice of even one human being."[3] Are we so important? How do we know?

You could say: we *just know*. But it is best to avoid *ad hoc* intuitionism for as long as we can. Haven't complacent assertions of intuitive superiority turned out wrong often enough before? Haven't we, for example, seen through the intuitions that purported to justify slavery and racism? We have come to see, I suppose, that we don't know (and *never did* know), that the life of a white is more important than that of a black, or that there is no number of slaves, however great, that is worth the sacrifice of even one slave owner. Now, what about the pig?

II

"Human beings," Mill tells us, "have faculties more elevated than the animal appetites and, when once made conscious of them, do not regard anything as happiness which does not include their gratification." How can we tell when one faculty is "more elevated" than another? Mill's criterion is well known. "Of two pleasures, if there be one to which all or almost all who have experience of both give a decided preference, irrespective of any feeling of moral obligation to prefer it, that is the more desirable pleasure." Mill no sooner enunciates this criterion than he proceeds to indicate how it can be used, not merely to rank pleasures roughly, but to place the "more elevated" pleasures beyond impeachability.

> If one of the two is, by those who are competently acquainted with both, placed so far above the other that they prefer it, even though knowing it to be attended with a greater amount of discontent, and would not resign it for any quantity of the other pleasure which their nature is capable of, we are justified in ascribing to the preferred enjoyment a superiority in quality so far out-weighing quantity as to render it, in comparison, of small account.

Thus, it is "better to be a human being dissatisfied than a pig satisfied; better to be Socrates dissatisfied than a fool satisfied." Note that Mill is not appealing just to the fact that *we* prefer human dissatisfaction to swinish satisfaction. Rather, he thinks that we are specially qualified to judge. The opinions of the fool and the pig are disallowed by Mill. "And if the fool, or the pig, are of a different opinion, it is because they only know their own side of the question. The other party to the comparison knows both sides." The inadequacy of Mill's discussion here has been much noted. Bertrand Russell makes the drollest comment, remarking that "utilitarians have been strangely anxious to prove that the life of the pig is not happier than that of the philosopher—a most dubious proposition, which, if they had considered the matter frankly, could hardly have been decided in the same way by all of them."[4] Mill assumes that *we*, unlike the pig, can be "competently acquainted with both" the pig's happiness and our own. That is doubtful. Socrates, in his learned ignorance, may not recognize where ignorance is bliss. How much more difficult is the case where we must deal, across species, with vastly different sensibilities and capacities. What reason is there to suppose that any human really knows anything about what it is like to be a pig, or a bat, or any other animal? As William Blake asks:

> How do you know but ev'ry Bird that cuts the airy way,
> Is an immense world of delight, clos'd by your senses five?[5]

In the really difficult cases, it may not even be *possible* to be "competently acquainted with both," since the capacities that make one pleasure possible may be exactly what make another impossible. The hedonist can't go slumming *everywhere*. Socrates cannot know the pleasures that the fool enjoys *in his foolishness*; at best, he can have an intellectual's *ersatz*. It is unreasonable to assume, as Mill does, that humans are *of course* acquainted with "animal" pleasures as well as with other, distinctively "human" pleasures. The availability of the "higher" pleasures may change everything, so that we are no longer in a position to have, or to judge, the "lower" ones. In that case, Mill's very justification for speaking of "higher" and "lower" disappears.

Mill also assumes that broader experience (if we can have it) always puts one in a *better* position to judge. But this overlooks the possibility of decadence or corruption: perhaps the enjoyment of some pleasures may put us in a *worse* position to judge among pleasures. As Rousseau says: "Slaves lose everything in their chains, even the desire of escaping from them: they love their servitude, as the comrades of Ulysses loved their brutish condition."[6]

III

In view of the difficulties attending any attempt to show that we humans are specially qualified to judge the value of animal lives, it is tempting to adopt a view that makes no such claim. Thus, E. B. McGilvary says this:

> It is better to be a Socrates unsatisfied—better for whom? For Socrates or for the pig? But a pig! Who would be a pig? Is he not loathly? Assuredly he is—*to us;* but *to himself* not so assuredly. Who knows what preciousness there may not be to pigs in unadulterated piggery? Who then shall decide? To what arbiter shall we appeal?
> It is strange that when such a question is asked, the fact is overlooked that it is not thrown out to the universe in general. It is we men and women who are asking the question; we are asking it of ourselves; why not answer it for ourselves? We are not particularly interested in the question whether pigs like to be pigs. It matters not if they do. We are concerned with the question what

we should like to be, what we should like to help our children become, what kind of civilization we shall lend our efforts to build up for the future.[7]

The same sort of view appears in Philip Devine's recent book on the ethics of homicide, where it is argued that:

> We need not be concerned with the relative value of human and animal life in the abstract, but only with their relative value in the context of decision making by human beings. Even supposing that Hume is right when he says that "the life of a man is of no greater importance in the universe than that of an oyster," where the decision maker is not an oyster or God (or the universe personified), but a human being, that kind of creature which shares certain essential traits with the agent is entitled to a kind of respect to which those who do not are not. Still further, human beings—or nearly all of them—are capable of a much richer kind of life than nonhuman animals on this planet enjoy, including the very moral agency presupposed in the asking of a moral question. To be deprived of this kind of life (or to have it impaired) is a much greater harm than to be deprived of a merely animal existence. Of course, one might say that human beings are unable adequately to judge the richness of the lives of spiders or dolphins, and thus to determine whether their lives are or are not as valuable as ours. But one is forced in any case to judge matters from one's own point of view (from what other point of view might one judge them?) and there is nothing inappropriate . . . in human actions being guided by the perceptions of human beings.[8]

It certainly sounds realistic to say that we "are concerned with the question what *we* should like to be," or that "one is forced in any case to judge matters from one's own point of view." But is this morally adequate? Imagine that *we* (members of a dominant race) were to offer an analogous justification for counting the lives of a subject race as of less importance than our own: "Of course, one might say that whites are unable adequately to judge the richness of the lives of blacks, and thus to determine whether their lives are or are not as valuable as ours. But one is forced in any case to judge matters from one's own point of view, and there is nothing inappropriate in the actions of whites being guided by the perceptions of whites." If such an argument would be nothing more than the specious rhetoric of racism, then it is difficult to see the sort of view espoused by McGilvary and by Devine as anything but self-congratulatory speciesism. If the former is morally inadequate, isn't the second as well?

IV

So far, I have rejected two views about how we are able to know that human lives are more important than nonhuman lives. The first view was that we are in a position to judge animals' lives, but they are not in a position to judge ours, because we (and not they) are, or can be, "competently acquainted with both." The second view was that we know that our lives are more important because *we* are the ones judging. I want now to consider a third view, which is a bit more complex. The basic idea is that we know that our lives are more important because we can know something about our lives that animals cannot know about their lives; according to this view, the complexity of human minds is not (necessarily) valuable in itself, but it allows us to value our lives in a specially important way. There are many versions of this view.

Kant holds that nonrational beings have "only a relative value as means and are consequently called *things*."[9] Animals, he says, "are not self-conscious and are there merely as a means to an end."[10] We have no direct duties to animals, he thinks, and it follows that they have no rights, in particular no right to life. Hegel says that animals "have no right to their life, because they do not will it."[11] He, too, denies that animals are ends in themselves, and calls them *things*, remarking that

> the thing, as externality, has no end in itself; it is not infinite self-relation but something external to itself. A living thing too (an animal) is external to itself in this way and is so far itself a thing.[12]

An animal lacks rationality, self-consciousness, infinite self-relation; it "lacks subjectivity" and so "is external not merely to the subject but to itself" as well. To say that an animal, as a thing, is external to itself is to say that it lacks some sort of mental complexity, some sort of reflexivity, that persons have. "An animal can intuit," says Hegel, "but the soul of an animal has for its object not its soul, itself, but something external." Henry Johnstone says this:

> The being of a person is reflexive in a way in which the being of an inert thing is not. One cannot be a person without knowing what it is like *to oneself* to be a person. It is entirely by virtue of this knowledge that persons place whatever value or disvalue they do on life . . . An animal . . . does not know what it is like *to itself*—from its own piscine, avian, feline, or canine point of view—to be a fish, bird, cat, or dog. While it enacts the behavior of its species, it does so without taking a point of view. The fish behaves like a fish—not to itself, but to us.[13]

Currently fashionable versions of this concern for reflexivity admit that animals (as conscious beings) have desires, but emphasize that humans have something more. Harry Frankfurt[14] and Richard Jeffrey[15] too, suggest that though animals have first-order desires they lack second-order (or higher-order) desires, volitions, or preferences. Animals want, but they don't want to want; they care about things, but they don't care what cares they have. Gary Watson holds that the key to understanding free agency lies in distinguishing two different sorts of motivation—desires and values—and writes: "In the case of the Brutes ... motivation has a single source: appetite and (perhaps) passion. The Brutes (or so we normally think) have no evaluational system."[16] Similarly, Richard Taylor (1976, p. 282) endorses the notion that

> human subjects are capable of evaluating what they are, and to the extent that they can shape themselves on this evaluation, are responsible for what they are in a way that other subjects of action and desire (the higher animals for instance) cannot be said to be.[17]

These are all different ways of saying that animals cannot adopt a view about what they are; they cannot accept or reject their wants, and thus mold their futures, in the way humans can; nor can animals use their future to give significance, retrospectively, to their past behavior (see Harman).[18]

Let us suppose, for the sake of argument, that there is a difference between humans and other animals of the sort that these various versions of concern about relexivity have tried to point to. Humans, let us say, are reflexive or self-conscious in a way that animals aren't. What moral weight should such a fact have? Why should reflexive lives matter more than unreflexive lives?

V

One answer would be that reflexive capacities allow their possessor to care about life, and to mind death, in a way that animals cannot. According to a common view, animals lack the concept of death, and so cannot mind death, any more than they mind not having a ticket to the opera. Rational creatures, however, can mind, and normally do, and this is the reason why it is wrong, *prima facie*, to kill them. Is such a view correct?

You can have an interest in avoiding death if you are capable of conceiving death, and so of minding it; you can have an interest in your own continued existence if you are capable of conceiving it, and so of wanting it. But you can also have an indirect or derivative interest in life that feeds off of your other interests. If a cow likes to chew her cud, then it is, other things being equal, in her interest to be allowed to do so.[19] She is benefited by having opportunities to satisfy her desires: the more the better. But does this not give the cow an interest in continued life? When to have a desire satisfied is to be benefited, isn't one benefited more, other things being equal, the more opportunities one has to satisfy it (perhaps—where this is relevant—up to some point of satiation)? This will be so even if one lacks the concept of a future, of personal identity over time, etc. Of course, if one does have such concepts, since one will then be able to *care* about the future, that will give one an additonal interest in living. But the lack of such concepts does not mean that one has *no* interest in, or claim to, life: the derivative sort of interest in life remains. Insofar as life seems likely to satisfy one's desires, fulfill interests that one has, one has an interest in life.

To make this more precise, we need to distinguish between negative and positive interests. Roughly, negative interests are those that would be satisfied if one suddenly ceased to exist. Avoiding pain is a negative interest. Experiencing pleasure is a positive one. By their very nature, negative interests give one no grip on future life, since they will be fulfilled just as well if one dies as they possibly can be if one continues to live. The fact that one has an interest in avoiding pain is not enough to give one an interest in living; indeed, in some cases it may give one an interest in dying. That is the point, sometimes, of suicide and euthanasia. Since nonhumans, as well as humans, can feel pleasure, they have an interest in living, when living can provide them with opportunities to enjoy their many natural pleasures.

This view explains how animals can have an interest in living, while at the same time explaining how the interest rational beings have in living is importantly different. Humans, like animals, have an interest in life derivative from their interest in other things. But humans also can have a quite independent interest in life, since they may care about the future. If an animal's future will be one of unrelieved pain, then it lacks an interest in life, and should be killed. But we cannot immediately draw the same conclusion in the case of a human. It is possible that a human's desire to continue living may outweigh the fact that her or his life will be on balance one of pain and frustration. In the normal case, humans will have both the sort of interest in life that depends on other interests *and* the sort that depends on caring about the future.

I suggested earlier that the satisfaction of an animal's (positive) interests is a benefit to it, and that more opportunity for satisfaction is better than less, and that consequently animals can have, in virtue of their interests, a further interest in living. But is this correct?[20] There are two ways of handling any desire: one can satisfy it or get rid of it. One way of getting rid of a being's desires is to kill it: it then no longer has any unfulfilled desires. Why not handle matters in this manner? In the case of humans, we can appeal to the fact that people *care* which way their unsatisfied desires (or some of them) are handled. But this sort of appeal is not possible in the case of animals, who lack (by hypothesis) the conceptual capacities necessary for higher-order desires. If it does not matter to an animal what desires it has, or what desires it acts on, how can it matter to it whether the desire is satisfied or extinguished? All that matters to the animal, it seems, is that it not go on having (on balance) unsatisfied desires. If so, there is no reason, as far as the animal's interests are concerned, why the animal should not simply be killed.

Notice, however, that it is not enough that persons just have higher-order desires or preferences that specify what they want to want. For the question will simply reappear at the level of the highest-order preference: Should we satisfy this meta-preference or extinguish it? All that would be true is that humans would have a more complicated preference structure than animals. If there is to be a real difference between persons and animals, then, it seems that persons cannot have a highest-order volition: meta-desires must recede infinitely. (One may see in this, perhaps, part of Hegel's motivation for talking of persons in terms of "infinite self-relation.")

This would be a dark doctrine. But even if one could accept the view that humans are interminably reflexive, and so different from animals on this matter, one would still have to deal with the stubborn intuition that removing an animal's desire is not, as a general policy, just as acceptable as satisfying the desire.

Views emphasizing human reflexivity may allow that nonrational creatures have an interest in life, but they insinuate that rational creatures have *more* of an interest in life, since a rational creature can be interested in continued existence in itself. It is not clear, however, that this provides a justification for preferring human to animal life in every case of conflict. We often judge that increasing one person's opportunities to satisfy interests is more important than satisfying specific desires of another person. I don't see that we can *assume* that any desire to live on the part of a human outweighs in itself the sort of interest in living that an animal can have.

VI

A reflexive being has a kind of interest in life that an unreflexive being lacks, but it is not clear exactly why this should give the reflexive being any greater claim on life, or make its life more valuable or important. Why should mental complexity count for anything? That it *does* count is an assumption common to speciesist and anti-speciesist alike. Even Peter Singer says that

> a rejection of speciesism does not imply that all lives are of equal worth. While self-awareness, intelligence, the capacity for meaningful relations with others, and so on are not relevant to the question of inflicting pain—since pain is pain, whatever other capacities, beyond the capacity to feel pain, the being may have—these capacities may be relevant to the question of taking life. It is not arbitrary to hold that the life of a self-aware being, capable of abstract thought, of planning for the future, of complex acts of communication, and so on, is more valuable than the life of a being without these capacities.[21]

Singer's rule of thumb for avoiding speciesism is that "we should give the same respect to the lives of animals as we give to the lives of those humans at a similar mental level . . ."[22] But why the qualification "at the same mental level"? Why does mental complexity count? One answer would be that mentally complex beings experience greater pleasure and pain than others. Another answer would be that mentally complex beings are capable of entering into relations with one another, in a way that simple souls are not; this view requires us to see morality as radically contractual in nature. A third answer would claim that mental complexity is intrinsically valuable.

I do not have time here to discuss the faults of each of these answers.[23] Instead, let me try to indicate as forcefully as I can the difficulty raised for moral reflection by this question of the comparative value of human and nonhuman lives.

I assume that animals are conscious.[24] I am willing to concede, for the sake of argument, that the consciousness of (most) animals is not self-consciousness, and that self-consciousness is a more "complex" state of mind than "mere" consciousness. But what moral weight does such complexity carry? I incline to the view that each mind can be valuable to itself. There need be nothing *intrinsically* wrong with the mentalities of those who are "mad," "retarded," or "childish." That they are not what I want for myself does nothing to show that they are not valuable to *those* beings. Shouldn't every mind have a voice, even if I cannot hear it? As Samuel Alexander says about children: "We like them because they are children, and not because they will be men."[25] Children are adorable, he suggests, because of, rather than despite, their mental simplicity. So, he says, is his dog. Once one starts down this path, it is difficult to know where to stop. The great microbiologist H. S. Jennings says that he is

> thoroughly convinced, after long study of the behavior of this organism, that if Amoeba were a large animal, so as to come within the everyday experience of human beings, its behavior would at once call forth the attribution to it of states of pleasure and pain, of hunger, desire and the like, on precisely the same basis as we attribute these things to the dog.[26]

And Richard Taylor, though on less empirical grounds, suggests this:

> Even the glow worms . . . whose cycles of existence over the millions of years seem so pointless when looked at by us, will seem utterly different to us if we can somehow try to view their existence from within.[27]

Consider, finally, the oyster, a much maligned creature. Plato argues that "if you were without reason, memory, knowledge, and true judgment, you would necessarily . . . be unaware whether you were, or were not, enjoying yourself . . . You would be living the life not of a human being, but of some sort of sea lung or one of those creatures of the ocean whose bodies are incased in shells" (*Philebus* 21b–c). Descartes argues as follows:

The most that one can say is that though the animals do not perform any action which shows us that they think, still, since the organs of their body are not very different from ours, it may be conjectured that there is attached to those organs some thoughts such as we experience in ourselves, but of a very much less perfect kind. To which I have nothing to reply except that if they thought as we do, they would have an immortal soul like us. This is unlikely, because there is no reason to believe it of some animals without believing it of all, and many of them such as oysters and sponges are too imperfect for this to be credible.[28]

Even Peter Singer excludes the oyster.[29] I have no idea whether oysters are conscious or not. My point is that, if they or any other creatures are, if there is reason to believe that they are, there is *no reason* to despise their consciousness as *in itself* of less value to them than our own is to us. In the essay of Santayana's that convinced Russell to give up his early belief in the objectivity of good and evil, Santayana[30] makes the following comment on that argument of Plato's:

It is an *argumentum ad hominem* (and there can be no other kind of argument in ethics); but the man who gives the required answer does so not because the answer is self-evident, which it is not, but because he is the required sort of man. He is shocked at the idea of resembling an oyster. Yet changeless pleasure, without memory or reflection, without the wearisome intermixture of arbitrary images, is just what the mystic, the voluptuary, and perhaps the oyster find to be good . . . Such a radical hedonism is indeed inhuman; it undermines all conventional ambitions, and is not a possible foundation for political or artistic life. But that is all we can say against it. Our humanity cannot annul the incommensurable sorts of good that may be pursued in the world, though it cannot itself pursue them. The impossibility which people labour under of being satisfied with pure pleasure as a goal is due to their want of imagination, or rather to their being dominated by an imagination which is exclusively human.[31]

If we base ethics on self-assertion, as McGilvary and Devine and (more profoundly) Santayana do, we can morally exclude oysters and pigs, which is gastronomically convenient, but we pay a price: those who are asserting themselves can, with equal justification, exclude Jews or Blacks, the retarded, me, or, even, you. One wants to draw a line here, but no rationale so far has worked. This result, if not surprising, is, for anyone who wants to believe in the coherence of ethics, deeply disturbing.

NOTES

1. Mill, John Stuart, *Utilitarianism* (1863). Many editions.
2. MacIver, A. M., "Ethics and the Beetle." *Philosophy* 44 (1948), p. 65.
3. Goodrich, T., "The Morality of Killing." *Philosophy* 44 (1969), p. 128.

4. Russell, Bertrand, *Autobiography* (London: Unwin Books, 1975), p. 162, quoting a letter of 1902.

5. Blake, William, "The Marriage of Heaven and Hell," in Geoffrey Keynes (ed.), *Balke: Complete Writings* (Oxford: Oxford University Press, 1966), p. 150.

6. Rousseau, Jean-Jacques, *The Social Contract*, Book One, Chapter Two (1762). Many editions.

7. McGilvary, Evander Bradley, *Toward a Perspective Realism* (LaSalle: Open Court, 1956), pp. 292–94.

8. Devine, Philip E., *The Ethics of Homicide* (Ithaca: Cornell University Press, 1978), p. 49.

9. Kant, Immanuel, *Grundlegung zur Metaphysik der Sitten* (1785). Many editions.

10. Kant, Immanuel, *Lectures on Ethics* (London: Methuen, 1930), p. 239.

11. Hegel, G. W. F., *Philosophy of Right* (Oxford: Oxford University Press, 1952), p. 237.

12. *Ibid.*, p. 236.

13. Johnstone, Henry W., Jr., "On Being a Person," in Carl G. Vaught (ed.), *Essays in Metaphysics* (University Park: Pennsylvania State University Press, 1970), p. 138.

14. Frankfurt, G., "Freedom of the Will and the Concept of a Person." *Journal of Philosophy* 68 (1971), pp. 5–20.

15. Jeffrey, Richard C., "Preference among Preferences." *Journal of Philosophy* 71 (1974), pp. 377–91.

16. Watson, Gary, "Free Agency." *Journal of Philosophy* 72 (1975), p. 220.

17. Taylor, Richard, *Good and Evil* (New York: Macmillan, 1970).

18. Harman, Gilbert, "Practical Reasoning." *Review of Metaphysics* 29 (1976), pp. 431–63.

19. I use "interest" in a broad sense. I have an interest in having my desires satisfied, or their satisfaction promoted, other things being equal. Also, if I desire that a particular state of affairs obtain, or a particular event or experience occur, I have an interest in the realization of that state of affairs, event, or experience, other things being equal. (But this is not a matter of what I "take an interest" in or "am interested" in.) Something is in my interest if it benefits me (or its absence harms me), if it is a good for me, if it is something I want (other things being equal). I have an interest in the things that make my life better, or prevent it from becoming worse. There may be narrower senses of "interest," but I would argue that my broad usage is perfectly legitimate.

20. I owe this objection to Susan Wolf.

21. Singer, Peter, *Animal Liberation* (New York: New York Review/Random House, 1975).

22. *Ibid.*

23. On the latter two especially, see my dissertation, *Species and Morality* (Princeton University, 1976), chapters four and five.

24. Griffen, Donald R., *The Question of Animal Awareness* (New York: Rockefeller University Press, 1976).

25. Alexander, Samuel, "The Mind of a Dog," in *Philosophical and Literary Pieces* (London: Macmillan, 1939), p. 115.

26. Jennings, H. S., *Behavior of the Lower Organisms* (New York: Columbia University Press, 1906), p. 336.

27. Taylor, Richard, *op. cit.*, p. 267.

28. Descartes, René, *Philosophical Letters*, translated by A. Kenny (Oxford: Oxford University Press, 1970), pp. 207–208.

29. Singer, Peter, *op. cit.*, p. 186.

30. Santayana's influence on Russell's recantation is documented in Bertrand Russell, *Portraits from Memory and Other Essays* (New York: Simon & Schuster, 1956), p. 96.

31. Santayana, George, *Winds of Doctrine* (New York: Charles Scribner's Sons, 1913).

RUTH CIGMAN

Why Death
Does Not
Harm Animals

To be a possible subject of misfortunes which are not merely unpleasant experiences, one must be able to desire and value certain things. The kind of misfortune which is in question here is death, and to discover whether this is a misfortune for an animal, we must ask whether, or in what sense, animals don't want to die. Of course, in some sense this is true of virtually all animals, which manifest acute fear when their lives are threatened. Yet blindly clinging on to life is not the same as wanting to live because one *values* life. This is the kind of desire for life of which persons are capable. It is this which gives sense to the claim that death is a misfortune, even a tragedy, for a person. Bernard Williams argues a view like this.[1]

Williams introduces the useful concept of a categorical desire. This is a desire which does not merely presuppose being alive (like the desire to eat when one is hungry), but rather answers the question whether one wants to remain alive. It may answer this question affirmatively or not. Williams discusses what he calls a rational forward-looking desire for suicide; this

Ruth Cigman studied philosophy at the University of Cambridge and has taught philosophy at Iona College.

Ruth Cigman, "Death, Misfortune, and Species Inequality," *Philosophy & Public Affairs* 10, no. 1 (Winter 1981). Copyright © 1981 by Princeton University Press. Reprinted with permission of Princeton University Press.

desire is categorical because it resolves (negatively), rather than assumes, the questions of one's continued existence. Alternatively one may resolve this question affirmatively with a desire, for example, to raise children or write a book. Such desires give one reason to go on living, they give life so-called point or meaning. Most persons have some such desires throughout substantial periods of their lives.

A person who possesses categorical desires of the second sort is, Williams suggests, vulnerable to the misfortune of death. . . . "To want something," says Williams, "is to that extent to have a reason for resisting what excludes having that thing: and death certainly does that, for a very large range of things that one wants." A subject of categorical desires, therefore, "has reason to regard possible death as a misfortune to be avoided, and we, looking at things from his point of view, would have reason to regard his actual death as a misfortune." The fear of death need not grow out of a confused conception of death as a state which is somehow suffered . . . it may be the entirely rational corollary of the desire to do certain things with one's life. Furthermore we often pity a person who has died on exactly the ground that death prevents the satisfaction of certain desires, and not merely . . . that death closes certain possibilities that the subject may or may not have wanted to realize.

It will be obvious from the earlier discussion that I reject the suggestion that a categorical desire, or anything of this nature, is attributable to animals. For consider what would have to be the case if this were so. First, animals would have to possess essentially the same conceptions of life and death as persons do. The subject of a categorical desire must either understand death as a condition which closes a possible future forever, and leaves behind one a world in which one has no part as an agent or conscious being of any sort; or he must grasp, and then reject, this conception of death, in favor of a belief in immortality. Either way, the radical and exclusive nature of the transition from life to death must be understood—it must at least be appreciated why people think in these terms—so that the full significance of the idea that "X is a reason for living" may be grasped.

One can only understand life and death in these ways if one possesses the related concepts of long-term future possibilities, of life itself as an object of value, of consciousness, agency and their annihilation, and of tragedy and similar misfortunes. It is only by an imaginative leap that possession of these concepts seems attributable to animals as well as to persons; this leap is all the more tempting, and therefore all the more dangerous, because it is not *obviously* absurd. It is certainly the case, for example, that some animals experience emotions of a relatively sophisticated nature, and that these emotions involve a kind of recognition of such things as human misfortune, impending danger to another, potential loss, and so on. I see no reason to withhold the ascription of sympathy, anxiety, even grief, to some animals; I only want to deny (what may be suggested by an anti-speciesist) that these emotions, and the range of awareness which they presuppose, give us a way into legitimately ascribing to animals an understanding of the finality, and potentially tragic significance, of death. Such understanding is necessary for a subject of categorical desires. . . .

NOTES

1. Bernard Williams, "The Makropolous Case." in *Problems of the Self.*

TOM REGAN

Why Death Does Harm Animals

The recognition that harms need not hurt has important implications regarding the death and killing of animals. It is sometimes said that so long as animals are put to death painlessly, so long as they do not suffer as they die, we should have no moral objection. This view frequently is advanced in debates about the "humaneness" of alternative methods of slaughtering animals for food and the ethics of using animals for scientific purposes. For example, in this latter case we frequently are told that if animals are anesthetized, so that they feel nothing and so do not suffer, and if, after the test, experiment or demonstration is completed, the animal is "sacrificed" before regaining consciousness, then everything is morally above board. . . . But this completely overlooks the other type of harm we may visit upon them—namely, the harm done by deprivation. And an untimely death *is* a deprivation of a quite fundamental and irreversible kind. It is irreversible because, once dead, always dead. It is fundamental because death forecloses *all* possibilities of finding satisfaction. Once dead, the individual who had preferences, who could find satisfaction in this or that, who could exercise preference autonomy, can do this no more. Death is the ultimate harm because it is the ultimate loss—the loss of life itself. . . .

Tom Regan, *The Case for Animal Rights.* Berkeley: University of California Press, 1983. Reprinted by permission of the University of California Press.

Professor Ruth Cigman disputes this way of viewing the death of an animal:[1] It will be instructive to examine her reasons. In order for death to be, in her terms, a "misfortune" for a given individual, that individual must have the capacity to have what Cigman, following Bernard Williams, calls "categorical desires."[2] Such a desire, she writes,

> is a desire which does not merely presuppose being alive (like the desire to eat when one is hungry), but rather answers the question whether one wants to remain alive. It may answer this question affirmatively or not. Williams discusses what he calls a rational forward-looking desire for suicide; this desire is categorical because it resolves (negatively), rather than assumes, the question of one's continued existence. Alternatively one may resolve this question affirmatively with a desire, for example, to raise children or write a book. Such desires give one reason to go on living, they give life so-called point or meaning. Most persons have some such desires throughout substantial periods of their lives.[3]

Animals, Cigman contends, although they "manifest acute fear when their lives are threatened," "blindly clinging on to life," lack the capacity to have categorical desires.[4] This is because animals lack the necessary understanding of life and death that having categorical desires presupposes. One cannot see death as a misfortune or harm unless "one possesses the related concepts of long-term future possibilities, of life itself as an object of value, of consciousness, agency and their annihilation, and of tragedy and similar misfortunes." Since "such understanding is necessary for a subject of categorical desires," and since animals lack this understanding and the capacity to have such desires, it follows that death for them is no misfortune—is no harm.[5]

There is a good deal that is unclear here, perhaps ineradicably so in some cases. For death to be a misfortune for a given individual, that individual, Cigman contends, must have a sense of "long-term future possibilities." But how long is "long-term"? The question is not idle. Grounds have been advanced . . . for viewing animals as having a sense of their own future; they act in the present with a view to bringing about the satisfaction of their desires in the future. Is their grasp of their future ever long enough to qualify as a grasp of "long-term future possibilities"? When, for example, wolves run for many hours, possibly even days, in a given direction and then, upon reaching a given place, stop and wait; and when in time the wandering herd of caribou comes into view, may we not parsimoniously describe and explain the wolves' behavior in terms of their sense of "future possibilities"?[6] If so, is their grasp of these possibilities sufficiently future-oriented to satisfy Cigman's requirement that they involve a sense of *long-term* possibilities? Clearly we cannot say one way or the other unless or until Cigman herself sheds some light on this shadowy idea.

Suppose, however, that animals fall short in this regard: their sense of future possibilities never involves their grasp of long-term future possibilities. What follows from this? What follows is that animals would be unable to make long-term plans or set themselves distant goals and then proceed to act in the present with the intention of actualizing these plans or fulfilling these goals. The writing of a book, to use Cigman's example, is a long-term project; one begins with a goal one sets before oneself, and one must work on the project as the future unfolds. If one had no sense, no understanding, of long-term future possibilities, one could not set such a goal for oneself. That much is reasonably clear. But it does not follow that individuals who lack any grasp of long-term future possibilities *have* no long-term future possibilities. On the contrary, even if we assume that animals fail to have a sufficiently rich grasp of long-term future possibilities, in Cigman's sense, animals do have a psychophysical identity over time. Barring unforeseen developments, Fido will be the same dog tomorrow, and tomorrow, and so on into the indefinite future, as he is today. The untimely death of such an animal, therefore, does cut that individual's life short, not only in the sense that a living organism ceases to be biologically alive, but, more pertinently, in the sense that a particular psychological being ceases to be. And it is this latter fact, not whether animals themselves have a sense of their long-term future possibilities, that is decisive in giving an account of the harm or misfortune death can be for them. Death for them is a misfortune, a harm, when death for them is a deprivation, a loss, and it is the latter when their death is contrary to their welfare-interests, even assuming that they themselves have no preference-interest in remaining alive or in avoiding death.

Aside from the inadequacy of Cigman's grounds for denying that death is a misfortune for *animals,* we ought also note how newly born and soon-to-be-born *human beings* fare, given her position. Everything turns on how she understands the notion of having (in her words) the *capacity* to have categorical desires. By this she could mean *potential,* so that, for example, human fetuses and young children have the capacity to have categorical desires although they have yet to have any. But she might mean, instead, *ability* to have such desires, so that one has the capacity to have categorical desires if, and only if, one actually has them. How she understands this crucial notion of capacity does make a difference. If the latter interpretation is the one she accepts, then not only human fetuses but also young children and many mentally enfeebled and senile humans would be in the same category regarding death as the one in which Cigman places animals: since, like animals, these humans lack the ability to have categorical desires, *their* death, like the death of animals, would be no misfortune. This is strongly counterintuitive. Few people would endorse the view that the untimely death of a young child is no harm, no misfortune. Most will find the untimely death of a young child the very paradigm of the tragic face of death—death's ugly sting at its worst. Cigman could accommodate this view by accepting the potentiality interpretation: since young children have the potential to have categorical desires, death is a misfortune for them. Unfortunately, this option would cause more problems than it would solve, given Cigman's position, since human fetuses, not just young children, have the potential to have categorical desires. And it is *quite* clear that Professor Cigman does not believe that death is a misfortune for the fetus.[7]

There is a still more fundamental question to be raised, however, and this concerns how Professor Cigman understands the central notion of death as a misfortune. Characteristically she writes of the misfortune of death in terms of its being a "tragedy," as something "tragic." To view death in this way is fairly certain to exclude the death of at least most animals from being a misfortune, since to view the death of each and every animal as a "tragedy," as "tragic," is to strain anyone's credulity. The inference we should draw from this, however, is not that the death of an animal can be no misfortune or harm to that animal; it is that there is something fundamentally unsatisfactory in requiring that death be "tragic" if it is to be a harm or misfortune.

To regard all *human* death as tragic is to cheapen the notion of tragedy. This is clearest in the case of those humans for whom death is a merciful release from a life of constant, untreatable pain and torment. It is the condition of their life, not their death, that is more aptly viewed as tragic. The fullness of one's life, especially when compared with one's promise, also makes a difference. Van Gogh's death was tragic: he had so much to give and so little time to give it. But no one looking for tragedy will find it in, say, Picasso's death. Mozart's death was tragic, but not Handel's. The deaths of the Kennedy brothers, tragic, but the death of the Wright brothers? What for many is the very paradigm of the tragedy of death, the death of young children, *is* tragic, when it is, because death irrevocably and irretrievably denies them any opportunity to have a full life. The tragedy of the death of these children, despite their inability to have "categorical desires" except potentially, shows that having such desires is not a necessary condition of one's death being a tragedy, just as the absence of tragedy in Picasso's death shows that having such desires, or dying before one fulfills them, is not a sufficient condition of death's being a tragedy.

It does not follow from this that deaths that are not tragic are not harms or misfortunes. These notions—tragedy, on the one hand, and harm and misfortune, on the other—are not equivalent. To say that Picasso's death was not a tragedy is not to say that it was not a harm or misfortune. It is quite possible that living longer would have been in Picasso's interests, in which case his death, whether painful or not, was a harm because of the loss it represented. But to apply the notion of tragedy to his death is to force it where it does not fit. All deaths that are tragic are harms or misfortunes, but not all deaths that are the latter are the former. Even assuming, then, that we were to grant to Professor Cigman her view that the death of an animal is never a tragedy (and it is unclear that we should make this major concession to her),[8] it would not follow that we are committed to denying that death can be, and frequently is, a harm or misfortune for individual animals. To bring about the untimely death of animals will not hurt them if this is done painlessly; but they will be harmed. And it is the harm that an untimely death is, not just the painful methods frequently used, that should occasion our ethical curiosity.

NOTES

1. Ruth Cigman, "Death, Misfortune and Species Inequality," *Philosophy and Public Affairs* 10, no. 1 (Winter 1980): 47–64. Excerpt reproduced in this volume.
2. Bernard Williams, "The Markropolous Case," in *Problems of the Self* (Cambridge: Harvard University Press, 1973).
3. Cigman, "Death, Misfortune," p. 58.
4. Ibid., p. 57
5. Ibid., p. 59. I assume that misfortunes and harms, when applied to humans and animals, are coextensive. It would not make any clear sense to say that something was a misfortune to Mary but that she was not harmed by it, or that, though she was harmed by something, she suffered no misfortune. Thus I assume that when Cigman denies that death is a misfortune for animals, she implies that it is not a harm for them either. My viewing matters in this way, whether sound or not, at least is not eccentric. In addition to Nagel ("Death"), see L. W. Sumner, "A Matter of Life and Death," *Nous* 10 (May 1976): 145–171.
6. Barry Holstum Lopez gives a number of examples of such behavior by wolves. See his *Of Wolves and Men* (New York: Scribners, 1978).
7. Ibid., p. 55.
8. Those who work to save the whale, for example, are unlikely to change how they talk because philosophers argue that "tragedy" is an idea that does not apply to the death of animals. These persons are likely to continue to think, and say, that the killing of whales by commercial whalers is tragic indeed. It must be a somewhat narrow analysis of tragedy that would preclude the propriety of using language in this way.

PART SIX
The Treatment
of Farm Animals

PETER SINGER

Down on the Factory Farm

For most humans, especially those in modern urban and suburban communities, the most direct form of contact with nonhuman animals is at meal time: we eat them. This simple fact is the key to our attitudes to other animals, and also the key to what each one of us can do about changing these attitudes. The use and abuse of animals raised for food far exceeds, in sheer numbers of animals affected, any other kind of mistreatment. Hundreds of millions of cattle, pigs, and sheep are raised and slaughtered in the United States alone each year; and for poultry the figure is a staggering 3 *billion*. (That means that about 5,000 birds—mostly chickens—will have been slaughtered in the time it takes you to read this page.) It is here, on our dinner table and in our neighborhood supermarket or butcher's shop, that we are brought into direct touch with the most extensive exploitation of other species that has ever existed.

In general, we are ignorant of the abuse of living creatures that lies behind the food we eat. Consider the images conjured up by the word "farm": a house, a barn, a flock of hens, overseen by a strutting rooster, scratching around the farmyard, a herd of cows being brought in from the

From Peter Singer, *Animal Liberation*. © New York Review of Books, 1975, and distributed through Random House, New York.

fields for milking, and perhaps a sow rooting around in the orchard with a litter of squealing piglets running excitedly behind her.

Very few farms were ever as idyllic as that traditional image would have us believe. Yet we still think of a farm as a pleasant place, far removed from our own industrial, profit-conscious city life. Of those few who think about the lives of animals on farms, not many know much of modern methods of animal raising. Some people wonder whether animals are slaughtered painlessly, and anyone who has followed a truckload of cattle must know that farm animals are transported in very crowded conditions; but few suspect that transportation and slaughter are anything more than the brief and inevitable conclusion of a life of ease and contentment, a life that contains the natural pleasures of animal existence without the hardships that wild animals must endure in the struggle for survival.

These comfortable assumptions bear little relation to the realities of modern farming. For a start, farming is no longer controlled by simple country folk. It is a business, and big business at that. In the last thirty years the entry of large corporations and assembly-line methods of production have turned farming into "agribusiness." . . .

The first animal to be removed from the relatively natural conditions of the traditional farms and subjected to the full stress of modern intensive farming was the chicken. Chickens have the misfortune of being useful to humans in two ways: for their flesh and for their eggs. There are now standard mass-production techniques for obtaining both these products.

Agribusiness enthusiasts consider the rise of the chicken industry to be one of the great success stories of farming. At the end of World War II chicken for the table was still relatively rare. It came mainly from small independent farmers or from the unwanted males produced by egg-laying flocks. Today "broilers"—as table chickens are now usually called—are produced literally by the millions from the highly automated factory-like plants of the large corporations that own or control 98 percent of all broiler production in the United States.[1]

The essential step in turning the chicken from a farmyard bird into a manufactured item was confining them indoors. A broiler producer today gets a load of 10,000, 50,000, or even more day-old chicks from the hatcheries and puts them straight into a long, windowless shed—usually on the floor, although some producers use tiers of cages in order to get more birds into the same-size shed. Inside the shed, every aspect of the birds' environment is controlled to make them grow faster on less feed. Food and water are fed automatically from hoppers suspended from the roof. The lighting is adjusted according to advice from agricultural researchers: for instance, there may be bright light 24 hours a day for the first week or two, to encourage the chicks to gain quickly; then the lights may be dimmed slightly and made to go off and on every two hours, in the belief that the chickens are readier to eat after a period of sleep; finally there comes a point, around six weeks of age, when the birds have grown so much that they are becoming crowded, and the lights will then be made very dim at all times. The point of this dim lighting is to reduce the effects of crowding. Toward the end of the eight- or nine-week life of the chicken, there may be as little as half a square foot of space per chicken—or less than the area of a sheet of quarto paper for a 3½ lb. bird. Under these conditions with normal lighting the stress of crowding and the absence of natural outlets for the bird's energies lead to outbreaks of fighting, with birds pecking at each other's feathers and sometimes killing and eating one another. Very dim lighting has been found to reduce this and so the birds are likely to live out their last weeks in near-darkness.

Feather-pecking and cannibalism are, in the broiler producer's language, "vices." They are not natural vices, however—they are the result of the stress and crowding to which the modern broilerman subjects his birds. Chickens are highly social animals, and in the farmyard they develop a hierarchy, sometimes called a "pecking order." Every bird yields, at the food trough or elsewhere, to those above it in rank, and takes precedence over those below. There may be a few confrontations before the order is firmly established but more often than not a show of force, rather than actual physical contact, is enough to put a chicken in its place. As Konrad Lorenz, a renowned figure in the field of animal behavior, wrote in the days when flocks were still small:

> Do animals thus know each other among themselves? They certainly do. . . . Every poultry farmer knows that . . . there exists a very definite order, in which each bird is afraid of those that are above her in rank. After some few disputes, which need not necessarily come to blows, each bird knows which of the others she has to fear and which must show respect to her. Not only physical strength, but also personal courage, energy, and even the self-assurance of every individual bird are decisive in the maintenance of the pecking order.[2]

Other studies have shown that a flock of up to 90 chickens can maintain a stable social order, each bird knowing its place; but 10,000 birds crowded together in a single shed is obviously a different matter.[3] The birds cannot establish a social order, and as a result they fight frequently with each other. Quite apart from the inability of the individual bird to recognize so many other birds, the mere fact of extreme crowding probably contributes to irritability and excitability in chickens, as it does in humans and other animals. This is something farming magazines are aware of, and they frequently warn their readers:

> Feather-pecking and cannibalism have increased to a formidable extent of late years, due, no doubt, to the changes in technique and the swing towards completely intensive management of laying flocks and table poultry. . . . The most common faults in management which may lead to vice are boredom,

overcrowding in badly ventilated houses ... lack of feeding space, unbalanced food or shortage of water, and heavy infestation with insect pests.[4]

Clearly the farmer must stop "vices," because they cost him money; but although he may know that overcrowding is the root cause, he cannot do anything about this, since in the competitive state of the industry, eliminating overcrowding could mean eliminating his profit margin at the same time. He would have fewer birds to sell, but would have had to pay the same outlay for his building, for the automatic feeding equipment, for the fuel used to heat and ventilate the building, and for labor. So the farmer limits his efforts to reducing the consequences of the stress that costs him money. The unnatural way in which he keeps his birds causes the vices; but to control them the poultryman must make the conditions still more unnatural. Very dim lighting is one way of doing this. A more drastic step, though one now almost universally used in the industry, is "debeaking." This involves inserting the chick's head in a guillotine-like device which cuts off part of its beak. Alternatively the operation may be done with a hot knife. Some poultrymen claim that this operation is painless, but an expert British Government committee under zoologist Professor F. W. Rogers Brambell appointed to look into aspects of intensive farming found otherwise:

> ... between the horn and the bone is a thin layer of highly sensitive soft tissue, resembling the "quick" of the human nail. The hot knife used in de-beaking cuts through this complex of horn, bone and sensitive tissue, causing severe pain.[5]

De-beaking, which is routinely performed in anticipation of cannibalism by most poultrymen, does greatly reduce the amount of damage a chicken can do to other chickens. It also, in the words of the Brambell Committee, "deprives the bird of what is in effect its most versatile member" while it obviously does nothing to reduce the stress and overcrowding that lead to this unnatural cannibalism in the first place. . . .

"A hen," Samuel Butler once wrote, "is only an egg's way of making another egg." Butler, no doubt, was being humorous; but when Fred. C. Haley, president of a Georgia poultry firm that controls the lives of 225,000 laying hens, describes the hen as "an egg producing machine" his words have more serious implications. To emphasize his business-like attitude Haley adds: "The object of producing eggs is to make money. When we forget this objective, we have forgotten what it is all about."[6]

Nor is this only an American attitude. A British farming magazine has told its readers:

> The modern layer, is, after all, only a very efficient converting machine, changing the raw material—feedingstuffs—into the finished product—the egg—less, of course, maintenance requirements.[7]

Remarks of this kind can regularly be found in the egg industry trade journals throughout the United States and Europe, and they express an attitude that is common in the industry. As may be anticipated, their consequences for the laying hens are not good.

Laying hens go through many of the same procedures as broilers, but there are some differences. Like broilers, layers have to be de-beaked, to prevent the cannibalism that would otherwise occur in their crowded conditions; but because they live much longer than broilers, they often go through this operation twice. So we find a poultry specialist at the New Jersey College of Agriculture advising poultrymen to de-beak their chicks when they are between one and two weeks old because there is, he says, less stress on the chicks at this time than if the operation is done earlier, and in addition "there are fewer culls in the laying flock as a result of improper de-beaking." In either case, the article continues, the birds must be de-beaked again when they are ready to begin laying, at around twenty weeks of age.[8]

Laying hens get no more individual attention than broilers. Alan Hainsworth, owner of a poultry farm in upstate New York, told an inquiring local reporter that four hours a day is all he needs for the care of his 36,000 laying hens, while his wife looks after the 20,000 pullets (as the younger birds not yet ready to lay are called): "It takes her about 15 minutes a day. All she checks is their automatic feeders, water cups and any deaths during the night."

This kind of care does not make for a happy flock, as the reporter's description shows:

> Walk into the pullet house and the reaction is immediate—complete pandemonium. The squawking is loud and intense as some 20,000 birds shove to the farthest side of their cages in fear of the human intruders.[9]

Julius Goldman's Egg City, 50 miles northwest of Los Angeles, is one of the world's largest egg producing units, consisting of 2 million hens divided into block long buildings containing 90,000 hens each, five birds to a 16 by 18 inch cage. When the *National Geographic Magazine* did an enthusiastic survey of new farming methods, Ben Shames, Egg City's executive Vice-President, explained to its reporter the methods used to look after so many birds:

> We keep track of the food eaten and the eggs collected in 2 rows of cages among the 110 rows in each building. When production drops to the uneconomic point, all 90,000 birds are sold to processors for potpies or chicken soup. It doesn't pay to keep track of every row in the house, let alone individual hens; with 2 million birds on hand you have to rely on statistical samplings.[10]

Nearly all the big egg producers now keep their laying hens in cages. Originally there was only one bird to a cage; and the idea was that the farmer could then tell which birds were not laying enough eggs to give an economic return on their food. Those birds were then killed. Then it was found that more birds could be housed and costs per bird reduced if two birds were put in each cage. That was only the first step, and as we have seen, there is no longer any question of keeping a tally of each bird's eggs. The advantages of cages for the egg producer now consist in the greater number of birds that can be housed, warmed, fed, and watered in one building, and in the greater use that can be made of labor-saving automatic equipment.

The cages are stacked in tiers, with food and water troughs running along the rows, filled automatically from a central supply. They have sloping wire floors. The slope—usually a gradient of 1 in 5—makes it more difficult for the birds to stand comfortably, but it causes the eggs to roll to the front of the cage where they can easily be collected by hand or, in the more modern plants, carried by conveyor belt to a packing plant.

When a reporter from the New York *Daily News* wanted to see a typical modern egg farm, he visited Frenchtown Poultry Farm, in New Jersey, where he found that

> Each 18 by 24 inch cage on the Frenchtown farm contains nine hens who seemed jammed into them by some unseen hand. They barely have enough room to turn around in the cages.
> "Really, you should have no more than eight birds in a cage that size," conceded Oscar Grossman, the farm's lessor. "But sometimes you have to do things to get the most out of your stock."[11]

Actually, if Mr. Grossman had put only eight birds in his cages they would still have been grossly overcrowded; at nine to a cage they have only ⅓ square foot per bird.

In 1968 the farm magazine *American Agriculturalist* advised its readers in an article headed "Bird Squeezing" that it had been found possible to stock at ⅓ square foot per bird by putting four birds in a 12 by 16 inch cage. This was apparently a novel step at the time; the steady increase in densities over the years is indicated by the fact that a 1974 issue of the same magazine describing the Lannsdale Poultry Farm, near Rochester, New York, mentions the same housing density without any suggestion that it is unusual.[12] In reading egg industry magazines I have found numerous reports of similar high densities, and scarcely any that are substantially lower. My own visits to poultry farms in the United States have shown the same pattern. The highest reported density that I have read about is at the Hainsworth farm in Mt. Morris, New York, where four hens are squeezed into cages 12 inches by 12 inches, or just one square foot—and the reporter adds: "Some hold five birds when Hainsworth has more birds than room."[13]

This means ¼ and sometimes ⅕ square foot per bird. At this stocking rate a *single sheet of quarto paper represents the living area of two to three hens.*

Under the conditions standard on modern egg farms in the United States and other "developed nations" every natural instinct the birds have is frustrated. They cannot walk around, scratch the ground, dust-bathe, build a nest, or stretch their wings. They are not part of a flock. They cannot keep out of each other's way and weaker birds have no escape from the attacks of stronger ones, already maddened by the unnatural conditions. . . .

Intensive production of pigs and cattle is now also common; but of all the forms of intensive farming now practiced, the quality veal industry ranks as the most morally repugnant, comparable only with barbarities like the force-feeding of geese through a funnel that produces the deformed livers made into *pâté de foie gras.* The essence of veal raising is the feeding of a high-protein food (that should be used to reduce malnutrition in poorer parts of the world) to confined, anemic calves in a manner that will produce a tender, pale-colored flesh that will be served to gourmets in expensive restaurants. Fortunately this industry does not compare in size with poultry, beef, or pig production; nevertheless it is worth our attention because it represents an extreme, both in the degree of exploitation to which it subjects its animals and in its absurd inefficiency as a method of providing people with nourishment.

Veal is the flesh of a young calf, and the term was originally reserved for calves killed before they had been weaned from their mothers. The flesh of these very young animals was paler and more tender than that of a calf that had begun to eat grass; but there was not much of it, since calves begin to eat grass when they are a few weeks old and still very small. So there was little money in veal, and the small amount available came from the unwanted male calves produced by the dairy industry. These males were a nuisance to the dairy farmers, since the dairy breeds do not make good beef cattle. Therefore they were sold as quickly as possible. A day or two after being born they were trucked to market where, hungry and frightened by the strange surroundings and the absence of their mothers, they were sold for immediate delivery to the slaughterhouse.

Once this was the main source of veal in the United States. Now, using methods first developed in Holland, farmers have found a way to keep the calf longer without the flesh becoming darker in color or less tender. This means that the veal calf, when sold, may weigh as much as 325 lbs., instead of the 90-odd lbs. that newborn calves weigh. Because veal fetches a premium price, this has made rearing veal calves a profitable occupation.

The trick depends on keeping the calf in highly unnatural conditions. If the calf were left to grow up outside, its playful nature would lead it to romp around the fields. Soon it would begin to develop muscles, which would make its flesh tough. At the same time it would eat grass and its flesh would lose the pale color that the flesh of newborn calves has. So the specialist veal producer takes his calves straight from the auction ring to a confinement unit. Here, in a converted barn or purpose-built shed, he will have rows of wooden stalls. Each stall will be 1 foot 10 inches wide and 4 feet 6 inches long. It will have a slatted wooden floor, raised above the concrete floor of the shed. The calves will be tethered by a chain around the neck to prevent them from turning around in their stalls. (The chain may be removed when the calves grow too big to turn around in such narrow stalls.) The stall will have no straw or other bedding, since the calf might eat it, spoiling the paleness of his flesh.

Here the calves will live for the next thirteen to fifteen weeks. They will leave their stalls only to be taken out to slaughter. They are fed a totally liquid diet, based on nonfat milk powder with added vitamins, minerals, and growth-promoting drugs. . . .

The narrow stalls and their slatted wooden floors are a serious source of discomfort for the calves. The inability to turn around is frustrating. When he lies down, the calf must lie hunched up, sitting almost on top of his legs rather than having them out to one side as he would do if he had more room. A stall too narrow to turn around in is also too narrow to groom comfortably in; and calves have an innate desire to twist their heads around and groom themselves with their tongues. A wooden floor without any bedding is hard and uncomfortable; it is rough on the calves' knees as they get up and lie down. In addition, animals with hooves are uncomfortable on slatted floors. A slatted floor is like a cattle grid, which cattle will always avoid, except that the slats are closer together. The spaces, however, must still be large enough to allow manure to fall or be washed through, and this means that they are large enough to make the calves uncomfortable.[14]

The special nature of the veal calf has other implications that show the industry's lack of genuine concern for the animals' welfare. Obviously the calves sorely miss their mothers. They also miss something to suck on. The urge to suck is strong in a baby calf, as it is in a baby human. These calves have no teat to suck on, nor do they have any substitute. From their first day in confinement—which may well be only the third or fourth day of their lives—they drink from a plastic bucket. Attempts have been made to feed calves through artificial teats, but the problems of keeping the teats clean and sterile are apparently too great for the farmer to try to overcome. It is common to see calves frantically trying to suck some part of their stalls, although there is usually nothing suitable; and if you offer a veal calf your finger he will immediately begin to suck on it, as a human baby sucks its thumb.

Later on the calf develops the desire to ruminate—that is, to take in roughage and chew the cud. But roughage is strictly forbidden and so, again, the calf may resort to vain attempts to chew the sides of its stall.

Digestive disorders, including stomach ulcers, are common in veal calves, as are chronically loose bowel movements.

As if this were not enough, there is the fact that the calf is deliberately kept anemic. As one veal producers' journal has said,

> Color of veal is one of the primary factors involved in obtaining "top-dollar" returns from the fancy veal market . . . "light color" veal is a premium item much in demand at better clubs, hotels and restaurants. "Light color" or pink veal is partly associated with the amount of iron in the muscle of the calves.[15]

So veal feeds are deliberately kept low in iron. A normal calf would obtain iron from grass or other forms of roughage, but since a veal calf is not allowed this he becomes anemic. Pale pink flesh is in fact anemic flesh. The demand for flesh of this color is a matter of snob appeal. The color does not affect the taste and it certainly does not make the flesh more nourishing—rather the opposite.

Calves kept in this matter are unhappy and unhealthy animals. Despite the fact that the veal producer selects only the strongest, healthiest calves to begin with, uses a medicated feed as a routine measure, and gives additional injections at the slightest sign of illness, digestive, respiratory and infectious diseases are widespread. It is common for a veal producer to find that one in ten of a batch of calves does not survive the fifteen weeks of confinement. Ten percent mortality over such a short period would be disastrous for anyone raising calves for beef, but the veal producer can tolerate this loss because of the high price restaurants are prepared to pay for his product. If the reader will recall that this whole laborious, wasteful, and painful process exists for the sole purpose of pandering to would-be gourmets who insist on pale, soft veal, no further comment should be needed.

NOTES

1. Harrison Wellford, *Sowing the Wind: The Politics of Food, Safety and Agribusiness* (New York: Grossman Press, 1971), p. 104.
2. K. Lorenz, *King Solomon's Ring* (London: Methuen and Co., 1964), p. 147.
3. Ian Duncan, "Can the Psychologist Measure Stress?" *New Scientist*, October 18, 1973.
4. *The Smallholder*, January 6, 1962; quoted by Ruth Harrison, *Animal Machines* (London: Vincent Stuart, 1964), p. 18
5. *Report of the Technical Committee to Enquire into the Welfare of Animals Kept under Intensive Livestock Husbandry Systems* (London: Her Majesty's Stationery Office, 1965), para. 97.
6. *Poultry Tribune*, January 1974.
7. *Farmer and Stockbreeder*, January 30, 1962; quoted by Ruth Harrison, *Animal Machines*, p. 50.
8. *American Agriculturist*, July 1966.
9. *Upstate*, August 5, 1973, report by Mary Rita Kiereck.
10. *National Geographic Magazine*, February 1970.

11. *Daily News,* September 1, 1971.

12. *American Agriculturist,* August 1968, April 1974.

13. *Upstate,* August 5, 1973.

14. Ruth Harrison, *Animal Machines,* p. 72.

15. *The Stall Street Journal,* published by Provimi, Inc., Watertown, Wisconsin, November 1973.

STANLEY E. CURTIS

The Case
for Intensive Farming
of Food Animals

INTENSIVE FARMING OF FOOD ANIMALS

Hundreds of millions of Americans must have food but choose not to grow it for themselves. Food production is a business and subject to the same economic forces as any business.[1] The chances of a turnaround in the trend to fewer, larger, more intensive animal farms are akin to those of a return to mom-and-pop grocery stores in the residential areas of every city and an independent fast-food restaurant on the main street of every town.

Intensive dairy, livestock, and poultry farms came on the scene soon after World War II. The movement of agricultural animals from dirt lots and pastures to confinement facilities accelerated markedly during the 1950s in the poultry and dairy industries and the 1960s in livestock production. It continues to this day. The most important reason for this did not revolve around the well-being of the animals. Admittedly, although there have been significant side-benefits of intensivism for the animals, there have been new problems, too.[2]

One major force leading to intensivism in animal agriculture had to do with responsible land management. Rearing animals extensively re-

Stanley Curtis teaches in the Department of Animal Sciences, the University of Illinois at Urbana-Champaign. His books include *Environmental Management in Animal Agriculture* (University of Iowa Press, 1983).

Curtis, S. (1986–1987). *Advances in Animal Welfare Science*. Washington, DC: Humane Society of the United States. Reprinted with permission of the publisher.

quires tremendous acreages, and in many parts of the United States it not only constitutes unsound stewardship of the soil, but it has proved economically unfeasible as well.

Another critical factor was labor. With the family farm goes the force of cheap workers upon which this kind of farming was based. Also, animal caretaking is a seven-day-a-week job, so to attain a living standard similar to that of society as a whole, outside help was needed. Today's poultry, livestock, and dairy producers increasingly need to hire workers from the general labor pool to do chores formerly assigned to family members. Of course, prevailing wages must be offered if workers are to be attracted. Despite relatively high rates of unemployment in many rural communities in recent years, the farmer often has had to provide unusual incentives to employees, because the work is hard, and in some respects, unappealing. Thus, animal producers have had to expand and specialize their operations to the extents necessary to justify increased outlays for hired help.

A third factor has been animal waste. Farm animals produce tremendous amounts of feces and urine. For example, one hog puts out as much waste as three adult humans. Of course, the magnitude of the waste-management task rises in parallel with the size of operation. Because of the keen interest in environmental protection over the past two decades, regulations have been put in place which in effect preclude animal production on many of the hills and in many of the valleys these animals roamed in days past. For practical purposes, waste containment is achievable only with a confinement-production facility.

Land, labor, and waste—these have been the principal socioeconomic forces behind the widespread adoption of intensive animal-production systems. The changes that have resulted from these forces have had impacts on the animals' welfare. At this point, let us mention those changes that have been beneficial for the creatures. For one thing, seasonal production cycles have been dampened considerably. It is easier to manage newly born or hatched animals—and juveniles and adults, too, for that matter—the year around in houses than in either natural surroundings or rudimentary artificial shelters typical of extensive production. This has been good for the animals. And the resultant changes in dairy, poultry, and livestock marketing increased economic efficiencies in food production, processing, and distribution. The ultimate beneficiaries of these efficiencies in our free-enterprise economy are the consumers of food products of animal origin.

More pluses have to do with biological management, with the animal's life per se. (1) Providing steady supplies of a well-balanced diet and sanitary water is easier in confinement than on range. (2) Predation of young and small animals by wild and feral carnivores is a tremendous problem in many parts of the United States. Intensive animal facilities such as sheep folds have been used to foil this aspect of the web of life since biblical times. (3) The perforated floors commonly used in animal facilities separate the beasts and birds from their own excreta, thus preventing them from practicing some unhygienic, obnoxious habits such as coprophagy and wallowing in their own excrement. Because enteric infections are major causes of disease and even death in all species of farm animals, the perforated floor improved the living conditions of these creatures greatly. (4) Caretakers can observe individual animals more thoroughly when they are close at hand, held singly, or in small groups. Injuries and disease can be detected more readily and remedial measures implemented more easily as a result.

Interestingly, despite technological changes, managers of large, intensive animal farms still consider sound animal care the keystone of profitability in animal production. Can anything else be imagined by anybody? Excellent animal husbandry is the sine qua non of successful animal production.

The advent of larger units also made it possible to upgrade management quality. On many farms, animal production is no longer a sideline activity or one of several enterprises competing for the manager's attention. More and more, managers of animal-production operations are multitalented professionals who devote all of their time to a single species. Demand for well-educated and -trained managers has led to the establishment of special curricula in intensive animal production.

Finally, with increasing size of operation come economies of purchasing and marketing in large lots, with more or less continuous flow (Halcrow 1980). While this generally enhances the profitability of an individual enterprise, again consumers of foods of animal origin are the ultimate beneficiaries in our kind of economy.

In agriculture, it is not sufficient to be interested only in physiological, behavioral, immunological, and anatomical indices of animals' environmental adaptability. The next question is: How much decrement in production is associated with residing in a particular environment? To learn the quantitative effects of a given environment on animal performance, we still must measure the productive traits themselves. An animal exhibiting obvious reaction to stress, as mentioned above, is generally assumed to be having depressed performance. But the performance loss may be reversible only by a modification of the environment that cannot be repaid in terms of increased animal productivity. Further, visible strain in an animal signifies that it is trying to compensate for an environmental impingement. These attempts might succeed, and they might interfere with performance only slightly. Of course, the question remains as to whether the stresses imposed by a certain production system comprise an unacceptable environment in terms of the animals' overall welfare, a point to be expanded upon later.

ABUSE, NEGLECT, AND DEPRIVATION

Animal production resembles other professions in that there are (in terms of humane treatment) good animal farmers and poor ones. When critics of animal farms cite examples of cruelty to animals, they are referring to farms run by poor producers. Inhumane treatment leads to unhealthy, unproductive animals, and consequently, financial losses. Poor stockmen are among the first animal farmers to go out of business in times of economic crisis.

It has been suggested that any suffering an animal experiences at the hands of a farmer falls into one of three categories: abuse, neglect, or deprivation.[3] Abuse refers to obvious, active cruelty, such as beating an animal with a stick. Neglect is obvious, passive cruelty; for example, confining an animal and then not providing it one or more vital resources, such as food or water. Everyone would agree that abuse and neglect are cruel, and state and federal legislation outlawing both was passed many years ago. Progressive animal producers neither condone nor encourage such cruelty, and any representation to the contrary comprises a calumny. Further, abuse and neglect constitute or lead to severe stress and thus are clearly counterproductive; their practice by farmers would be just as clearly irrational.

Deprivation is the most subtle form of cruelty, and thus the most difficult to assess. It involves the denial of relatively less vital resources, the actual requirements for which mostly have yet to be established. Whether or not farm animals in certain living situations in intensive production systems are suffering from deprivation is a major issue being discussed by humane activists, farmers, and scientists. If so, economical and practically feasible means of alleviating the deprivation will need to be discovered and developed for adoption by farmers. While it might be tempting to speculate anthropomorphically as to the stress perceived by animals when they are prevented by the nature of the environment in which they reside from performing some specific behavior, both humane and economic aspects of environmental design and management are better served when the scientific approach to needs identification and fulfillment is taken.

NEEDS: PHYSIOLOGICAL, SAFETY, AND BEHAVIORAL

It is axiomatic that, when an animals' needs are not being met, its welfare is more or less jeopardized. But here again it must be remembered—and this idea also will be expanded upon later—that a particular welfare decrement does not necessarily place the animal in an ethically unacceptable environment; perhaps the animal simply experiences less—but still an ethically acceptable amount—of well-being.

In any case, it has been suggested that agricultural animals have a hierarchy of needs along the lines of Abraham Maslow's scheme for humans, and that animals' basic needs are being met in most intensive production systems.[4] First and most basic are farm animals' physiological needs; for feed, physical and biological elements of the environment, and health care. These are already relatively well understood and fulfilled.

Intermediate are the animals' safety needs. Although the needs to be protected from harmful environmental elements are important, these safety needs are tended somewhat less rigorously than are the physiological needs. Weather accidents, predation, and poorly designed, manufactured, and operated equipment and facilities still exact reducible tolls in terms of both animal welfare and financial profits.[5]

Last in the hierarchy are the animals' behavioral needs. The question among most scientists is: Is there reasonable evidence supporting the existence of any behavioral need in any agricultural animal? Indeed, no such need has been established, although many scientists believe that they well might exist, however difficult they may be to elucidate.[6] Of course, fundamental to assessing welfare in a farm animal are answers to two questions, the second of which is proving to be exceedingly difficult to answer: (1) Does the animal have subjective feelings? (2) What indicators reveal any such feelings?[7] Knowledge of animals' mental activities can be gained only via indirect experimental evidence at this time, hence any conclusions must be considered tentative. . . .

SUMMARY AND CONCLUSIONS

Alas, farmers face an animal-welfare dilemma. They must decide on animal-production systems while constrained by humane concerns—both their own as well as those of the general citizenry—on one hand and by the realities of doing business in a free-enterprise milieu on the other. And the dilemma will be resolvable only if and when we know much more than we now know about animal suffering and thus about animal well-being. The question is not whether animals have feelings; there is general agreement up and down the line that they do. The question is: How does the animal feel, living in this production system or that? Ian Duncan and Marian Dawkins believe that there are " . . . indicators that with careful experimentation we may be able to accumulate indirect evidence about animals' subjective feelings. This should be our ultimate aim. There are many problems but they are not insurmountable."[8]

How can these problems be surmounted? How will it come to pass that we learn once and for all whether certain production systems cause farm animals to suffer? How will economically feasible, more socially acceptable systems of farm-animal production be discovered and developed? The answer: We can learn these things only from research.

The time is ripe for humane activists to support in all ways possible bona fide scientific investigations of farm animal welfare. This suggestion is not heretical, naive, or ridiculous. My reasoning follows, in the form of a brief recapitulation and juxtaposition of earlier points with a couple of new ones, together with pragmatic analysis and synthesis.

1. Consumer demand for human foods of animal origin is strong, and it will continue to be so for decades. The vast majority of consumers decide whether or not to eat these foods on the bases of nutritional factors, convenience, and flavor, not on the basis of ethical questions. It is folly to hope that animal farms will disappear from the U.S. scene. Those of us who want farm animals to experience as little suffering and as much well-being as possible ought to do what we can to ensure that these animals' needs and feelings are understood, and that the needs are fulfilled, the feelings protected.

2. Food-animal production is a business. As such, it is constrained by economic factors.

3. Society—including animal producers—requires that food animals not be caused to suffer in any way. Therefore, food animal production is also constrained by humane factors.

4. Economic and humane factors do not always work in tandem. Compromise between humane and economic constraints is inevitably necessary in terms of animal-production-system design. This compromise ocurs at the juncture of the welfare plateau and the range of marginally acceptable production systems.

5. Animal agriculture quickly adopts appropriate technologies, especially when the benefit/cost ratio is favorable.

6. Animal producers are at least as humane as members of society in general. Any representation to the contrary comprises a calumny.

7. If animal producers have adopted inhumane production technologies, it has been because they and those who advise them have been ignorant. Any such ignorance owes to lack of scientific evidence, not lack of concern for the animals' general well-being.

8. Those of us who care about animals and want to try to improve the welfare of food animals ought to do everything we can to learn more about what these animals need and how they feel. At the same time, we can be searching for improvements in terms of production equipment and facilities and husbandry systems designed to fulfill the animals' needs and support favorable feelings. Basic and applied research along these lines deserves the complete support of all who want to engender the highest level of welfare possible in food animals.

NOTES

1. Halcrow, H. G. 1980. *Economics of Agriculture.* New York: McGraw-Hill Book Co.
2. Curtis, S. E. 1983. *Environmental Management in Animal Agriculture.* Ames, IA: Iowa State University Press.
3. Ewbank, R. 1981. Alternatives: Definitions and doubts. In: *Alternatives to Intensive Husbandry Systems.* Potters Bar, United Kingdom: Universities Federation for Animal Welfare.
4. Curtis, S. E. 1985. What constitutes well-being? In: Moberg, G. P. ed. *Animal Stress.* Bethesda, MD: American Physiological Society.
5. Ibid.
6. Hughes, B. O. 1980. The assessment of behavioural needs. In: Moss, R. ed. *The Laying Hen and Its Environment.* Boston, MA: Martinus Nijhoff Publishers.
7. Duncan, I. J. and Dawkins, M.S. 1983. The problem of assessing "well-being" and "suffering" in farm animals. In: Smidt, D. ed. *Indicators Relevant to Farm Animal Welfare.* Boston, MA: Martinus Nijhoff Publishers.
8. Ibid.

BART GRUZALSKI

The Case against Raising and Killing Animals for Food

The important ethical view that one ought to live in such a way that one contributes as little as possible to the total amount of suffering in the world and as much as possible to the world's total happiness is called utilitarianism. In this paper I develop the classical utilitarian argument against raising and killing animals for food. I then examine this position in light of several arguments which have recently been raised to show that utilitarianism permits this use of animals. Throughout the paper I refer to nonhuman animals as animals, and to human animals as humans. Although such usage suggests an elitism that might offend some humans, the substantive arguments in the paper are better expressed if we follow ordinary usage, however unenlightened it may be.

THE UTILITARIAN ARGUMENT AGAINST RAISING AND SLAUGHTERING ANIMALS FOR FOOD

According to the classical utilitarianism of John Stuart Mill, actions are right insofar as they tend to produce the greatest happiness for the greatest

Bart Gruzalski teaches philosophy at Northeastern University. He is a frequent contributor to professional journals in moral, political, and social philosophy.

Bart Gruzalski, "The Case against Raising and Killing Animals for Food," pp. 251–263 in H. Miller and W. Williams (eds.), *Ethics and Animals*. Clifton, NJ: Humana Press, 1983.

number. For our purposes it will be helpful to interpret this general slogan as a specific principle regarding the foreseeable consequences of individual actions. In so doing we want to be responsive to the fact that most acts have several mutually exclusive foreseeable consequences that are of different values (e.g., rolling a die has six foreseeable consequences and we may value some more than others). One way to take these different contingencies into account is to assign a number to each foreseeable consequence to represent its desirability (or lack thereof). If we multiply the desirability of a foreseeable consequence by its probability and then sum these products of the likelihood and the desirability of each of the foreseeable consequences, we have the *expected desirability* of doing the action, which, roughly, tells us the odds that the action will produce consequences of a certain value. According to classical act utilitarianism so interpreted, an action is right if it is the best bet a person has to avoid producing painful consequences and to bring about pleasurable or happy consequences (more technically: if its expected desirability is no less than the expected desirability of any alternative).[1] In applying this view we will be using the standard conception of consequences: an event is a consequence of an action only if there is some other action the agent could have performed that would have prevented the occurrence of the event in question.[2] For example, my glass being full of water is a consequence of my holding it under the tap, since had I placed the glass on the counter, an alternative I could have performed, it would still be empty.

From the utilitarian viewpoint there are strong reasons for thinking that raising and slaughtering animals for food is wrong. When we raise animals they suffer because of confinement, transportation, and slaughter-related activities in ways they would not suffer were we not raising them for food. These actions are therefore wrong on utilitarian grounds unless there are other consequences which outweigh these sufferings inflicted on animals. Of course, there are other consequences of these acts besides the pain the animals experience. The most obvious of these consequences is that the animals become tasty morsels of food. But it is doubtful whether the enjoyment of those who are eating these animals can overcome the pain of captivity and slaughter. Does a family at a Kentucky Fried Chicken experience such pleasure from eating chicken that this pleasure overcomes the frustration, pain, and terror which the chicken had to undergo in order to wind up on a cole slaw garnished paper plate?

The plausibility of a utilitarian justification of raising animals for food is even weaker than the previous rhetorical question suggests. In order that the practice of raising and slaughtering animals for their flesh be justified, the animal's pain must not only be *outweighed* by the omnivore's pleasure, but *there can be no alternative act that would foreseeably result in a better balance of pleasure over pain.* Since eating plants is one alternative, and since this alternative produces the pleasures of taste and health without inflicting pain on animals, it follows that, if one is interested in contributing to the total amount of happiness in the world and not contributing to any unnecessary suffering, then one ought not to raise, slaughter, or eat animals, for by doing any of these actions one contributes to a kind of suffering that is unnecessary. Although the above argument may seem sound, some philosophers have raised objections to it while accepting the utilitarian defenses of using animals for food.

OBJECTION ONE: RAISING ANIMALS BENEVOLENTLY

According to the first utilitarian defense of raising and slaughtering animals, the use of animals for food can be justified on utilitarian grounds even if we take into account only the pleasures and pains of the animals involved. James Cargile states this defense of a carnivorous animal husbandry as follows:

> Every year I buy several pigs from a neighboring hog farm and raise them to slaughter for food. They are given lots of room and food, everything a pig could want for a good life but a short one. It would be nice if they could have longer lives. But I believe that their good, short lives are better than no life at all. . . . These animals are getting the best deal people are willing to give them, and I do not see the vegetarians as giving them even that much.[3]

Cargile concludes that he has done "more for the happiness of pigs than most vegetarians."

In his book *Animal Liberation,* Peter Singer claims that the argument Cargile raises, which I refer to as the animal husbandry argument,

> . . . could be refuted merely by pointing out that life for an animal in a modern factory farm is so devoid of any pleasure that this kind of existence is *in no sense a benefit* to the animal.[4]

Cargile does not overlook this important and ethically relevant consideration. He agrees that we should stop "cruel animal raisers." His, however, is not a cruel form of animal husbandry. If we raise animals in such a way that their lives are *more* of a pleasure than a burden, as Cargile does, then Cargile can claim that we do what will increase the amount of happiness in the world and so what is right on utilitarian grounds.

The animal husbandry argument rests on an assortment of claims:

1. The pleasures of the animals we raise would not occur if we did not raise them.
2. The pleasures of these animals increase the total amount of happiness in the world.

3. The burdens of these animals are outweighed by their pleasures (and, if not, then that sort of animal husbandry is immoral).
4. There is no alternative policy that would increase the foreseeable amount of happiness in the world.

It is reasonable for us to assume that (1), (2), and (3) are true. Importantly and realistically, (3) assumes that the animals raised for consumption suffer from their confinement and slaughter. But the core of the argument is that there is no alternative to a humane animal husbandry that would foreseeably produce more pleasure.[5] The alternative in question is vegetarianism. What can be shown is that vegetarianism produces more foreseeable pleasure *on the whole* and that, not unsurprisingly, the animal husbandry argument does not provide a utilitarian justification of raising animals for food.

If we adopted the vegetarian alternative and stopped raising marketable animals we would need to farm much less land to feed the same number of people we feed by raising such animals for food, since plants yield about ten times more protein per acre than meat.[6] Hence, if our concern is to feed the same number of people we now feed and produce as much animal pleasure as possible, there is an alternative available that would accomplish this better than raising any animals for food. The alternative is to allow 90 percent of the resources currently used to raise livestock to be idle. These resources—lands lying fallow, empty barns—which previously supported market-bound animals, would then support other sorts of animals: chipmunks, rabbits, snakes, deer, and similarly unmarketable animals whose numbers are currently restricted by our practices of animal husbandry. These other animals would use the resources we currently direct to the animals we butcher for market, and these other animals would experience the sort of pleasures experienced by Cargile's cattle and pigs without suffering from restricted movement and slaughter. Animals in the wild do not have to experience the frustrations and anxiety of confinement or the terror of waiting passively "in line" to be killed. Although it is true that by failing to raise pigs or chickens, we fail to produce *pig* pleasures and *chicken* pleasures, there is no reason to think that the pleasures of these animals is not on an even par with *chipmunk* pleasures, *rabbit* pleasures, *prairie dog* pleasures, and *snake* pleasures. This observation defeats the central idea behind the animal husbandry argument, the idea that the total amount of animal pleasure is best increased if we raise livestock, something we will not do unless we subsequently slaughter these animals for food.

The policy of allowing 90 percent of the resources we currently use to support livestock to lie idle may, however, be undesirable from a utilitarian point of view. Many of the peoples of the world are suffering and dying from protein deficiencies. In the United States during 1968, we fed to livestock (excluding dairy cows) 20 million tons of plant protein that could have been consumed by humans. Although the livestock provided 2 million tons of protein, the 18 million tons of protein "wasted" by this process would have removed 90 percent of the yearly world protein deficit. Thus, a more humane use of our farming resources would eliminate a great deal of human suffering without imposing any additional suffering on market-bound animals. It is generally thought that a policy of reducing the suffering of beings that do and will exist independently of our choice is a more efficient way of maximizing happiness than a policy that involves the creation of additional beings. If this is true, then using the resources we currently expend on livestock to feed starving peoples would be the policy justified on utilitarian grounds.

More likely than not, a move toward vegetarianism would involve a mix of both policies. The result would be the alleviation of human starvation as well as an increase in the number of wild animals. What is central to this criticism of the animal husbandry argument is that each of these alternative policies increases pleasure and decreases suffering without imposing any additional suffering on animals.

OBJECTION TWO: THE INSIGNIFICANCE OF ANIMAL PLEASURES AND PAINS

Although raising animals for food is not the best way to increase the amount of animal pleasure, it may be argued that it is the best way to increase the amount of animal *and* human pleasure.[7] In developing the classical utilitarian position on the use of animals for food, I claimed that it is implausible to think that the suffering an animal experiences from confinement, transportation, and slaughter-related activities are outweighed by the pleasures of eating these animals. The carnivorous utilitarian may object by claiming that I have overestimated the disutility animals experience as a result of our using them for food and that once this exaggeration of animal suffering is corrected, a utilitarian defense of eating meat can plausibly be made out.

One source of miscalculation may be thought to be my implicit assumption that animal suffering has the same objective disutility as human suffering and animal pleasure has the same objective value as human pleasure. Narveson has argued that human and animal pleasures are not on a par. His argument has two steps. The first is that human beings have higher capacities. These capacities are grounded in our ability to be acutely aware of the future stretching out before us, and of the past in the other direction, and so, unlike lower animals, a human has a

> . . . capacity to have a conception of oneself, to formulate long-range plans, to appreciate general facts about one's environment and intelligently employ them in one's plans, and rationally to carry out or attempt to carry out one's plans.[8]

In light of these "higher capacities," Narveson proceeds to the second step of his argument:

> Isn't it reasonable to hold that the significance, and thus the quality, and so ultimately the utility, of the sufferings of beings with *sophisticated* capacities is different from that of the sufferings of lesser beings? Suppose one of the lower animals to be suffering quite intensely. Well, what counts as suffering of like degree in a *sophisticated* animal—one like, say, Beethoven or Kierkegaard, or you, gentle reader? If we are asked to compare the disutility of a pained cow with that of a pained human, or even a somewhat frustrated one, is it so absurd to think that the latter's is greater?[9]

Narveson's tentative conclusion is that the pleasures and pains of sophisticated beings are more valuable than those of less sophisticated beings. Hence, if our livestock and poultry are unsophisticated in the crucial sense, then the human pleasures of eating meat, being the *very* significant pleasures of sophisticated beings, may outweigh the requisite suffering of the unsophisticated poultry and livestock.

But Narveson's argument is not successful. The fact that we as humans are able to anticipate the future in ways (we believe) that animals cannot does not show that we have a greater capacity for pleasure. One reason for doubt is that such abilities increase our capacity to fail to appreciate whatever is not present to our senses. The Narveson who is eating filet mignon while anticipating an upcoming philosophic exchange or a Beethoven concert is, precisely because of this future-oriented mental activity, unaware of some of the pleasure eating would have otherwise provided. But even if we assume that humans have some capacity to enjoy life more than animals, the capacity Narveson cites suggests that humans, because distracted by thoughts and fears, may well enjoy life less, and in particular enjoy eating less, which is the critical experience on the human side of this controversy. On the animal side, however, Narveson's considerations not only do not support the claim that animal pains are dim but, ironically, they support the conclusion that the pains animals experience due to confinement, transportation, or slaughter are keenly felt, for there are no future-oriented distractions to mitigate these powerful sensations! In short, as far as the relevant pleasures and pains are concerned, humans and animals are, as far as we can tell, on a par.

OBJECTION THREE: THE SIGNIFICANCE OF HUMAN PREFERENCES GIVEN THAT ANIMALS DIE ANYWAY

Although we cannot justifiably downgrade the value of animal experiences, there is a second reason one may think that I have overestimated the amount of animal suffering that results from our use of animals as food. Whether we raise animals or not, animals must die and experience whatever anguish is involved in dying. Hence, whatever animal suffering is generally associated with the death of an animal cannot be considered a result of our raising animals for food. This reduction in the amount of suffering attributable to our animal husbandry is significant, for the main source of suffering that remains is the suffering caused by the frustrations of confinement. Since this is a frustration of animal preferences, and since not eating meat is a frustration of human preferences, there seems to be no significant difference in terms of total pleasure between satisfying the animal preference for less confinement and satisfying the human preference for the taste of meat. Hence, it may seem that we cannot condemn eating meat on utilitarian grounds, for both eating meat and its alternative lead to a similar amount of pleasure and frustration.

A chief source of animal suffering is the animal frustration caused by various sorts of restrictions. Domestic animals, in order to be profitably raised at all, must be somewhat restricted. The restrictions will be on movement (do Cargile's pigs forage through the Blue Ridge Mountains?), on social intercourse (in packs of ten or twenty?), and diet (eating acorns?). Although domestic animals are selectively bred, it is reasonable to believe with the experts that

> . . . the natural, instinctive urges and behavioral patterns . . . appropriate to the high degree of social organization as found in the ancestral wild species . . . have been little, if at all, bred out in the process of domestication.[10]

Where there are animals being raised, even humanely, it is noncontroversial that there will be a good deal of frustration even under the care of humane animal husbanders. The issue is how much of such frustration is justified by the pleasure of eating meat. Would the frustration experienced by a young boy locked in a room be outweighed by the pleasure of a parent derived from watching an "adult" TV show? If that comparison cannot *clearly* be made out in favor of the satisfaction of the parent's preference, it becomes hard to imagine anyone reasonably claiming that satisfying the preference to eat meat outweighs the many months of animal frustration caused by space, diet, and socialization restrictions.

But there are two additional factors which make this allegedly utilitarian defense of eating flesh implausible. The first focuses on the kind and numbers of deaths domestic animals undergo to satisfy the meat eater's taste for flesh. The second raises the issue of whether the pleasures of taste that "justify" raising animals for food are not, in the final analysis, *trivial when compared with the animal suffering required to satisfy these tastes.*

Even in those slaughterhouses in which the animals are killed as painlessly as possible, the animal hears, sees, and smells the slaughter and becomes terrified. In terror, in an unfamiliar environment, the animal, physically healthy, is prodded along.[11] At that point, in these "humane" slaughterhouses, the animal is stunned by a captive-bolt pistol or an electric current before being killed painlessly. In smaller settings these stunning devices are too expensive and, in addition, skill at killing quickly is not as practiced. One would expect that the small farmer who clubs, slices, or shoots his animals must not infrequently confront an injured, squealing animal that by now is utterly terrified and even harder to kill.

Everything we have learned about animals suggests that in terms of experiencing terror, pain, grief, anxiety and stress these sentient beings are relevantly similar to humans. It is reasonable to believe that our knowledge of the quality of human dying will also tell us something about the dying process of other animals. For humans, the most horrible deaths involve terror. When this factor is not present, and especially when the process of dying is not unexpected for the dying person, dying can be peaceful. From this minimal observation about human dying and the observation that domestic animals are typically slaughtered in circumstances that are unfamiliar and terrifying for the animals, it follows that the experience of being slaughtered is no worse for these animals than the worst deaths experienced in the wild and significantly worse than the deaths of wild animals that die from disease or old age in familiar and unterrifying surroundings. In addition, because the life of an adult animal raised for food is much shorter than the life of a similar animal in the wild, there will be more dyings per total adult population among these animals than among wild animals of similar species. Hence, both in quantity and quality of deaths, rearing animals for food produces a great deal of death-related anguish and terror that is directly a consequence of humans using them for food.

These are some of the foreseeable disutilities that are a consequence even of a "humane" animal husbandry.[12] In order to justify our producing this foreseeable animal suffering, we must ask whether it is plausible to believe that these foreseeable bad consequences are outweighed by the foreseeable pleasures of eating meat. But we must first clarify this question for, as stated, it suggests that whatever pleasures we derive from eating meat are to be compared with whatever sufferings animals experience solely as a result of farming practices. But that is not an accurate interpretation of this crucial question. Rather, we are *only* interested in *the amount of pleasure that would occur were we to eat meat and that would not occur were we to eat tasty vegetable dishes instead.* That is the amount of pleasure which is a consequence of our eating meat (as opposed to eating in general). Since much of the world's population finds that vegetarian meals can be delightfully tasty, there is good reason for thinking that the pleasures many people derive from eating meat can be completely replaced with pleasures from eating vegetables. Hence, the pleasures to be derived from the eating of meat are so minimal as to be insignificant. It follows that any defense of flesh-eating along the above lines is totally unacceptable for the utilitarian.

OBJECTIONS FOUR AND FIVE: THE INCONVENIENCES OF A VEGETARIAN CUISINE

Two additional issues are relevant to any attempt to defend eating meat on utilitarian grounds. The first is raised by Narveson, who points out "that the vegetarian diet is more limited, since every pleasure available to the vegetarian is also available to the carnivore."[13] Although Narveson concedes that this will not be a decisive consideration for most of us, it is worth asking whether it should be decisive even for a person who attaches a high value to greater esthetic variety in diet and who feels that meatless eating would be boring. At issue is whether it is justifiable to cause animal suffering in order to satisfy the tastes of those who prefer a diet with a variety only available by including meat. On the animals' side of the argument there is a concise but powerful reason for thinking that satisfying this preference does not justify the requisite animal suffering. Part of the suffering we inflict on animals is the frustration and intense boredom of a monotonous diet. To claim that *this* intense animal boredom is outweighed by the pleasure of increased variety for humans would be to assume what is unreasonable: that avoiding some human frustration justifies producing a great deal of animal frustration, even when the frustrations are causally identical (viz., lack of variety in diet). When we take into consideration *all* the kinds of animal suffering produced in order to maintain the variety meat adds to a diet, there are *no* reasonable grounds for thinking that satisfying this preference for variety could compensate for the animal suffering involved.

The second additional issue relevant to a utilitarian appraisal of eating meat is that eating meat is, for most omnivores, a deeply engrained habit. Since changing habits is always difficult, it follows that whatever inconvenience and frustration a person experiences as he or she shifts to vegetarianism are a cost that can be avoided by continuing to eat meat. But there are several reasons for thinking that this cost does not justify continuing to eat meat.

One is that this cost is a relatively short-term affair, whereas the avoidance of unnecessary animal suffering is a very long-range and ongoing consequence. Once the change of eating habits is accomplished, not only will the new vegetarian not contribute to the unnecessary suffering of animals, but most likely neither will any of the vegetarian's progeny, whose vegetarian habits would make eating meat difficult. Hence, although creativity, exploration, and initiative are required to change eating habits in this fundamental way, the payoff is avoiding years and even decades of animal suffering, and such a large good seems to outweigh by far the inconvenience of changing habits. Secondly, it is important to point out that the adventure of such a change of eating habits is, for many people, an exciting and deeply satisfying adventure. Part of the adventure is the discovery of new sources of culinary delight. For many people it is not only liberating to be able to cook without having to rely on meat, but it is also fun to discover that vegetables are more than soggy garnishes. In addition, there is the satisfaction of eating and knowing that one is not contributing to the suffering of animals. Finally, there is the adoption of a way of eating that in many ways is far more healthy than a diet relying on animal flesh.[14]

It is time to bring these observations to bear on our central question: are there any pleasurable consequences of raising and eating animals which would outweigh the frustration, terror, and pain these animals had to undergo in order for us to experience these pleasures? Once we properly focus our attention only on those pleasures that are not replaceable by an alternative style of eating, it is not plausible to believe that there are any.

OBJECTION SIX: THE IMPOTENCY OF THE INDIVIDUAL TO AFFECT ANIMAL SUFFERING

A final attempt to defend eating meat on utilitarian grounds rests on the claim that, for those of us who do not raise our own animals, there is no chance that any one of us will make a difference in the total amount of animal suffering by failing to buy and eat meat. Suppose that I buy meat from a retailer who is supplied by the giant meat industry. Because the meat suppliers are so large, if I stop eating meat, my action will have no effect on the number of animals raised. Hence, if I am concerned to prevent suffering, there is no animal suffering I prevent by becoming a vegetarian. But if I enjoy eating meat, and if becoming a vegetarian would cause me to suffer, then I ought to eat meat, for by continuing to indulge this habit I produce my own pleasure without producing any avoidable suffering for any other sentient being.

The problem is not that the odds are very small that my action will have an effect on industry production. For if I only had a small chance of changing industry production, then one of the foreseeable consequences of my action would be the prevention of a great amount of animal pain. Such an action would be a good gamble for preventing animal suffering, i.e., a small sacrifice for a great gain, and so it would be obligatory on act utilitarian grounds. The problem, rather, is the much more severe problem of individual impotency in large market situations. The defender of eating meat claims that only a large number of actions can produce a change in the production of meat and that no single person's actions are or would be necessary for this change to take place. Since meat production will remain constant or will change *regardless* of what I do, any change in meat production cannot be considered a consequence of *my* action and, hence, my action has no foreseeable effect on the suffering of domestic animals being raised for food. It follows, according to this objection, that if I am an act utilitarian and assess my acts in terms of their own foreseeable consequences, or if, what amounts to the same thing, I am concerned to do what will contribute as little as possible to the amount of suffering in the world, then there is no reason for me to take into account the suffering inflicted on animals by the meat industry when I am choosing between continuing to eat meat or becoming a vegetarian.

One reply to this utilitarian defense of eating meat begins with the assumption that my eating meat, or failing to eat meat, will not alter the consumption behavior of others, i.e., others will not eat either more or less meat if I change my eating habits. This assumption permits the utilitarian to argue that by becoming a vegetarian I diminish the demand for meat and so there will be an eventual diminishment in meat production and, significantly, a diminishment of the corresponding suffering of animals.[15] The assumption that my becoming a vegetarian will not influence the consumption of others is crucial, for it prevents the defender of eating meat from claiming that the meat I fail to eat will eventually be eaten by those who previously ate less meat, or none at all.

But this assumption must be rejected, partly because it denies what is at the core of the utilitarian defense of eating meat, and—not irrelevantly—because it is blatantly unrealistic.[16] Profit margins in various parts of the meat industry are so small, for example, that the amount of meat "wasted" by even one person becoming a vegetarian would in fact be recycled into other markets, even if only fertilizer markets or pet food markets.[17] Of course, once we abandon the assumption that my failing to eat meat will not alter the meat consumption of others, the act utilitarian can bring a new consideration into the discussion, viz., the ripple effect on others caused by my example of becoming a vegetarian. But the utilitarian defender of eating meat will reply that other markets and other consumers will absorb what any single person or a few persons do not consume, and so my failing to eat meat, even if conjoined with the acts of those who follow my example, will make no difference in the amount of animal suffering produced by the meat industry. A key issue in this controversy is whether one person's example of becoming a vegetarian has a foreseeable possibility of altering the meat consumption of others to such an extent that animal suffering is reduced. Although I think it is true that one person's example has a real chance of being efficacious in this way, even if true, that would hardly close the issue. For instance, should many people become vegetarians, the resulting meat surplus would temporarily depress the price of meat. One result would be that those who previously could not afford meat would enter the market, thereby becoming meat consumers, and some of these new consumers would likely continue purchasing meat after the price rose back to normal. But even if the price of meat were depressed for a long time, that in itself would not guarantee a reduction in animal production and a corresponding reduction in animal suffering. A price reduction might have the undesirable consequence that some meat producers, given the reduced price for meat, would intensify even further their methods of factory farming in order to make a profit, and these methods would cause even more suffering since they would involve additional diet and movement restriction for the animals. Obviously if *enough* people stopped eating meat and the price became depressed *enough*, then the businessman-farmer would cease producing meat and so cease causing suffering to animals. But such a line of argument is sufficiently dependent on long-range and controversial economic probabilities that, on the face of it, the strongest criticism that could be made against the defender of eating meat is that he is willing to take a chance, perhaps an infinitesimal one, of causing intense animal suffering for the sake of convenience, pleasure, or out of habit. Since this criticism packs little force if the odds are truly infinitesimal, it is time we examined two arguments that do not depend on these economic contingencies and yet show that our consumption of meat is causally related to animal suffering.

Each of these arguments depends on the general idea that if a number of acts together produce some group result of value or disvalue, a proportion of the value or disvalue of that group result is causally attributable to each of the contributing individual actions. Consider the following example of David Lyons:

> If it takes six men to push a car up a hill and, not knowing this, eight lend a hand and do the job, what are we to say? If all pushed, and pushed equally hard, and delivered equal forces, are we to say that only some of them actually contributed to the effects because fewer *could* have done the job?[18]

As long as we cannot distinguish those acts that are necessary for the result from those acts that are not (and this is the hypothesis of interest to us), Lyons' conclusion is that each of these acts does contribute causally to the group effect. Lyons does not attempt to analyze the concept of "contributory causation," and that is a task too large to attempt here. But surely it is reasonable to think that, when a number of actions contribute equally to an effect, we are to causally attribute part of the value of the effect to each individual action. In whatever way the account of contributory causation is worked out, what it would account for is the claim that when many acts contribute to some common result, there is some consequential value to be attributed to each of these actions because each does, in fact, contribute to that result. (More technically, we will assume that if n acts equally contribute to E, and the value of E is V, then the value of the consequences of each act is a function of the value of V/n.)

The first "contributory account" of why an individual is not impotent in the marketplace involves two steps. *Step one:* we assume that a large number of persons do become vegetarians, that this results in a reduction in the demand for meat, that no particular action was necessary for this result to take place, and that the reduction in demand reduces animal suffering by curtailing meat production. Since the reduction of animal suffering is of positive value, the cause of this reduction—the reduction in demand for meat—is also of positive value. It is at this point that the contributory causation analysis is operative. Since many acts have contributed to the valuable result of lower demand for meat, there is a consequential value to be attributed to each act of becoming a vegetarian because each does, in fact, contribute to the lower demand for meat. Hence, given our assumptions, the value of the consequences of each act includes part of the positive value of the reduction of animal suffering. That's step one. *Step two* requires that we replace the *unrealistic* assumption that enough people *will in fact* become vegetarians to alter meat production with the *realistic* assumption that there is *some chance* that enough people will become vegetarians to alter meat production. Whatever probability there is that enough people will become vegetarians to reduce meat production is also the probability that an individual person, by becoming a vegetarian, will contribute to the good of a significant reduction of animal suffering. Hence, that is the probability that a person by becoming a vegetarian will be performing actions with positive consequential value. Since by becoming vegetarians we may prevent, or at least help prevent, some of the suffering that animals would otherwise have had to experience because of confinement and the terrors of slaughter, we must do so on act utilitarian grounds.

There is a second "contributory" rebuttal to the objection that one's own actions are impotent to increase or decrease the suffering of animals. This second reply has the virtue of not relying on any probability assessments about people becoming vegetarians. Rather, this second argument focuses squarely on a central aspect of act utilitarianism: an action is right only if *there is no alternative action* that is a better bet to avoid painful consequences or to bring about pleasurable or happy consequences. In the current market situation the person who eats meat is contributing to the demand for meat. But this demand itself is a cause of meat production and, hence, is a cause of the terrible animal suffering involved in meat production. Because causes are evaluated in terms of the value of what they cause—a mudslide that kills twenty people is thereby bad, whereas a rainfall that ends a famine-causing drought is good—the general demand for meat is of great negative value because of the animal suffering it causes. Since individual acts of buying meat contribute to this great evil (the demand for meat), some negative consequential value is attributable to each act of buying meat, for each such act causally contributes to the general demand that causes animal suffering. Significantly, becoming a vegetarian is an alternative that avoids this contribution to the suffering of animals. Hence, one should become a vegetarian if one is trying to do what has the best bet of not bringing about consequences that are pain-producing or of negative value. In short, a person who is trying to live in such a way as to contribute both as little as possible to the total amount of suffering in the world, and as much as possible to the total amount of the world's happiness, will not purchase meat in today's marketplace, for any such act contributes to the brutal and exploitative practice of raising and slaughtering other sentient beings for their flesh.[19]

NOTES

1. Although Bentham's and Mill's interpretation of utilitarianism in terms of expected or foreseeable consequences has for a time lost favor in the twentieth century, this interpretation, which I adopt in the text, has been recently adopted by Richard Brandt, *A Theory of the Good and the Right* (Oxford: Clarendon Press, 1979), pp. 271ff, and defended by me in "Foreseeable Consequence Utilitarianism," *Australasian Journal of Philosophy*, 59, No. 4, June 1981.

2. Those who discuss this notion of consequences include Lars Bergstrom, *The Alternatives and Consequences of Actions* (Stockholm: Almqvist and Wiksell, 1966), p. 91, D. Prawitz, "A Discussion note on utilitarianism." *Theoria* 34 (1968), p. 83, and J. Howard Sobel, "Utilitarianisms: Simple and General." *Inquiry* 13 (1970), pp.398–400.

3. James Cargile, "Comments on 'The Priority of Human Interests,'" p. 249 in *Ethics and Animals*, H. Miller and W. Williams (eds.) (Clifton, NJ: Humana Press, 1983).

4. Singer, P. *Animal Liberation* (New York: Random House, 1975) p. 241. Those unfamiliar with how animals are turned into meat will find Chapter Three of Singer's book enlightening.

5. On utilitarian grounds the animal husbandry argument can be made even stronger. In "Killing humans and killing animals" (*Inquiry* 22, 1979, pp. 145–156), Peter Singer modifying some of what he, in *Animal Liberation*, distinguishes between self-conscious beings who have preferences, including the preference to stay alive, and beings which, though sentient, do not have such preferences. When a creature without preferences is killed, the only disutility which occurs is the disutility of the pain of dying and the disutility of the loss of future pleasures. Hence, if we can minimize the pain of dying and prevent the loss of future pleasures by replacing the killed animal with another animal, a humane Cargile-style animal husbandry will produce foreseeable pleasure. As Singer says:
   Some of the animals commonly killed for food are not self-conscious— chickens could be an example. Given that an animal belongs to a species incapable of self-consciousness, it follows that it is not wrong to rear and kill it for food, provided it lives a pleasant life and, after being killed, will be replaced by another animal which will lead a similarly pleasant life and would not have existed if the first animal had not been killed (p. 153).
   What Singer calls the replaceability argument is, however, objectionable for the same reasons that defeat Cargile's animal husbandry argument.

6. Or consider the following from Frances Moore Lappé, *Diet for a Small Planet* (New York: Ballentine Books, 1975), p. 14:
   To imagine what this means in practical, everyday terms simply set yourself at a restaurant in front of an eight-ounce steak and then imagine the room filled with 45 to 50 people with empty bowls in front of them. For the "feed cost" of your steak, each of their bowls could be filled with a full cup of cooked cereal grains!

7. Any such argument must deal with the objection that human pleasure would be maximized by feeding starving people the grain that would otherwise be fed to livestock. One

reply to this objection is that feeding starving peoples will only encourage them to propagate themselves even further, and so feeding some starving peoples now only produces many more starving peoples later. If the objection were accurate, then using livestock grain to feed starving humans would not be a good way of producing the best consequences in the long run, and so the question of maximizing human pleasure by raising livestock could still arise. (There are alternatives besides eating meat and letting the undernourished starve. For example, a mixed policy of food aid, agricultural support, and birth control might save lives without condemning future generations to starvation, and so would be the utilitarian policy of choice.) The question of whether human pleasure justifies some animal suffering could also be raised under a more optimistic scenario: assuming that the world deficiency of protein for human consumption were alleviated, would it then be permissible to raise animals to satisfy a human taste preference?

8. Jan Narveson, "Animal rights." *The Canadian Journal of Philosophy* 7 (1979), p. 166.

9. *Ibid.*, p. 168.

10. W. H. Thorpe in the Brambell Report, quoted in Singer, *Animal Liberation*, p. 135.

11. Richard Rhodes, who regards such killing as "necessary," reports what he felt and observed in a slaughterhouse that was doing its job of slaughtering pigs "as humanely as possible." He writes:

    The pen narrows like a funnel: the drivers behind urge the pigs forward, until one at a time they climb onto the moving ramp. . . . Now they scream, never having been on such a ramp, smelling the smells they smell ahead. I do not want to overdramatize because you have read all this before. But it was a frightening experience, seeing their fear. ("Watching the Animals," *Harper's*, March 1979, quoted in Singer, *Animal Liberation*, p. 157.)

12. There are two other foreseeable disutilities of an animal industry, even a "humane" one. The first is that it is only a small step from the perception of animals as beings we kill to satisfy human tastes to a perception of animals as meat-producing mechanisms, a perception that is part and parcel with the cruel practices of today's meat industries. Hence, among the foreseeable consequences of even a "humane" animal industry is the sort of cruelty imposed on animals daily under the guise of meat production. The other foreseeable disutility of the meat industry is the horrible suffering animals experience when they are transported. The following account is typical: "For an 800-lb. steer to lose seventy pounds, or 9 percent of his weight, on a single trip is not at all unusual" (Singer, *Animal Liberation*, p. 118). This loss, not only from the fleshly parts of the animal but also from the head and shanks, indicates "a severe amount of otherwise unmeasurable stress on these animals" (p. 120). This account is not one of the horror-stories of animal transportation, but is typical and indicates the amount of anxiety and fear animals experience in trucks and trains.

13. Jan Narveson, "Animal rights," p. 14.

14. A vegetarian diet tends to be low in cholesterol and animal fats, high in fiber content and without the dangerous additives that are often used in livestock feed (for example, hormones to stimulate growth and antibiotics to decrease stress-related disease).

15. I am indebted to Jan Narveson for this argument.

16. But note that in 1973 the average American consumed 175 pounds of red meat and over 50 pounds of chicken (*Information Please Almanac*, 1975)!

17. It follows, as an editor of Humana Press suggested, that pet owners should try to avoid using meat products as far as possible. Note that the three chief ingredients in commercial dry cat foot and dry dog food are corn, wheat, and soy. It also follows that people should try to avoid using meat products to feed birds. For example, peanut butter may be substituted for suet in order to feed such birds as woodpeckers.

18. David Lyons, *Forms and Limits of Utilitarianism* (Oxford: Clarendon Press, 1965), p. 39.

19. I am indebted to Henry West for encouraging me to write the hedonistic act utilitarian's account of our duties toward animals; to William DeAngelis, Michael Lipton, Stephen

Nathanson, and others who commented on an earlier version I read at a colloquium for the Department of Philosophy and Religion, Northeastern University, December, 1979; and to the editors of Humana Press for many helpful suggestions. I am also grateful to Sharon B. Young for her many helpful comments on earlier versions of this paper as well as for sharing with me her active exploration of vegetarian cuisine. Finally, I am pleased to thank Barbara Jones and Walter Knoppel for initially introducing me to vegetarianism in an intelligent, effective, and tasty manner.

JAN NARVESON

A Defense
of Meat Eating

The tendency in the past few years has been to take John Rawls' well-known theory of justice as the model of contractualist moral theory. I must therefore begin by explaining why that is a mistake.

On the contract view of morality, morality is a sort of agreement among rational, independent, self-interested persons, persons who have something to gain from entering into such an agreement. It is of the very essence, on such a theory, that the parties to the agreement know who they are and what they want—what they in particular want, and not just what a certain general class of beings of which they are members generally tend to want. Now, Rawls' theory has his parties constrained by agreements that they would have made if they *did not* know who they were. But if we can have that constraint, why should we not go just a little further and specify that one is not only not to know *which* person he or she is, but also whether he or she will be a person *at all:* reason on the assumption that you might turn out to be an owl, say, or a vermin, or a cow. We may imagine that *that* possibility would make quite a difference . . . (Some proponents of vege-

Jan Narveson teaches philosophy at the University of Waterloo, Canada. His most recent book is the *Libertarian Idea* (Temple University Press, 1989).

Jan Narveson, "Animal Rights Revisited." Pp. 56–59 in H. Miller and W. Williams (eds.), *Ethics and Animals*. Clifton, NJ: Humana Press, 1983.

tarianism, I believe, are tempted by it, and do extend the veil of ignorance that far.)

The "agreement" of which morality consists is a voluntary undertaking to limit one's behavior in various respects. In a sense, it consists in a renunciation of action on unconstrained self-interest. It is, however, self-interested overall. The idea is to come out ahead in the long run, by refraining, contingently on others' likewise refraining, from certain actions, the general indulgence in which would be worse for all and therefore for oneself. There are well-known problems generated by this characterization, and I do not claim to have solutions for them. I only claim that this is an important and plausible conception of morality, worth investigating in the present context.

A major feature of this view of morality is that it explains why we have it and who is a party to it. We have it for reasons of long-run self-interest, and parties to it include all and only those who have *both* of the following characteristics: (1) they stand to gain by subscribing to it, at least in the long run, compared with not doing so, and (2) they are *capable* of entering into (and keeping) an agreement. Those not capable of it obviously cannot be parties to it, and among those capable of it, there is no reason for them to enter into it if there is nothing to gain for them from it, no matter how much the others might benefit.

Given these requirements, it will be clear why animals do not have rights. For there are evident shortcomings on both scores. On the one hand, humans have nothing generally to gain by voluntarily refraining from (for instance) killing animals or "treating them as mere means." And on the other, animals cannot generally make agreements with us anyway, even if we wanted to have them do so. Both points are worth expanding on briefly.

(1) In saying that humans have "nothing generally to gain" from adopting principled restraints against behavior harmful to animals, I am in one respect certainly overstating the case, for it is possible that animal food, for instance, is bad for us, or that something else about animals, which requires such restraint from us, would be for our long-term benefit. Those are issues I mostly leave on one side here, except to note that some people may think that we gain on the score of purity of soul by treating animals better. But if the purity in question is moral purity, then that would be question-begging on the contractarian conception of morality. In any case, those people are, of course, welcome to treat animals as nicely as they like. The question is whether others may be prevented from treating animals badly, e.g., by eating them, and the "purity of soul" factor cannot be appealed to in that context.

A main motive for morality on the contract view is, of course, diffidence. Humans have excellent reason to be fearful about each other. Our fellows, all and sundry, are quite capable of doing damage to us, and not only capable but often quite interested in doing so; and their rational (or at least, calculative) capacities only make things worse. There is compelling need for mutual restraint. Now, animals can, many of them, be harmful to us. But the danger is rather specialized and limited in most cases, and in those cases we can deal with it by such methods as caging the animals in question, or by shooting them, and so on. There is no general need for moral methods, and there is also the question whether they are available. In any case, we have much to gain from eating them, and if one of the main planks in a moral platform is refraining from killing merely for self-interest, then it is quite clear that such a plank, in the case of animals, would not be worth it from the point of view of most of us. Taking our chances in the state of nature would be preferable.

(2) What about the capability of entering into and keeping such agreements? Animals have been pretty badly maligned on this matter in the past, I gather. Really beastly behavior is a phenomenon pretty nearly unique to the human species. But still, when animals refrain from killing other animals or people just for the fun of it, there is no good reason to think that they do so out of moral principle. Rather, it is just that it is not really their idea of fun!

There remains a genuine question about the eligibility of animals for morality on the score of their abilities. A very few individuals among some animal species have been enabled, after years of highly specialized work, to communicate in fairly simple ways with people. That does not augur well for animals' entering quite generally into something as apparently sophisticated as an agreement. But of course agreements can be tacit and unwritten, even unspoken. Should we postulate, at some such inexplicit level, an "agreement" among humans, it is largely tacit there. People do not enter into agreements to refrain from killing each other, except in fairly specialized cases; the rule against killing that we (virtually) all acknowledge is one we adopt out of common sense and antecedent inculcation by our mentors. Still, it is reasonable to say that when one person does kill another one, he or she is (among other things) taking *unfair advantage* of the restraint that one's fellows have exercised with regard toward one over many years. But can any such thing be reasonably said of animals? I would think not.

On the whole, therefore, it seems clear that contractarianism leaves animals out of it, so far as rights are concerned. They are, by and large, to be dealt with in terms of our self-interest, unconstrained by the terms of hypothetical agreements with them. Just exactly what our interest in them is may, of course, be matter for debate; but that those are the terms on which we may deal with them is, on this view of morality, overwhelmingly indicated.

There is an evident problem about the treatment of what I have called "marginal cases" on this view, of course: infants, the feeble-minded, and the incapacitated are in varying degrees in the position of the animals in relation to us, are they not? True: but the situation is very different in several ways. For one thing, we generally have very little to gain from treating such people badly, and we often have much to gain from treating them well. For another, marginal humans are invariably members of families, or members of other groupings, which makes them the object of love and interest on the part of other members of those groups. Even if there were an interest in treating a particular marginal person badly, there would be others who have an interest in their being treated well and who are themselves clearly members of the moral community on contractarian premises. Finally, it does have to be pointed out that there is genuine question about the morality of, for instance, euthanasia, and that infanticide has been approved of in various human communities at various times. On the whole, it seems to me not an insurmountable objection to the contractarian account that we grant marginal humans fairly strong rights.

It remains that we may think that suffering is a bad thing, no matter whose. But although we think so, we do not think it is so bad as to require us to become vegetarians. Here by "we," of course, I mean most of us. And what most of us think is that, although suffering is too bad and it is unfortunate for animals that they are turned into hamburgers at a tender age, we nevertheless are justified on the whole in eating them. If contractarianism is correct, then these attitudes are not inconsistent. And perhaps it is.

PART SEVEN
The Treatment
of Animals
in Science

SIDNEY GENDIN

The Use of Animals
in Science

Although each year only about 5 percent of all animal deaths at the hands of human beings result from the use of animals in science, the number killed—in the neighborhood of 500 million—is not inconsiderable.[1] If we are to make an intelligent judgment about the ethics and scientific wisdom of permitting this many animals to be used in scientific settings, we must begin to inform ourselves at least about the broad contours of their use: for what purposes they are used, under what conditions, and with what legal protection, for example. . . .

1. CATEGORIES AND NUMBERS

Product Testing

Animals are routinely used to test the safety of consumer products. Acute and chronic toxity tests are carried out on animals to establish toxic effects of low or high doses of such items as insecticides, pesticides, antifreeze,

Sidney Gendin teaches philosophy at Eastern Michigan State University. He is a frequent contributor to professional journals in moral, political and social philosophy.

Gendin, S. "The Use of Animals in Science," in *Animal Sacrifices: Religious Perspectives on the Use of Animals in Science,* ed. Tom Regan. Philadelphia: Temple University Press, 1986. Reprinted by permission of the publisher.

brake fluids, bleaches, Christmas tree sprays, silver and brass polish, oven cleaners, deodorants, skin fresheners, bubble baths, freckle creams, eye makeup, crayons, inks, suntan lotions, nail polish, zipper lubricants, paints, food dyes, chemical solvents, and floor cleaners. The test animals may be force-fed these products or have them rubbed or injected into their skin or dropped into their eyes. . . .

Behavioral Research

Behavioral research using animals may or may not involve pain. In many cases the experiments are the classic learning experiments in which mice or rats are required to run through mazes, move levers, or perform some comparable task. These may involve reward and punishment for success and failure. If the animal does not move the proper lever or does not move it quickly enough, it may not be fed or it may receive a small shock. Other psychological experiments typically performed on larger animals (usually primates) differ. For example, chimpanzees may be taken from their mothers, and a soft chimplike toy may serve as a surrogate mother. The baby chimps may experience different discomforts, while the scientist observes their degree of reliance on the mother-substitute.

Instructional Purposes

Animals are used for study in the classroom. High school students learning some elementary anatomy frequently dissect frogs. The frogs are often dead, but sometimes the students themselves must first deliver the *coup de grâce*. High school students, and particularly college students, are not limited to frogs. Mice, rats, hamsters, guinea pigs, and cats are used to teach students, the majority of whom have no plans to become biologists, the elementary facts of anatomy by way of "hands-on" learning. . . .

In Vivo Tests

Animals are used whole and alive in so-called *in vivo* tests in the pharmaceutical industry. New drugs and vaccines are routinely tested on animals for their efficacy and safety before they are made available to humans.

Emergency Medicine

Animals are used in emergency medical situations. For example, primates have been killed and their organs have been immediately transplanted into humans to serve as very short-term support until satisfactory donors arrive. . . .

Long-Term Medical Research

Animals are used in long term medical research, including research on cancer, AIDS, and herpes.

Biological Research

Animals are used in "pure" biological research. Frequently investigators have no particular medical aims in mind but, rather, are trying to advance scientific knowledge. It is a commonplace in science that some of the most important medical advances have come about serendipitously in the course of pure research.

A statistical tabulation of the number of animals used for scientific purposes in any country can at best be only a good estimate. Despite claims to the contrary, nobody is keeping very close count. What is counted, in the United Kingdom for example, are the number of animals used in experiments that are funded by government agencies and, to a lesser extent, the number of animals used by pharmaceutical companies. In the United States, the convention is to estimate the number of animals used for such purposes at about 70 to 90 million per year. Some estimates, however, are as low as 15 million per year. Yet there are a few persons who claim that the best estimate is 120 million per year.[2] . . .

2. BEHIND THE STATISTICS

Besides statistics, the details of some uses of animals need our attention. The Draize test, an eye irritancy test, will concern us first. Then, in turn, we will examine some specific uses of animals—and the controversies they have inspired—in behavioral research, drug testing, and cancer research. Our aim is not to resolve but to better understand the ethical and scientific divisions these uses engender.

The Draize Test[3]

In the cosmetics industry, one of the more commonly used methods to screen products for their safety is the Draize test, named after its inventor, John Draize, who developed the method in 1944. The test consists of placing rabbits in stocks that immobilize their heads and then dropping the substance to be tested into one eye, using the other eye as a control. The testing takes place over several days and may lead to opacity of the cornea, hemorrhage, ulceration, blindness, and nearly always to considerable irritation and pain. Indeed, the pain is sometimes so great that rabbits have been known to break their backs in efforts to free themselves from the stocks.[4] Rabbits are particularly well suited for this experiment because their tear ducts are too inefficient to wipe away or dilute the product being tested.

In the United States, retail cosmetics sales amount to about $10 billion per year and there are approximately 24,000 different cosmetics containing about 8,000 ingredients. . . . Indeed, there are hundreds of small firms, such as the by-now well known Beauty Without Cruelty, that produce lines of cosmetics, toiletries, and clothing that are neither tested on animals nor made from animal parts.

Behavioral Research

Although behavioral research is not the exclusive domain of psychologists, and although psychologists sometimes report their findings in nonpsychological journals, we shall limit the survey to what appears in psychology journals because that is the area in dispute.[5]

In a 1975 paper in the *Journal of Abnormal Psychology*,[6] researchers reported investigations of the facial expressions and social responsiveness of blind monkeys. First, the eyes of five macaque monkeys were removed prior to the 19th day of life. The young monkeys were then separated from their mothers, who were placed in separate cages. Upon the mothers' uttering calls of alarm, the time required for the monkeys to contact their mothers' cages was measured. These interactions were compared with those of young monkeys who were not blinded. The researchers concluded that all the usual facial expressions of sighted monkeys are also observed in blinded ones.

Cats are often used in brain lesion experiments. Several such experiments are reported in the *Journal of Comparative and Physiological Psychology* in 1977. A team of researchers from the Department of Psychology at the University of Iowa offered this report:

> Because an abnormal grooming behavior that is mediated by the superior colliculi is elicited from cats with pontile lesions, an ablation study of the structures was conducted to specify quantitatively the changes in grooming behavior. Cats that underwent the surgical procedure except for the lesion and cats with lesions of the auditory and visual cortices served as control groups.[7]

The researchers found that "grooming behavior in cats with pontile or tectal lesions [was] deficient in removing tapes stuck on their fur."

Experiments at Harvard University utilized squirrel monkeys trained to press a lever under fixed-interval schedules of food or electric shock presentation. The purpose was to compare hose biting induced by these two methods of scheduling. The monkeys were strapped in restraining chairs and a bite hose was mounted in front of them. Shocks were administered to the monkeys' tails and the frequency, duration, and pressure of biting were measured. The responses were compared with those induced by food presentations in various sophisticated ways. The animals were also studied under a range of doses of amphetamines. Various findings were duly reported in the *Journal of Experimental Analysis of Behavior,* vol. 27, 1977.[8]

At the Veteran's Administration Hospital, Perry Point, Maryland, dogs were placed in an experimental chamber and restrained on a table. They had to press a response panel to escape electric shock. Later their bladders were removed and ureters were externalized so that urine samples could be taken without storage in the now missing bladders. After surgery, the "animals were subjected to lengthy experience with various aversive schedules." In fact, they were subjected to 140 sessions of unavoidable shock with an intensity of 8.0 mA. The sessions lasted five hours per day, five days per week. Tranquilizers were administered, and the researchers concluded that "chlorpromazine consistently reduced avoidance response rates in dogs, producing consequent increases in shock rate." They also discovered that heart rate and urinary volume "showed no consistent pattern of results in response to drug administration."[9]

Drs. Steven Maier and Martin Seligman did "learned helplessness" studies on 150 dogs over a four-year period in which inescapable shock was studied. These responses were compared with responses in cats, rats, primates, and other species. It was noted that when response is totally debilitated and nothing can be done to escape pain, then "the learned helplessness effect seems rather general among species that learn."[10] Elsewhere it is argued that learned helplessness serves as a laboratory model of depression in humans. The effects of uncontrollable events influence a person's self-concept, assertiveness, aggressiveness, and even spatial localization. It is argued that to the extent that a person's depression makes him deficient in these various traits "the learned helplessness model is confirmed or disconfirmed."[11]

Behavioral research on animals remains one of the most controversial areas even within the psychology community itself. . . .

Drug Testing

Drug testing is a central part of medical research, and the former use of the drug thalidomide highlights most dramatically the grave problems encountered in this area. Thalidomide was introduced to treat morning sickness in pregnant women and tested on a wide range of animal species before being made available to humans. Its use by pregnant women caused severe abnormalities in newborn babies. . . .

As the thalidomide tragedy illustrates, there is an inherent difficulty in trying to predict adverse reactions to humans from studies in experimental animals. One simply cannot automatically extrapolate information from animal studies that yields either necessary or sufficient conditions concerning their safety for humans. In other words, drugs that are harmless or positively beneficial to other species of animals sometimes prove highly dangerous to us. Penicillin is an interesting example of a drug that is fatal to guinea pigs even in very low doses. Other drugs useful to humans that are deadly to many animals include epinephrine, salicylates, insulin, cortisone, and meclizine. Drugs are not only dose-specific but species-specific. Species specificity is a function of differences in absorption, metabolism, excretion, gestation periods, and a host of other common biological functions.

A second problem inherent in toxicity testing of drugs on animals is that the animals cannot describe their experiences, including the aches and pains that are sometimes the side effects of drugs. For example, they cannot inform us of headache, giddiness, and feelings of nausea. Finally, animal tests are nearly all short term, and some chemicals may take the length of a human life time to produce their delayed effects. . . .

Cancer Research

The most feared of all diseases is cancer, and for that reason I shall focus the medical discussion exclusively on animal cancer research, but to a great extent the following remarks are generalizable throughout the entire area of medicine.

The infectious and nutritive-based diseases that ravaged the people of previous centuries are now in decline. It is generally conceded that progress made against infectious diseases owes most to personal hygiene and community-wide sanitation, the concern for these factors having been inspired by the discovery of germs. The foundation of nutritional science was the discovery of vitamins, and their role in health owes almost nothing to animal experimentation.[12] In any case, the decrease of these diseases has meant the rise of deaths attributable to other causes. Today, about one in three deaths in middle age is due to cancer. There are of course many kinds of cancers and these tend to affect specific parts of the body: the breast, lung, lymph glands, pancreas, esophagus, rectum, and stomach are the principal areas. Over the last 30 years or so, the incidence of cancer of the rectum and stomach has declined but most of the other cancers have increased. The greatest increase is in lung cancer. In England there was a 136 percent increase from 1951 to 1975. Yet even as far back as 1914 epidemiology successfully identified the causes of a variety of cancers. About 85 percent of them are environmentally induced: excessive exposure to sunlight (skin cancers), smoking cigarettes (lung cancer), smoking pipes (lip and tongue cancers), industrial pollution (a range of blood, lung and other cancers), and carcinogenic food additives (a similar wide range). Smoking accounts for 40 percent of cancers in men. Meat consumption has been found to be associated with cancer of the colon, and breast cancers are related to dietary fats. Asbestos, vinyl chloride, and benzene are examples of industrial carcinogens. X-rays used to counter cancer (radiation therapy) and anticancer drugs are ironically also implicated in the production of cancers.

How was all this discovered? Not by animal experimentation but mainly by studies in epidemiology. Accordingly, many see a bitter irony in the experimental production of cancers in animals. In the vast majority of cases, they claim, the tested substances are *already known* to be carcinogenic to humans. . . .

Moreover, critics allege that animal-based research, despite public relations to the contrary, tends to be unproductive. The favorite cancer research animal is the mouse. Since 1955 the National Cancer Institute (NCI) has screened about half a million chemicals on mice in its search for a useful drug against cancer. NCI does not just test chemicals on mice to see if they are effective; it also uses these chemicals to induce cancers in the animals. But most mouse cancers are sarcomas (cancers arising in the bone, connective tissue or muscle), while most human cancers are carcinomas (cancers arising in membranes). Thus, although the screening has had some good results, critics claim that none of the drugs discovered as a result of it are as effective or useful as the ten major anticancer drugs discovered before the screening began.[13]

3. ALTERNATIVES

Those critical of the use of animals in science do not argue that we ought to forgo science. Rather, they insist that we must explore alternatives. What are these alternatives and what are their possibilities? Here, briefly, is a list of the major ones:

1. Mathematical and computer modeling of anatomy-physiology relationships.
2. The use of lower organisms, such as bacteria and fungi, for tests of mutagenicity.
3. The development of more sophisticated *in vitro* techniques, including the use of subcellular fractions, short-term cellular systems (cell suspensions, tissue biopsies, whole organ perfusion), and tissue cultures (the maintenance of living cells in a nutritive medium for 24 hours or longer).
4. More reliance on human studies, including epidemiology, postmarketing surveillance, and the carefully regulated use of human volunteers.

I shall discuss only the first three of these because it is in these areas that scientists who use animals in medical research have been the most skeptical. . . .

Models

Computer simulations are often mentioned as a better model for scientific purposes than any animal. Although this claim may be a bit of hyperbole, the fact is that for many purposes they are as good, and future dependency on them can only result in their becoming much better. In particular, where physiological systems are well understood and definable in mathematical terms, good programs are already available. (In the ensuing discussion, a number of examples will be offered.) Some complex systems are poorly understood and therefore programs don't exist in these areas. Of course, in such cases, critics claim that relying on animals as models cannot be much better. But unlike the programs, the animals are already available.

It is important to understand that when mathematicians speak of computer models, they do not mean tiny replicas of large things. Mathematicians construct systems that they hope will mirror biological systems. Although the mathematical details are intricate, we can at least say this: These systems consist of equations into which biological data are input and analyses of data are output. Perhaps an example will elucidate. It is from a report by Dr. Alan Brady of the Bowman Gray School of Medicine, Winston-Salem.[14]

According to Brady, the glucose tolerance test is an example of something that may be simulated by a computer in a way that actually facilitates research. The computer model offers researchers the opportunity to explore situations that are not practical or ethical with animal experiments. Computer simulation also organizes material more systematically than animal experiments do and thus is better suited for teaching physiology students. A computer user first enters starting and stopping times for glucose infusion, the rate of glucose utilization, and the initial insulin concentration, then data on blood pressure and certain rate constants. The programmed algorithms manipulate the figures to generate the simulated results. Plainly, glucose tolerance can be calculated more quickly, for a vaster array of "animals," and over a range of values far more inclusive than would occur in real life. As an added benefit, Brady points out that computer simulations in physiology are much cheaper than animal experiments because costs are pretty much limited to initial outlay for program development. . . .

Opponents of animal experiments who cry out for greater reliance upon computer simulations frequently exaggerate what is currently available, but those who are content simply to insist upon the current limitations perhaps reveal their own biases as well as a failure of the imagination. . . .

Some anatomy departments have begun interesting experiments in simulation. They have found that they can teach dissection and a host of other important surgical techniques to medical students using pseudo-animals. These can bleed, blink, cough, vomit, simulate gas exchange, and even "die" when necessary. Recently, Dr. Charles Short, Chief of Anesthesiology at Cornell Veterinary College, developed a dog mannequin called Resusci-Dog. It responds to a broad range of techniques necessary for practicing and refining "hands-on" cardiopulmonary skills. For example, if a student applies excessive pressure while doing cardiac massage, a certain signal bleeps; if pressure is misplaced, there is a different bleep; and a white light indicates proper massage. Typically, veterinary students induce heart attacks in real dogs and only then begin to practice their resuscitation skills. Death may show they have done the massage poorly. Resusci-Dog has a femoral pulse, and it can also be used for practice in certain syringe injections.[15]

The Use of Lower Organisms

The best known of all tests on lower organisms as a replacement for animal tests is the Ames test, developed by Dr. Bruce Ames at the University of California at Berkeley. Although the Ames test actually discovers mutation-causing substances (mutagenicity), Ames believes it also screens for cancer-causing substances (carcinogenicity). This idea is based on the view that most carcinogenic substances are also mutagenic. Ames takes the suspected cancer-producing substance and puts it into a nutrient medium in which a strain of *Salmonella* bacteria is growing. If the tested substance really is mutagenic, then the *Salmonella* will develop the indicated mutations. About 80 percent of the carcinogens tested this way have resulted in mutation. When substances known not to be carcinogens are tested this way, only about 10 percent of them result in mutations. This corroborates the very close association of carcinogenicity and mutagenicity and makes the Ames test an excellent way of screening presumptive cancer-producing agents.[16] The Ames test, however, is not quite what some critics of animal-based tests claim it is. The medium in which the *Salmonella* grow is actually treated with a rat liver preparation first. Some liver preparation or other is needed at this point in the development of the test, but it need not be rat liver. In fact, Ames has used human liver obtained from autopsies, and his preference for rat liver is dictated by convenience. Nevertheless, the humane killing of a rat to induce mutagenic changes in *Salmonella* is much preferred by many opponents of animal tests to inducing cancers in rats themselves. The test is now fairly standard in about 3,000 laboratories.

Another interesting use for bacteria is in tests of water pollution. The standard procedure is to immerse fish in different concentrations of the effluent to be tested and observe what concentration kills 50 percent—one more variation of the LD-50 test. But Beckman Instruments company uses a strain of luminescent bacteria as the bioassay organism. The light-producing metabolism of the bacteria is six times more sensitive to toxicants than are fish, and the test takes half an hour in contrast to the 96-hour test used for fish.[17]

Finally, work has begun in utilizing plants both for synthesis of useful drugs and as the subjects of *in vivo* research. Indeed, recent progress has been so significant that it has been argued that "there are sufficient numbers of bioassay techniques described in the current literature so that almost any biological activity of interest can be studied without utilizing intact animals."[18] The National Cancer Institute has now screened over 40,000 species of plants for *in vivo* antitumor activity and has identified many that are highly active antitumor agents. Of course, their safety is first screened on animals before they are allowed to be included in clinical trials on humans. But Dr. Robert Sharpe has argued that plants themselves can have cancer induced into them. In particular, he claims, there is research supporting the replacement of mice by potatoes in traditional tests of leukemia.[19] Although NCI has been doing plant tumor research for 25 years, it remains a fairly exotic frontier.

Tissue Cultures

Tissue culture research requires keeping cells alive outside a total organism. Animal cells have been cultured in laboratories since the 1920's. In the early days, the possibility of bacterial contamination imposed immense limitations on the use of tissue cultures. Today, antibiotics have removed those restrictions and tissue culture is available in nearly all research institutes in the world.

A tissue cell is typically cultivated in a medium such as a salt solution supplemented by various plasmas and serums to make the environment as natural as possible. The establishment of cell lines out of tissue cultures is essential for modern virology. Most viruses grow nicely in these media, enabling biochemists to observe all their changes. This, of course, is exactly what is needed for clinical diagnosis of viral disease. The best-known commercial application of virology is the production of vaccines for the polio virus, originally grown in kidney cells of monkeys but now normally grown in human cells. Rabies vaccines also are now grown in human diploid-cell cultures rather than in live animals.

Cell cultures are important in cancer research. For example, we can study the effect of certain hormones on tumor cells in cultures that have been obtained by the surgical removal of a cancerous breast. If the hormone inhibits the growth of the cells, this would be a promising sign for therapy. Another promising piece of research involves putting known cancer cells into a fertilized hen's egg. This causes the embryo to put outgrowths of cells toward the cancer cells, and the extent of the growth is related to the malignancy of the tumor. Some researchers maintain that the standard practice of introducing cancer cells into live animals to observe the development of the malignancy is not as sensible, since tumor development in animals is far slower than in fertilized eggs. . . .[20]

Advances are being made. For example, the liver is the main site of drug metabolism, and it is possible to incubate a drug with a liver preparation before putting it into a tissue culture. Some recent work has been successful in testing for a drug's carcinogenic activity. Hence the reliance on living creatures with livers may be overcome. In fact, it is the opinion of Dr. Philip Hanawalt, biology professor at Stanford University, that that day has already arrived. Hanawalt maintains that studies utilizing only cultured cells can elucidate the differences in how mouse cancers and human cancers originate. "New experimental techiques such as the analysis of cloned DNA from one cell to another, and the use of hybrid cells are particularly powerful and now render obsolete many approaches that have utilized animals to study mechanisms of carcinogenesis."[21]

NOTES

1. This is an estimate of the number of animals killed for scientific purposes throughout the world. No figures are released by either the U.S.S.R. or China. Estimates for the United States range as low as 15 million to as high as 200 million. Conventional estimates are approximately 70 to 120 million. Among nations releasing data, Japan ranks second, with 19 million. My own estimate assumes that figures for the U.S.S.R. and China are comparable to those for the United States.

2. For a "traditional" estimate of 70 million, see Scientists Center for Animal Welfare (SCAW) *Newsletter* (June and October, 1984), p. 2. For 100 million, see B. E. Rollin, *Animal Rights and Human Morality* (Buffalo: Prometheus Books, 1981), p. 91 (hereafter referred to as Rollin, *Animal Rights*). For 200 million, see R. Ryder, *Victims of Science* (London: National Anti-Vivisection Society, 1983), p. 24 (hereafter referred to as Ryder, *Victims*). Ryder only reports this estimate, he does not endorse it. He suggests 120 million. For the low estimate of 15 million, see Perrie Adams, "The Need to Conduct Scientific Investigations," address to the American Psychological Association, 1984 (hereafter referred to as Adams, "Need").

3. The Draize test is one of the two major commercial tests that have aroused the ire of animal welfare and animal rights groups. The other is the LD-50 test. LD stands for lethal dose. In this test, animals are force-fed a dose of a substance that is being screened for toxicity. The amount of the dose is gradually increased to the point at which 50 percent of the test animals succumb. Further details may be gleaned from the aforementioned books by Rollin and Ryder.

4. T. Ward and L. Hunt, "Animal Rights in the Classroom," *National Anti-Vivisection Bulletin* (Fall–Winter, 1983), p. 19.

5. More details of all five cases reported under Behavioral Research, including author citations, can be found in Jeff Diner, *Physical and Mental Suffering of Experimental Animals* (Washington, D.C.: Animal Welfare Institute, 1979), (hereafter referred to as Diner, *Suffering*). Diner's survey of over 200 experiments covers just the years 1973–1978.

6. Diner, *Suffering*, p. 6.

7. Diner, *Suffering*, pp. 59–60.

8. Diner, *Suffering*, p. 81.

9. Diner, *Suffering*, pp. 105–107.

10. Diner, *Suffering*, pp. 111–117.

11. Diner, *Suffering*, p. 116.

12. Among dozens of skeptics and their publications concerning medicine's role in reducing infectious diseases are Rick Carlson, *The End of Medicine* (New York: Wiley, 1975), James Giles, *Medical Ethics* (Cambridge: Schenkman, 1983), and Victor Fuchs, *Who Shall Live?* (New York: Basic Books, 1975).

13. Reines, "Cancer Research with Animals," *NAVS* Bulletin (Summer, 1984), p.5.

14. Alan Brady, Scientists Center for Animal Welfare, *Newsletter* (September, 1983), p. 8.

15. American Fund for Alternatives to Animal Research, *News Abstract* (Winter, 1984–85 and several earlier issues).

16. Bruce Ames is the author of over 140 articles on the subject of mutagenicity. I am indebted to him for having sent me a considerable number of these. Among the more recent are "A New Salmonella Tester Strain, TA97, for the Detection of Frameshift Mutagens: A Run of Cytosines as a Mutational Hot-Spot," *Mutation Research* (no. 94, 1982), pp. 315–330; "Revised Methods for the Salmonella Mutagenicity Test," *Mutation Research* (no. 113, 1983), pp. 173–215; and "A New Salmonella Tester Strain (TA 102) with A:T Base Pairs at the Site of Mutation Detects Oxidative Mutagens," *Proceedings of the National Academy of Science, USA* (no. 79, 1982), pp. 7445–7449.

17. Dallas Pratt, *Alternatives to Pain in Experiments on Animals* (New York: Argus Archives, 1980), p. 214.

18. N. R. Farnsworth and J. M. Pezzuto, "Practical Pharmacological Evaluation of Plants," *Lord Dowling Fund Bulletin* (no. 21, Spring, 1984), pp. 26–34.

19. Robert Sharpe, "Science Now," *Lord Dowling Fund Bulletin* (no. 20, Autumn 1983), pp. 40–44.

20. The claim these researchers are making is not necessarily true of brain cancer but it is true of the far more common cancers of the breast and the lung.

21. Quoted by Dr. Robert Sharpe in "Cancer Research: Moves Away from Laboratory Animals," *Animals' Defender* (July–August, 1982), p. 62.

C. R. GALLISTEL

The Case for Unrestricted Research Using Animals

A bill called the "Research Modernization Act" is now before Congress, where it is picking up influential support. The bill would ban most surgical experiments using live animals, on the theory that the same knowledge may usually be gained by computer simulations, experiments on bacteria, and so on.[1] The bill would establish a review committee that would allow *at most* one experiment of a given type to be done on live animals. The proponents of this legislation claim that the law is a moral imperative and that it would not cause serious harm to research in the life sciences. I wish to argue that this bill would devastate behavioral neurobiology and that it is an affront to moral sensibility.

Behavioral neurobiology tries to establish the manner in which the nervous system mediates behavioral phenomena. It does so by studying the behavioral consequences of one or more of the following procedures: (a) destruction of a part of the nervous system, (b) stimulation of a part, and (c) administration of drugs that alter neural functioning. These three techniques are as old as the discipline. A recent addition is (d) the recording of

C. R. Gallistel teaches in the Psychology Department at the University of Pennsylvania. He is a frequent contributor to professional journals in psychology.

C. R. Gallistel, *American Psychologist, 36* (4), 357–362. Copyright © 1981 by The American Psychological Association. Reprinted by permission of the publisher and author.

electrical activity. All four procedures cause the animal at least some temporary distress. In the past they have frequently caused intense pain, and they occasionally do so now. Also, they often impair the animal's proper functioning, sometimes transiently, sometimes permanently.

From the beginning, this enterprise has provoked moral censure, to which the experimentalists have often reacted defensively. The terms of this debate have changed hardly at all in 200 years. Consider the following passage, written shortly after 1800:

> Before I close this introduction, I wish in some degree to exculpate the physiologists who make experiments upon living animals, from the reproaches of cruelty, so frequently uttered against them. I do not pretend wholly to justify them. I would only remark, that the most part of those who utter these reproaches may be deserving of the same. For example, do they not go, or have they never gone a hunting? How can the sportsman, who for his own pleasure mutilates so many animals, and often in so cruel a manner, be more humane then the physiologist who is forced to make them perish for his instruction? Whether the rights we assume over those animals be lawful or not, it is certain that few people scruple to destroy, in a variety of ways, such of those animals as cause them the least inconvenience, though ever so trifling; and that we only feed the most part of those that surround us, to sacrifice them to our wants. I can scarcely comprehend that we should be wrong in killing them for our instruction, when we think we are right in destroying them for our food.
>
> I own that it would be barbarous to make animals suffer in vain, if the object of the experiment could be obtained without it. But it is impossible. Experiments upon living animals are one of the greatest lights of physiology. The difference between the dead and the living animal is infinite. If the ablest mechanician is unable to discover all the effect of a machine after having seen it work, how could the most learned anatomist devise, by the study only of the organs, the effect of a machine as prodigiously complicated as the body of an animal. To find out its secrets, it is not enough to observe the simultaneous exercise of all the functions in the animal, while in health; it is above all important to study the effect of the derangement, or the cessation of such or such a function. It is in determining by this analysis what the function of such or such an organ is, as well as its relation with the other functions, that the art of experiments upon living animals consists. But to be able to do it with some degree of precision, it is indispensably necessary to multiply the victims, on account of the variety of circumstances and accidents which may render their result uncertain or inconclusive. I should be tempted to say of physiological experiments, what has been said of charities: *perdenda sunt multa; ut semel ponas bene.* SENECA. [Translation: Many are a waste, that one may come out well.][2]

The passsage just quoted seems to me to contain most of the basic facts and positions in the debate between behavioral neurobiologists and antivivsectionists. Let me first summarize what I take to be matters of fact:

1. Experimental surgery causes pain and distress to animals.
2. Researchers are well aware of this pain. Since the discovery of ether in 1847,

they have used anesthetics to reduce or prevent the pain, wherever such reduction or prevention does not affect the conclusions that can be drawn from the experiment.

3. There is no way to establish the relation between the nervous system and behavior without some experimental surgery.

4. Most experiments conducted by behavioral neurobiologists, *like scientific experiments in general,* may be seen in retrospect to have been a waste of time, in the sense that they did not prove anything or yield any new insight.

5. There is no way of discriminating in advance the waste-of-time experiments from the illuminating ones with anything approaching certainty. Such judgments are necessarily made under conditions of high uncertainty. As shown by the theory of signal detection, a necessary consequence of this uncertainty is that any attempt to reduce the number of neurobehavioral experiments by prior evaluation of their possible significance will necessarily give rise to many "false negatives," without eliminating "false positives." That is, prior restraints on neurobehavioral experiments will lead to rejection of experiments whose results would in fact have been important and allowance of experiments whose results will prove unimportant. This will be true no matter how stringent and cumbersome the a priori evaluation. . . .

These five statements must be taken as fact: Any attempt to advance a pro- or antivivisectionist position by denying one or another of these statements evades the ethical question by denying the very circumstances that give it force. The force of these circumstances can best be appreciated by the study of specific historical cases. One case that should be analyzed at length by anyone contemplating restricting neurobehavioral experiments is the discovery that the dorsal and ventral roots of the spinal cord are sensory and motor, respectively.

In 1822 François Magendie discovered that in young puppies the dorsal and ventral roots of the peripheral nerves come together outside the spinal column, so that they can be separately severed with relative ease. Magendie had been wondering for some time what would be the effect of cutting one or another root on the behavior of the limb or body segment served by the nerve. In the other animals he was familiar with, the roots fused before exiting from the spine. They could only be cut individually after breaking open the spine, which, in the days before anesthesia, was all but impossible to do without damaging the spinal cord. Soon after discovering the favorable anatomical disposition of the roots in young puppies, Magendie began exposing the spines of 6–8-week-old puppies and cutting either the dorsal or the ventral roots of one or more nerves. After several such experiments he was able to publish his famous three-page communication in which he concluded that the dorsal roots carried sensory signals while the ventral roots carried motor signals.[3]

Magendie's experiments place the ethical problems posed by neurobehavioral research in sharp relief for the following reasons: (a) The results were of the utmost importance. (b) The animals used were puppies and the pain of the necessary surgical procedure was both intense and unalleviated by anesthetics, whose discovery lay 25 years in the future. (c) Other very similar experiments had been conducted by some of the leading neuroscientists of the day—most notably the English anatomist Charles Bell—without yielding the decisive all-important insight. (d) The experiments, because they rapidly became well-known and because they were sometimes performed in public, incurred widespread moral censure and helped fuel the antivivisection movement in 19th century England.

Let me elaborate on these points. First, as regards the significance of the results, I can do no better than quote from the introduction to a recent book by Cranefield on the history of the Bell-Magendie precedence dispute:

> The discovery that the dorsal and ventral roots are the sensory and motor roots is one of the most important in the history of biology. The importance of the discovery has never been doubted; as E. H. Ackerknecht has recently written to me, "it is, after Harvey, probably the most momentous *single* discovery in physiology, and it had a more immediate influence on practical medicine than Harvey's discovery. Romberg's book on neurology, the first of its kind, is unthinkable without it."
>
> A comparison with Harvey is by no means idle, since just as no rational physiology of the cardiovascular system was possible before Harvey's discovery, so no rational physiology of the nervous system was possible before the discovery of the separate functions of the roots of the spinal nerves. It was the first unequivocal localization of function in the nervous system and it made possible and led directly to the study of the spinal reflex. The study of the spinal reflex culminated in the work of Sherrington, work that led to our modern concepts of the physiology of the entire central nervous system.[4]

As regards the pain caused the animals—the other horn of the dilemma, so to speak—little elaboration is necessary, except to note that the pain was hideous, that there was no way known to the science of the day of mitigating it, and last, for the reasons already explained, that the animal of choice was the one most likely to arouse human sympathy—the puppy.

The third point, the similar but inconclusive experiments conducted by other leading neuroscientists of that time, requires considerable elaboration. The elaboration is rich both in its irony and in its implications for the question of whether antivivisectionist sentiment may be appeased without doing serious damage to the progress of neuroscience. In 1811, in a privately circulated pamphlet,[5] Charles Bell reported the results of experiments on rabbits involving the sectioning of dorsal and/or ventral roots. The report of these experiments is sketchy, and the wording of the conclusions is diffuse and obscure; but, in essence, Bell concluded erroneously that the ventral roots subserved voluntary behavior while the dorsal roots subserved involuntary behavior. Bell's conclusions were steered in the direction of error by a theory of nervous system function that he had derived from his anatomical studies. In subsequent publications Bell made brief allusions to these results and to related results from experiments involving the sectioning of cranial nerves in donkeys; but he did not give any clear statement of their implications, nor did he attach much importance to them *until* Magendie published his paper in 1822. Immediately thereafter Bell and his students began a clamorous, unprincipled, but largely successful campaign to claim priority for what was properly Magendie's discovery.

In the course of this campaign, Bell advanced more or less self-contradictory claims. He repeatedly reproached Magendie for the cruelty of the experiments, claiming that the experiments were unnecessary and counterproductive and that the correct conclusion could be reached by anatomical observation alone. On the other hand, he argued that he, himself, had performed the crucial experiment first in 1811 and that Magendie had been inspired to "replicate" it by one of Bell's pupils, who demonstrated the related cranial nerve experiment to Magendie in late 1821. Bell even reissued "improved" versions of his earlier publications, in which crucial passages were reworded so as to appear to anticipate Magendie's conclusions.

Bell's reproaches and his claims that experiments were unnecessary were picked up by antivivisectionists and helped to get passed the laws that to this day make neurobehavioral work more difficult in England than in America or on the Continent. The claim that experiments on living animals are unnecessary finds its echo today in the claim made by antivivisectionists that it is possible to do neurobehavioral research by computer simulation, without ever cutting into a living animal.

These claims are absurd and nothing illustrates their absurdity better than the case at hand. There is nothing in anatomical observation per se that can do more than faintly suggest the functions of the roots. Bell himself knew that the results from the experiments on living animals were central to his claim of priority. Without them he had no claim, which is why—after 1822—he repeatedly emphasized his experiments on rabbits and donkeys. The irony is that Bell's erroneous inferences from anatomical observation played no small role in misleading his interpretation of his vivisection experiments. If anatomical observations are of little use, computer simulation is of still less use. What is there to simulate? You can make a computer whose input and output wires are segregated; you can make one in which they are intertwined; you can even make one in which the same wires are used for both functions. None of this modeling will tell you what the case is with the dorsal and ventral roots of mammalian nerves.

The sorry story of Bell's attempt to claim priority also illustrates the undesirability of setting up committees to pass in advance on whether the results to be obtained from a given experiment performed by a given experimenter are sufficiently important to outweigh the pain to be inflicted. Bell was one of the most important neuroscientists of his day. Furthermore, his vivisection experiments were inspired by a very general if vague and murky (in retrospect!) theory. Magendie was also a scientist of great stature, but he had no theory; indeed, he mistrusted and eschewed the system building that Bell was addicted to. Magendie just wanted to see what would happen. In Bell's hands, the crucial experiment led only to vague conclusions, to which Bell himself attributed little importance. In Magendie's hands, the experiment led to a clear conclusion whose importance was immediately obvious to all of the leading neuroscientists of his time.

Had Bell and Magendie simultaneously submitted proposals for the experiment to a Humane-Vivisection Committee for its permission, it is hard not to believe that they would have given the nod to Bell rather than to Magendie, assuming they gave either permission. If Magendie in 1822 had asked permission of a committee that happened to be aware of Bell's 1811 work—which is to assume an unusually well-informed committee—they would no doubt have refused permission on the grounds that the experiment had alredy been done by a first-rate researcher with meaningless results.

In summary, the debate over the ethics of surgical experiments on animals in behavioral neurobiology must come to grips with the following two dilemmas:

1. While it is true that these experments cause pain and/or distress to the animals, it is equally true that the science cannot progress without them.
2. While it is true that most of the animals which suffer in the course of neurobehavioral research suffer in vain, it is equally true that there is no way to restrict experimentation only to those experiments that will yield meaningful data.

A consideration of the Bell–Magendie case makes it clear why restricting research on living animals is certain to restrict the progress in our understanding of the relation between the nervous system and behavior. Therefore, one should advocate such restrictions only if one believes that the moral value of this scientific knowledge and of the many human and humane benefits that flow from it cannot outweigh the suffering of a rat.

It is an affront to my own ethical sensibility to hear arguments that the suffering of animals is of greater moral weight than are the advancement of human understanding and the consequent alleviation of human suffering. Like Le Gallois, I can scarcely comprehend how it can be right to use animals to provide food for our bodies but wrong to use them to provide food for thought. But, of course, I place a very high moral value on the advancement of human understanding. Those for whom science has no moral value will find my argument without force, assuming that they are also unmoved by the prospect that such understanding will alleviate human suffering.

NOTES

1. Broad, W. J. Legislating an end to animals in the lab. *Science*, 1980, *208*, 575–576. (News and Comment)
2. Le Gallois, M. *Experiments on the principle of life* (N. C. Nancrede & J. G. Nancrede, Trans.). Philadelphia, Pa: Thomas, 1813, pp. 19–21.
3. Magendie, F. Expériences sur les fonctions des racines des nerfs rachidien. *Journal de Physiologie Expérimentale et Pathologique*, 1822, 2, 276–279.
4. Cranefield, P. F. *The way in and the way out: François Magendie, Charles Bell and the roots of the spinal nerves*. Mount Kisco, N. Y.: Futura, 1974, p. xiii.
5. Bell, C. *Idea of a new anatomy of the brain*. London: Strahan & Preston, 1811.

MARY MIDGLEY

The Case for Restricting Research Using Animals

I shall say nothing here about how we should deal with situations in which animals are killed for vital human interests, for life and limb, as in essential medical research. I shall concentrate instead on asking how we should value all that range of research which does *not* affect those vital interests. What sacrifices should be made for it? More generally, what sort of justification does knowledge itself, pursued for its own sake, provide for sacrificing anything, including animals? This topic may look like a soft option, but I think it has to be handled before the tougher and rarer direct conflicts can be approached. . . .

The question is, then, where does knowledge stand in the hierarchy of human values? Are there any limits to the price we ought to pay for it? Someone from another planet, glancing over our civilization, would see at once that we do prize it highly. Still, most of us would say that there are limits, that it must take its place among other values. What is that place?

Since we certainly do want to place it high, let us start by looking at the extreme position which George Steiner took in his Bronowski lecture called

Mary Midgley formerly taught philosophy at the University of Newcastle on Tyne. Her books include *Beast and Man* (Harvester Press, 1979) and *Animals and Why They Matter* (Penguin Books, 1983).

Reprinted from "Why Knowledge Matters" from E. Sperlinger (ed.), *Animals in Research*. New York: John Wiley, 1981, pp. 319–331.

"Has truth a future?"[1] Steiner there celebrated the intense disinterested search for theoretical truth which is one characteristic of our culture. He distinguished this search from the mere prudent collecting of useful knowledge for practical convenience. Knowledge, he said, may not be useful at all, it may even be dangerous, but if we are really disinterested, that danger ought not to stop us pursuing it. . . .

Now part of this is true and important. Knowledge *is* an end to be pursued for its own sake. But it is not the only end; there are others. What could commit us to making *unlimited* sacrifices of all those other ends for knowledge? . . .

Again, in Norse mythology, Odin gave his right eye for wisdom, but it was his own right eye. It is not heroic to sacrifice other people, even if we leave animals out of the picture. In the second place, even scientists who experiment on themselves have to avoid suicide if they are serious in their search, since there can be no knowledge if there is nobody left to own it. . . .

Now this relativity of knowledge to knowers has a profound effect on the notion of *disinterested* knowledge. Certainly the search for knowledge should be free from irrelevant inducements like ambition or cash. But it cannot be free from interest in the sense in which "interest" is opposed to the boring and the pointless. Someone who incessantly counts the sand on the beach, and collects and weighs pebbles, and calculates the relative frequency of different shapes among them just for the hell of it is certainly "pursuing knowledge for its own sake." He passes Steiner's grandiloquent test for the scholar: "his addiction is with the abstract, the inapplicable, the sovereignly useless." But this addiction will not make him a scholar. Uselessness alone is not enough. The sort of knowledge which *is* worth pursuing is not just miscellaneous units of information. It is understanding. Real enquiry is highly selective. Obsession is often its servant, but never its master. It does not aim at collecting indiscriminately all the facts there are. (There are an infinite number, so if it did, the number still uncollected would never grow less.) It aims at making life more *intelligible* by finding explanatory structures which underlie and shape its apparent confusion. In a clear sense therefore enquiry cannot be, and should not try to be, totally disinterested. It has to be directed to some questions rather than others, and the ones it ought to choose are those centrally important to the human race, those required for understanding the things which we most need to understand. We have to find the central questions, and distinguish them from the trivial ones.

I have paid attention first to discussing the kind of value knowledge has, because that seems necessary before we can ask what other valuable things ought to be given up for it. Few people, perhaps, will want to sign up for Steiner's extreme and romantic vision of the final victory of knowledge, of the whole human race well lost for the solution to a few problems in genetic engineering or comparative intelligence-testing. But during both these debates I have heard people give defences quite as extreme of the right of scientists to pursue, quite unhindered and regardless of consequences, any enquiry which they happen to have taken up. They find this position plausible because they unthinkingly take for granted the view which leads Steiner to his crazy conclusion—namely, that all truths are of equal and incomparable value. When we are considering the cost of research, whether in money, in animal suffering, or in any other kind of resource, we tend to speak in the abstract about our aims. What justifies this sacrifice, we say, is Science, Discovery, Research, the Advancement of Knowledge. We oppose the particular price that must be paid directly to these large abstract values. How can the interest of a few rats—or even a few human deaths in epidemics—possibly matter when weighed against such sublime ends? But we need also to ask about the importance of the actual limited enquiry involved, about the centrality of *this* particular issue, and about whether this experiment is the best or only way of illuminating it. To an alarming extent, judgments about this are determined by habit, by the methods that have become familiar in recent research and by the tradition of the journals.

What then should our view be when a particular piece of research is in fact trivial?

Non-scientists may be surprised at this question; whatever may be said of the arts, they may say, surely scientific research is never trivial? Scientists will not be surprised at it. Every serious scientist knows that there is a great deal of trivial research going on, not his own, but other people's. This is not surprising. Experiments are trivial if they are designed to test hypotheses which are themselves trivial, or hypotheses which are important but whose truth or falsity is already sufficiently established, or if they make unwarrantable background assumptions which vitiate their method. They are also trivial if they are badly designed, if they will not prove what they are meant to prove, or if what they are meant to prove is itself something obscure and incoherent, an idea not properly worked out by its begetters. Avoiding all these disasters is very hard, and the skills needed for it are not prominent in the education of scientists.

There is, unfortunately, no single unifying entity called Science, which inevitably gains by all scientific work and whose gain is always transmitted to the human race. We have a real dilemma here. We hesitate to prune. We find it natural to think that, as Mill urged in his *Essay on Liberty*, every important and life-enhancing activity should be allowed to proliferate as widely and luxuriantly as possible. But there must be some limits. Moreover, activities do not always thrive on this treatment. The example of the US cancer research programme, which has had virtually unlimited funds, is not encouraging. There has been a great deal of waste and corruption, and the cost, naturally, is not only in terms of money:

The General Accounting Office also found that staff, equipment and animals paid for by the National Cancer Institute were used on private contracts. Finally, Eppley bred far too many animals; of 84,300 bred during 1976, 50,015 were killed without any research use. Yet, until GAO stepped in, NCI was about to fund a substantial increase in Eppley breeding facilities. On top of all this, the GAO found that NCI hardly looked at Eppley's results.

One could mention also the duplication of drugs by competing firms and the statutory tests for poisons. Examples in his own field will probably leap to the mind of any working scientist. All research produces knowledge, but a good deal of it does not seem worth producing. . . .

Some issues, we all agree, are more important than others. And most of us would also agree that it is wrong to cause suffering for an entirely trivial issue. (For instance, in the case of the US cancer programme, it seems pretty uncontroversial that it is wrong to commission the performing of experiments on animals when you care so little about the results that you scarcely bother to look at them.) Justification must therefore rest on importance. But *an important issue is by definition a pervasive one.* It is not an isolated matter, it is something far-reaching which crops up in many contexts and has many widely varied effects. If this is so, it can be tested in many ways. So it is impossible that tests which involve inflicting suffering on animals are the only ones, and unlikely that they are the best ones, by which an important issue can be settled.

An obvious example of this is the series of isolation experiments on infant monkeys, carried out by Harry S. Harlow and his colleagues from 1961 onwards, which established the presence of strong and specific social tendencies in these babies, and showed how the frustration of those tendencies in solitude could permanently warp the creatures' nature and destroy their sanity. These experiments were originally of great interest because they played a large part in breaking the hold of unrealistic behaviourist theories, widely held throughout the social sciences, which attributed social development both in men and the higher animals entirely to conditioning. That was an important issue. The error that was exploded was a serious one, damaging both in theory and in practice. Did this automatically justify all that was done to the monkeys? To do so, it is not enough to show that the research proved its point. We need also to show that it was the best or only available way to prove it. But because of the very generality and importance of the point proved, it could not be the only way. Crude behaviourism was so bad a theory, so thoroughly at odds with experience, that there were countless other ways of refuting it. What seems to have been needed in the first place was an advance in understanding, a clear, logical argument to show the incoherence of the theory, a critique of its basic concepts. Chomsky provided this when he pointed out that the capacity for speech must have an innate basis. Beyond this, there was also a need to show how behaviourism conflicted with the ordinary observed facts of life. Anyone with experience of children or of other young animals could have done this. But social scientists did not readily listen to such people. Common observation had to be strengthened by thoroughly systematic studies of spontaneous behaviour, supplemented by non-brutal experiments where these were actually necessary. This was in fact done by many observers of human children, such as Eibl-Eibesfeldt, Bowlby, and Blurton-Jones. The skills needed to observe spontaneous behaviour methodically had already been worked out by Konrad Lorenz and his followers; the notion that such observation must be merely "anecdotal" was already exploded, and ethologists already knew enough about the behaviour of young animals to make the points which Harlow and his collaborators made. This information could easily have been supplemented, where necessary, both from further studies in the wild and from less drastic studies of caged animals. . . .

Curiosity of some kind, after all, *is* the proper motive for science; what marks off the damnable and detestable kind? The simple and natural answer seems to be, its limited object, and its bias towards drama. Curiosity about pain and destruction *for their own sake*—rather than as aspects in some larger topic—is identical with cruelty. Children pulling flies to pieces are genuinely curious; they really do want to know what will happen next, and they are in a way quite disinterested. It is the topic that makes their curiosity illicit, and there are plenty of other examples of this. I may be genuinely curious about your private life. I may really want quite badly to read your letters, listen to your conversations, test your pain threshold, and find out how you react to simulated bad news, and this simply for the sake of it, without expecting any advantage. But it is my business to control this feeling. Curiosity in itself gives no sort of general licence for action, and the expectation of excitement makes it worse, not better.

This point will probably look surprising today, not only to scientists but to academics generally, because the thrust of most public debate on this question is to distinguish pure from applied research and to exalt the pure kind. Against powerful commercial and political pressures, intellectuals have quite rightly and repeatedly insisted that knowledge has direct value as an end, not just as a means. They may well be inclined to think it follows that we ought to pursue every kind of knowledge. . . . Pleasure, peace, and fulfilment too have, equally with knowledge, their value as ends in themselves. But the man who finds pleasure, peace, and fulfilment either in interminably counting pebbles or in working as a torturer has chosen badly. Quite apart from enquiries which are politically dangerous . . . , there are plenty which are genuinely trivial and valueless, and—still more remarkably—others which are intrinsically iniquitous *simply from the topic*. A professional torturer, for instance, may (though his employers usually are not) be motivated simply by disinterested curiosity. He may actually acquire a great deal of physiological and psychological knowledge about strains and endurances, and an intellectual interest in these may really be the main source of his job satisfaction. Since, however, curiosity here runs counter to every other value we recognize, we condemn his way of life completely. And this condemnation is not based merely on his being practically dangerous; it protests against his curiosity as such, against the direction of his attention. . . .

I mention this extreme, but by no means isolated, case of "bad knowledge" simply to complete the argument which, in its more familiar stretches, deals mostly with triviality and worthlessness. Researchers usually meet this charge by some variation of the "spin-off" arguments, pointing out —justly—that discoveries of real practical and theoretical value have often resulted by chance from enquiries which did not in themselves look at all important. There is much in this, but the trouble is that it proves too much. If what we are talking of is not a hunch about some real, specific, possible application, but pure, unadulterated, blind luck, then it might hit us in the course of any enquiry whatever, and it seems to follow that no research project should ever be rejected or abandoned. Everything must be investigated. We might simply draw lots for laboratory space, or concentrate on pebble-counting, or (alternatively) do as I have been suggesting and favour particularly projects whose conceptual relevance is fully and carefully argued. If we are really gambling, our expectations are no less in one case than in the other. But of course we are not just gambling. In the hot competition which reigns between projects, there have to be priority systems and standards of choice. And it is the principles of these which we are now discussing.

The spin-off argument cannot excuse research which does not even pretend to have a point. Scientists sometimes like to boast that their work is useless, and if they only mean that it has no practical application, this can be quite in order. If it means lack of theoretical application, it cannot. Long shots are legitimate; shots quite at random are not. The opening and closing sections of scientific papers, in which the importance of the work is discussed, ought to be extremely carefully thought out and extremely rigorously criticized. This sounds uncontroversial. But in practice the standard is often amazingly low. A remarkable, but by no means exceptional example is Suomi and Harlow's article on "Depressive behaviour in young monkeys subjected to vertical chamber confinement."[2] This describes the isolation of infant monkeys in what the authors call "the well of despair"—that is, a vertical stainless steel chamber, in which the monkey is left entirely alone for 45 days. Just what theoretical problem the experimenters were trying to solve when they designed this particular apparatus never clearly emerges. They speak initially of "the implications of these findings for the production *and study* of depressive behaviour in monkeys," but throughout they write as if production rather than study were their central business, as though they were primarily technicians designing apparatus to produce something already agreed to be obviously desirable:

> These (earlier) findings indicated that the vertical chamber apparatus had potential for the production of depressive-like behaviours, and the following study was performed to further investigate the chamber's effectiveness in production of psychopathology.

Not surprisingly, this treatment reduces the monkeys to a state of incurable social paralysis much deeper even than that found in controls who had merely been isolated in wire cages. When released, they show symptoms such as "increases in self-clasp and huddle, decreases in locomotion and exploration, and a paucity of activity directed towards peers" which are also found in human infants who have lost a parent or parent-substitute. This for some reason surprises the experimenters, who comment, "it is intriguing that a non-social manipulation can apparently produce behavioural components paralleling those resulting from a manipulation clearly social in nature." Since these are simply typical, general responses to misery in solitary young primates, and ordinary symptoms of regression, one would like to know what intrigues them. They are not, however, sufficiently intrigued to explain the presuppositions which make this behaviour seem surprising, or to try to devise others which might make it understandable. They do not discuss the relation between an animal's social instincts and the rest of its nature at all. If the point of the experiment is to distinguish between social and other kinds of deprivation, it should surely proceed by putting members of one group in a full natural environment—in woodland—but singly, without company, and those of the other in monotonous confinement, but together. Now that they are intrigued, if not before, you might expect the experimenters to do this, but their conclusion is far simpler—just more of the same. I quote their last paragraph:

> Clearly, chamber confinement early in life rapidly and effectively produces profound and persistent deficits of a depressive nature in young monkeys. Whether this capabilty can be traced specifically to variables such as chamber size, duration of confinement, age at time of confinement, prior and/or subsequent social environment . . . remains the subject of further research.

Anyone who is inclined to think unguided, spontaneous curiosity the best guide to the choice of a research topic might like to ponder its tendency to roll instantly, like this, down the groove provided for it. . . .

NOTES

1. Steiner, G. (1978). 'Has truth a future?', *The Listener*, 99, 42–46.
2. Suomi, S. and Harlow, H. S. (1972). 'Depressive behavior in young monkeys subjected to vertical chamber confinement', *Journal of Comparative and Physiological Psychology*, 80, 11–18.

R. G. FREY AND SIR WILLIAM PATON

Vivisection, Morals, and Medicine: An Exchange

R. G. FREY

I am not an antivivisectionist, and I am not in part for the same reason most people are not, namely, that vivisection can be justified by the benefits it confers. I do not believe it is widely realised, however, to what those who employ this reason are committed. Since many medical people also employ it to justify animal experiments, I think some discussion of the most important of these commitments is in order here. That members of the medical profession will almost certainly find this commitment repugnant in the extreme is perhaps reason enough for making sure that they are aware of it and of why they are in need of some means of avoiding it. (In order to stress this commitment, I am going only to sketch some matters and to avoid some others which, in a fuller treatment of vivisection, would have to be explored. My remarks are non-technical and will be familiar to those knowledgeable of recent controversies involving utilitarianism and the

R. G. Frey teaches philosophy at Bowling Green State University. His books include *Interests and Rights: The Case against Animals* (Oxford, 1980).

Sir William Paton has made major contributions in the area of pharmacology. Among his books are *Man and Mouse: Amimals in Medical Research* (Oxford University Press, 1984) where this topic is further discussed.

Reprinted with permission from the *Journal of Medical Ethics,* Vol. 9, no. 2, pp. 94–97, 102–104.

taking of life and of the work on vivisection of Peter Singer, one of the utilitarians involved in these controversies.)

I

Most people are not antivivisectionists, I suspect, because they think that some benefit or range of benefit can justify experiments, including painful ones, on animals. Increasingly, there are some things such people do not think; for example, that they are committed (i) to regarding simply anything—another floor polish, another eye shadow, for which animals have suffered—as a benefit, (ii) to approving of simply any experiment whatever on animals, in the hallowed name of research, (iii) to foregoing criticism of certain experiments as trivial or unnecessary or a (mere) PhD exercise, (iv) to halting the search for alternatives to the use of animals or to refraining from criticism of scientists who, before commencing experiments, conduct at best a perfunctory search for such alternatives, (v) to approving of (extravagant) wastage, as when twenty rabbits are used where five will do, and (vi) to refraining, in the case of some painful experiments, from a long, hard look at whether even *this* projected benefit is really important and substantial enough to warrant the infliction of *this* degree of pain.

Who benefits? Sometimes animals do, and sometimes both humans and animals do; but, not infrequently, indeed, perhaps typically, the experiments are carried out on animals with an eye to human benefit.

Some antivivisectionists appear to reject this appeal to benefit. I have in mind especially those who have, as it were, a two-stage position, who begin by objecting to painful animal experiments and eventually move on to objecting to animal experiments *per se*. Among other reasons for this move, two are noteworthy here. First, vivisectionists may well seek to reduce and eliminate the pain involved in an experiment, for example by redesigning it, by dropping parts of it, by adopting different methods for carrying it out, by the use of drugs and pain-killers (and by fostering new developments in drugs, pain-killers, and genetic engineering), by painlessly disposing of the animals before they come to feel post-operative pain, and so on. The point, of course, is not that the vivisectionist must or will inevitably succeed in his, or her, aim but rather that, if he did, or to the extent that he does, the argument from pain would, or does, cease to apply. Thus, giving up painful experiments may well not be the only or the only effective way of dealing with the pain they involve. So, it is tempting to shift to a condemnation of animal experiments *per se*, which at once reduces the manoeuvrings of the vivisectionist over pain to nothing. Second, and, to a great many antivivisectionists, possibly even more importantly, the pain argument has nothing to say to the countless millions of painless and relatively painless animal experiments performed each year throughout the world; and these, I should have thought, vastly outnumber the painful ones. So, in order to encompass them in one's antivivisectionism, it is once again tempting to shift to a condemnation of animal experiments *per se.*

The above in no way denies, of course, that the antivivisectionist may want to deal first with painful experiments, before turning to look at any other; but turn he will, if those I have talked to are representative. For, in the end, *it is the use of animals as experimental subjects at all,* not just or possibly even primarily their use as subjects of painful experiments, that I have found lies at the bottom of their antivivisectionism.

To the vivisectionist, the antivivisectionist would appear to think that *no* benefit is important and substantial enough to justify painful animal experiments and, eventually, that *no* benefit is important and substantial enough to justify animal experiments. And this position, the vivisectionist will think, is very unlikely to recommend itself to many people. It is obvious why. Would your view of Salk vaccine simply be turned on its head, if it came to light that it was tested on monkeys or that some monkeys suffered pain (perhaps even intense pain) in the course of testing it or that it is made by cultivating strains of a virus in monkey tissue?

It would be silly to pretend that all animal experiments are of vast, stupendous importance; it would be equally silly, however, to deny that benefit has accrued to us (and sometimes to animals) through animal experimentation. (Often, the problem is that a series of experiments, at different times, by different people, enable still someone else to build upon those experiments to yield a benefit; for this reason, it is not always easy to tell of a particular experiment what its ultimate significance will be). If informed, concerned people do not want animal research carried out without guidelines as to animal welfare, since animals are not merely another piece of equipment, to be manipulated however one will, neither do they want our laboratories closed down until, assuming such a time comes, all experiments can be carried out on bacteria, or, more generally, on non-animal subjects.

II

I believe this vivisectionist I have sketched represents what a great many people think about animal experimentation and antivivisectionism. To be sure, it represents what they think only in its most general outline; but even this much shows the central role the appeal to benefit plays in their thinking.

Now there is a feature of this appeal which, though perfectly straight-forward, is nevertheless not widely appreciated, a feature which has implications for the medical profession. Michael W. Fox, a long-serving member of the animal welfare movement, comes out against antivivisectionism[1]:

"Some antivivisectionists would have no research done on animals. This is a limited and unrealistic view since in many cases it is the only way to test a new vaccine or drug which could save many lives—human and animal. Often the drugs being tested will treat or alleviate disease in both animal and human." Fox might have posed a sterner test for himself and vivisectionists generally if he had drawn the example so that the vaccine benefited only humans but was tested, and tested painfully, only on animals; but this is by the way. The important point is Fox's entirely false presumption that the only alternative to not testing the vaccine and reaping the benefit is to test it upon animals; it could, of course, be tested upon human beings. There is absolutely nothing about the appeal to benefit which precludes this; so far as this appeal is concerned, if securing the benefit licenses (painful) experiments on animals, it equally licenses (painful) experiments on humans, since the benefit may be secured by either means. Moreover, we must not forget that we have already a powerful reason *for* human experiments: we typically experiment upon animals with an eye towards benefiting humans, and it seems only sensible, if we want to find out the effect of some substance upon humans, that we test it upon humans. This is especially true, as doubts increasingly arise about whether extrapolations from the animal to the human case are not very prone to error and to the effects of in-built differences between animals and humans. (The saccharin controversy is sometimes cited as a case in point.) In some cases, such extrapolations may be positively dangerous; I have in mind cases where a substance has far less marked or severe effects in animals than in humans. (I have heard thalidomide, and what testing was done with it, cited in this connection.)

What I am saying, then, is that someone who relies upon the appeal to benefit to justify (painful) experiments on animals needs one more shot in his locker, if he is to prevent the appeal from justifying (painful) experiments upon humans. Specifically, he needs some reason which demarcates humans from animals, and which shows why we are not justified in doing to humans what we in our laboratories do to animals.

A great many things could be said at this point (the claim that animals do not feel pain is hardly one of them, since, whatever else may be said about this claim, the experiments in question could be painless), but I do not have space for even a few of them. I propose to leap, therefore, to what I think would be widely held, upon reflection, to be the reason to allow the appeal to benefit in the case of animals but to disallow it in the case of humans. Quite simply, human life, it will be said, is more valuable than animal life. Not only is this something which is widely thought, but it is also something which even such a fervent defender of animal liberation as the philosopher Peter Singer accepts.[2]

What is the source of this greater value? To some, it may be traced to their religious beliefs; but to the ever increasing numbers of non-believers, which I presume include some medical people as well as others, this appeal to religion is unavailable. I am not myself religious, and I cannot in good faith maintain that humans have souls but animals do not, that humans have been granted dominion over the beasts of the earth, that human life is sacred or sanctified whereas animal life is either not similarly blessed or blessed to a far less extent, and so on. So, what is left? One might try to appeal to some non-religiously grounded principle of respect or reverence for life; but, *prima facie*, such a principle does not cede human life greater value than animal life but rather enjoins us to revere life or living things *per se*. Accordingly, a person who adopts the appeal to benefit and who accepts a respect or reverence-for-life view still has no reason for thinking the benefit may only be secured through animal and never through human experiments.

Ultimately, though many twists and turns of argument have to be disposed of first, I think the non-religious person who thinks that human life is more valuable than animal life will find himself forced back upon our complex make-up to find the source of that value. What I mean is this. If we ask ourselves what makes our lives valuable, I think we shall want to give as answers such things as the pleasures of friendship, eating and drinking, listening to music, participating in sports, obtaining satisfaction through our job, reading, enjoying a beautiful summer's day, getting married and sharing experiences with someone, sex, watching and helping our children to grow up, solving quite difficult practical and intellectual problems in pursuit of some goal we highly prize, and so on. Within this mixed bag, there are some activities we may well share with animals; but our make-up is complex, and there are dimensions to us which there are not to animals. When we think in these terms, of dimensions to us which there are not to animals, we are quite naturally led to cede our lives more value *because of the many more possibilities for enrichment they contain.*

To think in this way is very common; it is, I believe, the way many non-religious people find greater value in human life. It should be obvious, however, that those who think this way must eventually confront an undeniable fact: not all human lives have the same enrichment or scope for enrichment. (There are babies, of course, but most people seem happy to regard them as leading lives which have the relevant potentialities for enrichment). Some people lead lives of a quality we would not wish upon even our worst enemies, and some of these lives have not the scope for enrichment of ordinary human lives. If we regard the irreversibly comatose as living human lives of the lowest quality, we must nevertheless face the fact that many humans lead lives of a radically lower quality than ordinary human lives. We can all think of numerous such cases, cases where the lives lack enrichment and where the scope, the potentialities for enrichment are severely truncated or absent, as with spina bifida children or the very, very severely mentally enfeebled.

If we confront the fact that not all human life has the same quality, either in terms of the same enrichment or the same scope for enrichment, and if we are thinking of the value of life in these terms, then we seem compelled to conclude that not all human life has the same value. And, with this conclusion, the way is open for redrawing Fox's vaccine example in a way that makes it far less apparent that we should test the vaccine on animals. For, as opposed to testing it on quite ordinary and healthy animals, with a reasonably high quality of life, the alternative is to test it on humans whose quality of life is so low *either* as to be exceeded by the quality of life of the healthy animals *or* as to approach their quality of life. On the former alternative, and it is as well to bear in mind that a great many experiments are performed upon healthy, vigorous animals, we would have a reason to test the vaccine on the humans in question; on the latter alternative, we would again find ourselves in need of a reason for thinking it justified to test the vaccine on animals but not on humans.

III

Where, then, are we? If we are not to test the vaccine on humans, then we require some reason which justifies testing it on animals but not on humans. If we purport to find that reason in the greater value of human life, then we must reckon with the fact that the value of human life is bound up with and varies according to its quality; and this opens the way either for some animals to have a higher quality of life than some humans or for some humans to have so low a quality of life as to approach that of some animals. Either way, it is no longer clear that we should test the vaccine on animals.

So, in order to make this clear, what is needed, in effect, is some reason for thinking that a human life, no matter how truncated its scope for enrichment, no matter how low its quality, is more valuable than an animal life, no matter what its degree of enrichment, no matter how high its quality. (Bear in mind that those who have this need are those who, for whatever reason, are not religious and so cannot escape the need that way). I myself have and know of nothing with which to satisfy this need; that is, I have and know of nothing which enables me to say, *a priori*, that a human life of any quality, however low, is more valuable than an animal life of any quality, however high. Perhaps some readers think that they can satisfy this need; certainly, I am receptive to suggestions.

In the absence of something with which to meet the above need, we cannot, with the appeal to benefit, justify (painful) animal experiments without justifying (painful) human experiments. We seem to have, then, two directions in which we may move. On the one hand, we may take the fact that we cannot justify animal experiments without justifying human experiments as a good reason to re-examine our whole practice of (painful) animal experiments. The case for antivivisectionism, I think, is far stronger than most people allow: so far as I can see, the only way to avoid it, if you are attracted by the appeal to benefit and are not religious, is *either* to have in your possession some means of conceding human life of any quality greater value than animal life of any quality *or* to condone experiments on humans whose quality of life is exceeded by or equal to that of animals. If you are as I am and find yourself without a means of the required sort, then the choice before you is either antivivisectionism or condoning human experiments. On the other hand, we may take the fact that we cannot justify animal experiments without justifying human experiments as a good reason to allow some human experiments. Put differently, if the choice before us is between antivivisectionism and allowing human experiments, can we bring ourselves to embrace antivivisectionism? For, consider: we find ourselves involved in this whole problem because we strongly believe that some benefit or range of benefits can justify (painful) animal experiments. If we choose antivivisectionism, we may very well lose the many benefits obtained through vivisection, and this, at times, even if we concede, as we must, that not every experiment leads to a Salk vaccine, may be a serious loss indeed. Certainly, it would have been a serious loss in the past, if we had had to forego the benefits which accrued through (and which we presently enjoy as a result of) vivisection. Scientific research and technological innovation have completely altered the human condition, occasionally in rather frightening ways, but typically in ways for which most people are thankful, and very few people indeed would look in the face the benefits which medical research in particular has conferred upon us, benefits which on the whole have most certainly involved vivisections. If the appeal to benefit exerts its full attraction upon us, therefore, we may find ourselves unable to make the choice in favour of antivivisectionism, especially if that meant a good deal of serious research in serious affairs of health had either to be stopped until suitable, alternative experimental subjects were developed for a full range of experiments or, if nothing suitable for a full range of experiments were developed, to be stopped entirely.

Accordingly, we are left with human experiments. I think this is how I would choose, not with great glee and rejoicing, and with great reluctance; but if this is the price we must pay to hold the appeal to benefit and to enjoy the benefits which that appeal licenses, then we must, I think, pay it.

I am well aware that most people, including most medical people, will find my choice repugnant in the extreme, and it is easy to see how I can appear a monster in their eyes. But I am where I am, not because I begin a monster and end up choosing the monstrous, but because I cannot in good faith think of anything at all compelling that cedes human life of any quality greater value than animal life of any quality. It might be claimed by some that this shows in me the need for some religious beliefs, on the assumption that some religious belief or other will allow me to say that any human life is more valuable than any animal life. Apart from the fact that this appears a rather strange reason for taking on religious beliefs (for example, believing in the existence of God and of God's gifts to us in order to avoid having to allow experiments on humans), other questions about those beliefs, such as their correctness and the evidence for their truth, intrude. I may well find that I cannot persuade myself of the beliefs in question.

Is there nothing, then, that can now be cited which, even if we accept that we are committed to allowing human experiments, would nevertheless serve to bar them? I think all I can cite—I do not by this phraseology mean to undercut the force of what follows—are the likely side-effects of such experiments. Massive numbers of people would be outraged, society would be in an uproar, hospitals and research centres would come under fierce attack, the doctor-patient relationship might be irrevocably affected, and so on. (All of us will find it easy to carry on with the list.) Such considerations as these are very powerful, and they would have to be weighed very carefully, in deciding whether actually to perform the experiments. Perhaps their weight would be so great that we could not proceed with the experiments; certainly, that is possible.

But what I meant by saying that such important side-effects of human experiments are "all I can cite" in the present context is this: it is an utterly contingent affair whether such side-effects occur, and their occurrence is not immune to attempts—by education, by explaining in detail and repeatedly why such experiments are being undertaken, by going through, yet again, our inability to show that human life is always more valuable than animal life, etc.—to eliminate them. It is this last fact especially, that such things as outrage and harm to the doctor-patient relationship can be affected by education, information, and careful explanation, that poses a danger to those who want actually to bar human experiments by appeal to side-effects. So, I do not play down the importance of side-effects in deciding whether actually to perform human experiments, I only caution that they do not provide a once-and-for-all bar to such experiments, unless they survive any and all attempts to mitigate and eliminate them.

NOTES

1. Fox, M. *Returning to Eden: animal rights and human obligations.* New York: Viking Press, 1980: 116.
2. Singer, P. *Animal Liberation.* London: Jonathan Cape, 1976.

SIR WILLIAM PATON: A REPLY TO FREY

It would be best to start by summarising what (for this comment) I take to be the essential points of Dr Frey's interesting, and I believe novel, argument. 1) A major justification of animal experiment, commonly accepted, is the benefit that results. 2) This justification is rejected by some, initially on the grounds that the benefit does not justify the pain inflicted; but when it is noted that experiments may be painless, or that steps are taken to minimise the pain, the fundamental ground of rejection is revealed by a shift to the statement that the use of animals for these purposes is *absolutely* wrong. 3) Those who argue this way will accept the loss of the benefits. 4) But is it necessary to forego these benefits? Why not, in order to retain them, be willing to use man for these experiments? 5) If it is said against this that man is more valuable than animals, in what way is this so? 6) Dr Frey does not believe in "souls," nor does he accept the "dominion" of man, and he can only identify "capacity for enrichment" as a suitable defining characteristic of humanity. 7) He finds that this criterion does not separate man from animals; for instance, he concludes that some animals may possess *more* of this capacity than some humans (for example, the very, very severely mentally enfeebled or spina bifida children). 8) He therefore accepts (with great reluctance) that human experiment should be permissible, with due precaution, in order to obtain the benefits concerned. 9) While acknowledging that the side-effects of such experiment (society's outrage, damage to doctor-patient relations) might prevent particular experiments, their occurrence would be "utterly contingent," and would not negate the general principle of permissibility.

It is not always clear whether Dr Frey himself holds the views expressed, or is doing no more than presenting them for discussion. In the latter spirit, anything which follows refers to what Dr Frey happens to be voicing, and not to whatever may be his actual opinions.

Before coming to the specific question of human experiment, two general points arise. The first concerns the method of argument. It is an old one: that of reviewing a section of experience (in this case, experience of other people's opinion; reports, regrettably hearsay, about experimental work—thalidomide, saccharin, and experience of the life of animals and of handicapped humans); and then of abstracting from this experience particular propositions which then become the subject of the discourse. A single instance (the tree in the quad, or the visual experience of a red patch) has sometimes sufficed to create such a proposition. This is a blameless, indeed common activity. The problem comes with "re-entry" to the experiential world. The proposition may be combined with others to yield further propositions. One such result here is: "It is not possible to say, *a priori*, that a human life of any quality, however low, is more valuable than an animal life of any quality, however high." (Dr Frey does not put it so bluntly, but says only that nothing enables *him* to say this. I believe, however, that he is not merely wishing to report on his own psychological state, but wishes the proposition to be considered generally.) What *use* is this proposition? None that I can see. It explicitly assumes that there are scales of human and animal life, and explicitly compares the lower extreme of one with the upper extreme of the other; yet it gives no criterion as to where (or whether) the scales end. Even given these, and comparing (say) an anencephalic fetus with a favourite sheep-dog, over which people could make up their minds, all that has been done is to discuss extreme cases. What then? Few would accept that because a particular instance of animal life is more valuable than a particular instance of human life, therefore no human life is more valuable than animal life. The general proposition merely ends by regurgitating the sort of special case from which it originated.

This links with a second general point, the general philosophical mayhem created by continuity. The type of argument by which Dr Frey fails to find a "dimension" by which humans differ from animals is one that can also be used to fail to distinguish between light and dark, sweet and sour, motion and immobility. Yet this does not prevent (for instance) the specification of a well-lit factory or an efficient dark-room, or the formulation of successful cooking recipes, or the measurement of velocity. The idea of continuity in the "scale of creation" is an old and cogent one. It is true that individual species represent discrete steps, but within each species, variation is such as to blur the absolute demarcation in respect of any chosen character between neighbours. Dr Frey could have gone further, and added that no one has yet produced any logically rigorous principle of division at any point in the scale from the inanimate, through bacteria, protozoa, vegetables, insects and animals to man—whether reproduction, complexity, or evidence of responsiveness, purposiveness or sentience is considered. Even the leech will respond to morphine. But the recognition of continuity does not debar the drawing of *operational* divisions.

This brings us to the specific question of whether such operational distinctions can, or cannot, be drawn between humans and animals, particularly distinctions to which "value" can be attached. Dr Frey's strongest candidate is "self-enrichment," exemplified chiefly by a capacity for enjoyable experience. But he has to reject this as a discriminant between man and animal because he believes that a very, very severely mentally enfeebled person or a spina bifida child has less capacity for enrichment than a healthy animal. It is a comment on moral philosophy today that "capacity for enrichment" should be advanced as the strongest index of value in human activity. In such a context, one cannot expect that other indices, such as capacity for goodness, altruism, responsibility, or forgiveness, would be admissible. But one need not resort to these. There is one respect in which the human has come increasingly to distance himself from the animal—namely the capacity to accumulate his experience by the spoken and (especially) by the written and printed word. This means that successive generations build on their predecessors' achievements, not (as with a crystal, an anthill, or a coral reef) more and more of the same, but continually changing what they build. The scratches in the Lascaux caves lead to the Renaissance; Pythagorean harmonics in time grow up to the Bach fugue; Archimedes's method of exhaustion, transmuted in the 17th century to the calculus, becomes O-level mathematics for today's schoolboy. Man's mastery of the environment, initially little more than adequate for survival, is now so great as to arouse his deepest sense of responsibility and his deepest questions of meaning and purpose. Nor must this human capacity be linked only to the "normal" human in perfect health. Human achievement owes much to the deformed, diseased, epileptic and insane; but perhaps only those familiar with the handicapped know that achievement is not restricted to geniuses, but can pervade all levels of personal and social relationships. (There is the medical point, too, that one must not assume a present handicap to be necessarily permanent; the cretin used to be a striking example of severe handicap, seemingly irreversible in 1890, but curable by 1900. Phenylketonuria provides a more recent example.)

If we accept that man can accumulate his experience (not only that of other men: he can and does accumulate his experience of animals) how does that affect the argument? It is not necessary to argue that an absolute distinction from the animal has been found. Indeed there is some evidence (though it remains inconclusive) for vestiges of a capacity to build a language and to frame abstract thought in the higher primates, although it is hard to see evidence of the use of these for progressive cumulation. But all that is needed is to recognise a quantitative distinction between man and animal sufficiently great to be accepted in practice as qualitative. That this is the case seems to me, whether or not the reasons are articulated, the general consensus. The capacity to accumulate, and thus to build on the past and to look to the future, is a quality, too, to which value can be attached, and a value which looks beyond personal enjoyment to the needs of other individuals. This constitutes an answer to the question 5) in my initial summary of Dr Frey's argument, and a rebuttal to 6) and 7), after which 8) and 9) lapse.

One might stop there, but Dr Frey's paper—from which an uninformed reader might suppose that no human experiment had hitherto taken place—calls for something more. One can now identify three approaches to such experiment: (a) The one argued above, which gives a greater value to the human than to the animal; this does not debar human experiment, but only introduces a coefficient to be applied to the choices to be made. (b) At the opposite extreme is an equation of human and animal value. This, too, fails to debar human experiment. The question becomes instead that of choosing animals or human beings for experiments, presumably simply by practical criteria such as scientific suitability (large animals such as man would need much larger apparatus), cost, and availability. The question of availability is interesting; it would entail consent on the part of a human subject. How does one obtain the consent of an animal? It is not possible for a human to speak for it, for that would deny the postulated human-animal equivalence. The question illustrates the crucial character of one's view of human and animal relationships. (c) In between, it seems, is Dr Frey's position, which appears to accept that there *are* different scales of value for human beings and animals, but argues that they overlap. Thus Beethoven is more valuable than a mouse, but the severely handicapped human is of less value than a healthy "higher" animal. The implications of this are not worked out; but such a calculus would appear to legitimise the use especially of the diseased and mentally deficient. I doubt if this is what he intends.

More important, perhaps, is to make clear how much human experiment has been, and is being, done. I do not believe Dr Frey would have written as he has if he had adequately consulted the original medical literature, or medical scientists. Human experiment has a long and honourable, though still unwritten history. Some is severely *ad hoc:* experiments on effects of acceleration on the human body, leading to ejector seats; or on oxygen poisoning, high pressure, carbon dioxide poisoning, and the "bends," to make diving safer. Some is to help to improve medical understanding: the cardiologist first passing a cardiac catheter on himself; self-curarisation; the paralysis of nerves by local anaesthesia, or nerve section, or vascular occlusion, to throw light on neurological problems. Much takes place in pharmacological work: early trials of metabolism, pilot studies on dose-level, analyses of mechanism of action. Unlike animal experiment no licence is needed, no annual return of the numbers of human experiments is needed, and no government office counts them. Thus it is not easy to estimate their number. But some indication is given by a single issue of just one monthly journal, the *British Journal of Clinical Pharmacology* which contained 20 papers, covering 124 experiments on normal human subjects (both young and old) and 99 experiments on patients. Scale this up, and one may well doubt if there is scope for much more human experiment than is already conducted.

Dr Frey's argument raises yet other issues. One can well argue that if no distinction can be drawn between man and animals, then neither can it be drawn between the animal and the vegetable world. So one could ask, as one contemplates the insectivorous plants *Drosera,* responsive to sun, rain, and the nutrients of the soil, and exquisitely sensitive to chemicals, and watches it close a leaf around and digest an insect caught on its hairs, "Can anyone say that this plant is *less* enriched by its experience than a lion as it devours a buck, or a man enjoying his dinner?" But this merely emphasises again the importance of one's view of man's relation to the rest of creation.

But these are not the issues at the heart of the debate about animal experiment. In practice, I take the most important to be the assessment of the scientific value of an experiment, of the knowledge or benefit to be gained, and of the suffering (if any) involved, and the question of how to balance these. It is ultimately a moral problem, and a question of responsibility borne both by the scientist and by the rest of society in the characteristically human task of removing ignorance and minimising suffering.

RESPONSE: R. G. FREY

Professor Paton would have us believe that man's capacity to accumulate his experience by the spoken, written and printed word confers greater value on his life; but this generalisation does not help over the problem I posed.

A medical scientist engaged in serious work needs to perform experiments on retinas, experiments which in the end involve loss of sight and not in some accidental fashion; he may use the retinas of perfectly healthy rabbits or those of severely mentally-enfeebled humans. To put the matter somewhat elliptically, the scientist can blind the rabbits or blind the humans. How is this choice to be made? Presumably, Professor Paton would point to the humans and maintain that they belong to a species that has the capacity to make significant advance on any number of fronts as a result of accumulated experience; but exactly how does this fact help with the case before us? These same mentally-enfeebled humans belong to a species capable of producing Beethovens, Mozarts and Schuberts, but that in no way makes *them* composers or confers on *their* lives any value. So exactly how is the fact that our species has been capable of great wonders supposed to help out in the cases of those humans far removed from any such wonders? Professor Paton writes: "Few would accept that because a particular instance of animal life is more valuable than a particular instance of human life, therefore no human life is more valuable than animal life." Of course not; nor did I suggest anything so silly. But the people to be used by the scientist are not fully normal humans but seriously defective ones, who are still such—they have eyeballs—as to be suitable experimental subjects. Clearly, Professor Paton has given us no reason for not carrying out the experiment upon the humans in question; for, to repeat, the mere fact that my species can produce a Beethoven does not *per se* make *my* life any more valuable than that of a mouse.

Professor Paton writes at one point about our having to obtain the consent of human subjects and of our having no means of obtaining consent from animals; but I should have thought he was unwise to make much of this. Animals may not be able to consent, but that does not appear to stop Professor Paton using them as experimental subjects; whereas, though it makes no sense to speak of obtaining the consent of the severely mentally-enfeebled, I presume he would recoil from *their* use as subjects for blinding. Why? What makes him hesitate in their case but go ahead in the case of rabbits? My strong suspicion is that he intuitively accepts human life as more valuable than animal life, even when all the grandiose talk of our capacities and accomplishments is inapplicable, and it would be interesting to know how he justifies this intuition.

Professor Paton speaks of my use of hearsay, my failure to consult medical reports, my making it appear as if no human experiments have been performed; well, here is his chance to nail down his accusations. I can point to a number of instances where rabbits with good eyesight have knowingly been blinded in the course of experimental work; I ask him if he can point to a single instance where a human subject, with otherwise good or perfect eyesight, has knowingly been blinded by a medical experimenter. If he can, then let him name names; if he cannot, then he might justly be accused of having failed to take my point, which, as readers will know, is that we do not do to defective humans all that we presently do in our laboratories to quite healthy animals. My interest is in why we do not. If the justification is that we think human life of greater value than animal life, then we must be prepared to face the facts, at least on the grounds I suggested, that (i) not all human life is of the same value and (ii) some human life has a value so low as to be exceeded by some animal life.

PART EIGHT
The Treatment
of Wildlife

PAUL AND ANNE EHRLICH

Extinction

The Passenger Pigeon was a fascinating creature. A pretty, graceful pigeon with a slate-blue back and deep pink breast, it didn't coo like a dove, but produced "shrieks and chatters and clucks."[1] Its greatest claim to fame was the gigantic size of its populations; it may have been the most abundant bird ever to exist. Audubon observed a flock of passenger pigeons passing over a period of three days. Sometimes, he estimated, they went by at a rate of over 300 million birds an hour. The passage of large flocks created a roar of wings that could be heard a half-dozen miles away.[2] Alexander Wilson, who with Audubon founded American ornithology, estimated another flock to contain 2 billion birds. The pigeons nested in long narrow colonies that could be forty miles long and several miles across. Their droppings in favorite roosting areas piled inches thick, killing all herbs and shrubs and eventually the trees themselves.

The birds occurred throughout eastern North America, where they fed on the fruits of forest trees—especially acorns and beechnuts. The

Paul and Anne Ehrlich both are biologists by training. Among their many jointly authored books is *Ecoscience: Population, Resources, Environment* (W. H. Freeman, 1977).

Reprinted from Paul R. Ehrlich and Anne H. Ehrlich, *Extinction: The Causes and Consequences of the Disappearance of Species*. Random House, New York, 1981. By permission of the authors.

reason for their flocking behavior is not known for certain. It may have helped them to find food; it may also have been a predator defense.

Early settlers in the United States, though, had no trouble adding the Passenger Pigeon to their diets. The nesting grounds were so crowded that the adults were always being injured or killed and the succulent squabs knocked out of the nests. All that was required was to wander through the colony picking up dinner. As the human population increased, however, two things began to happen. Railroads pushed through the wilderness, opening avenues for market hunters to ship the birds to centers like New York, and the great oak and beech forests in which the birds nested began to be cleared.

The market hunters devised ingenious ways of killing large numbers of the birds. The pigeons were suffocated by burning grass or sulfur below their roosts; they were fed grain soaked in alcohol and picked up dead drunk, batted down with long sticks, blasted with shotguns, or netted (after which their heads were crushed with a pair of pincers). One ingenious trapping device depended on a decoy pigeon with its eyes sewn shut, tied to a perch called a stool. "Stool pigeon" thereby became part of the language.

The demise of the pigeons was startlingly rapid. After the Civil War, many millions were shipped from the Midwest to New York—so many that live birds were used as targets in shooting galleries. But the huge flocks were by then gone from the coastal states, and by the 1880s they were dwindling everywhere. In 1878 one hunter shipped some three million birds from Michigan, the Passenger Pigeon's last stronghold. The last wild bird was seen in that state just eleven years later, and the last captive bird died in the Cincinnati Zoo in 1914.[3] Her name was Martha.

Economic extinction preceded biological extinction. The last birds in the wild were not killed by hunting, which became unprofitable as soon as the great flocks were gone. And there are still large areas of forest extant in the eastern United States that would serve as suitable habitat. But apparently the ability to form huge flocks was essential to the survival of the pigeons. When their population sizes became too small to maintain sufficiently large breeding colonies, nesting failures, inbreeding, and mortality from predation must have escalated and pushed the species to extinction.[4]

The fate of the Passenger Pigeon illustrates very clearly that enormous numbers do not guarantee the safety of a species. Under the right circumstances, species can move from superabundance to extinction with astonishing speed. The fate of the American Bison (inaccurately called the buffalo) is another example. The eastern U.S. populations, sometimes considered a separate race, were hunted to extinction by the early 1830s, and the Oregon race by midcentury. The northern Wood Bison still lives in relatively large numbers in the forests of Alberta and the Northwest Territories of Canada.

The prairie populations of bison were huge almost beyond belief. In vast numbers they blackened the plains, an estimated 30 to 40 million individuals. They showed clearly that at least part of the megafauna could thrive in the presence of skilled hunters. Native Americans made little use of bison until they obtained horses from the Spaniards. Once mounted, some tribes based their economies on the shaggy beasts—eating their meat and making multiple use of their hides. But they made no discernible dent in the bison population; apparently the number they took each year was less than the annual production.[5]

The arrival of the settlers from Europe, and especially of the railroads in the 1860s, signaled the start of the great bison slaughter. Professional hunters shot the animals primarily for their tongues and hides, leaving the carcasses to rot. Later, others collected the bleached bones that whitened the plains and shipped them east for use as fertilizer. Perhaps 2.5 million bison were killed annually between 1870 and 1875 by white hunters, and in 1883 the last significant herd, numbering perhaps 10,000 bison, was slaughtered. At the turn of the century only about 500 Plains Bison remained—finally under legal protection.

The bison was luckier than the Passenger Pigeon—it was pulled back from the brink. Today there are perhaps 25,000 in North America, scattered through parks and in private herds, but no prairie bison exist "in the wild." Humanity may have been lucky, too. A fertile hybrid has now been produced between cattle and bison by a California rancher. The hybrids, called "beefalo," are reported to be very tasty, leaner, and more productive than beef. Beefalo are easier to raise than cattle, grow faster, and require no grain feed. At best, if accepted, beefalo could make meat cheaper and healthier, with less fat; at the least it could add variety to human diets.[6]

ENDANGERING FOR FOOD TODAY

Wild species of animals are still hunted by human beings for food on land, just as whales and fishes are hunted in the sea. Deer hunters in Pennsylvania, Bushmen stalking gazelles in Namibia, or people in western China hunting the Chinese Giant Salamander are simply carrying on an ancient human tradition. Throughout much of the world, the level of predation from hunting is low and has little or no effect on the populations cropped. But in some cases, for instance if the prey is rare (as is the salamander) or the hunting turns to slaughter, populations and species go under.

Sometimes wildlife suffers overexploitation as a result of unusual political or economic circumstances. One serious and grotesque incident occurred in Uganda in early 1979 when Tanzanian troops massacred wildlife in what had been one of Africa's most bountiful game reserves—Ruwenzori National Park. Troops out of control of their commanders butchered the wildlife, and the meat was purchased by Ugandan business-men. American biologist Karl Van Orsdal was an eyewitness to some of the murders at Lake Edward: "Two Tanzanian soldiers stood laughing while a third, lying on the ground, fired off rapid bursts at a large group of hippos out in the water . . . a group of seven or eight Ugandan civilians [were] butchering a dead hippo with axes and machetes a few hundred feet farther down the shore."[7]

There was a lot of money to be made. A dead hippopotamus can yield as much as 1,875 pounds of meat worth over a dollar a pound. At the end of three and a half months, when Van Orsdal left, he estimated that about 30 percent of the park's 46,500 large animals had been killed—6,000 hippos, 5,000 Uganda Kob, 2,000 buffalo, 400 Topi, 100 elephants, and 70 lions. If the slaughter stopped soon thereafter, most of the species would probably recover, although some concern has been expressed about the kob.

Events following the establishment of the Islamic Republic in Iran have taken a course not unlike that in Uganda. Wildlife has been extermi-nated indiscriminately. Poachers on motorcycles have machine-gunned ga-zelles that were once protected; sturgeon have been dynamited in the Caspian Sea. Thousands of acres have been cleared of hardwoods for conversion to grazing or farming. Many animals that had been carefully protected during the Shah's regime are now so tame that they quickly fall prey to hunters with automatic weapons. Some of the most seriously threat-ened mammals in the world—including the Caspian Tiger, the Wild Ass, and the Persian Fallow Deer—are now in even greater jeopardy.[8]

Such slaughters are not restricted to developing nations in turmoil. In the tightly controlled Soviet Union society, meat is in such short supply that wildlife has been attacked at an unprecedented level. In the spring of 1976, after three hundred young ducks were banded on a Siberian lake, all three hundred bands were returned to the ornithologists responsible. Hunters had bagged every bird. Poaching on Soviet reserves is rampant. The ani-mals of the Kyzyl-Agach Reserve on the Caspian Sea have been subjected to periodic assaults by groups of army officers operating from helicopters, all-terrain vehicles, and even tanks. Not surprisingly, little wildlife remains. Difficult as it is to believe, a Soviet division stationed near Lake Baikal for years reportedly has been using heat-seeking missiles to hunt deer.[9]

Perhaps the most repugnant and compassionless hunting practiced on our planet recently was not in the wilds of Africa or on the steppes of Russia, but in Australia. Australian graziers have long killed every kanga-roo they could because they compete with their sheep for grass. As early as 1863, the great naturalist and artist John Gould feared that the Red Kan-garoo and some other "fine species" of marsupial would be exterminated by the stockmen.[10] He was wrong—the Red Kangaroo remained common in drier areas where the sheep could not thrive.

Then in the late 1950s, a market was discovered for kangaroo meat as pet food, substandard sausage, and kangaroo-tail soup. The result was a stampede to hunt the kangaroos. The standard technique was to "spotlight" them from cars at night. The kangaroos would freeze in the light and were shot with rifles. Some were killed immediately, but some hunters purposely just wounded them—sometimes leaving them to suffer for hours or days so that their meat would remain fresh until they could be collected. The night hunts were treated as "sporting events," even though neither courage nor skill on the part of the hunters was required. In 1980 a new hunting method became popular: two people chase them on a motorcycle, one steering, the other gunning down the fleeing animals.

Since the founding of the country, about one million kangaroos have been slaughtered annually in Australia. The killing continues today, although fortunately the large kangaroos that are hunted seem to be holding their own. In contrast, some of the smaller species are succumbing to habitat destruction.

Many excuses for killing the kangaroos have been made, especially by graziers, and are related to their misconceptions about the impact of the kangaroos on pastures that the stockmen themselves have often ruined by overgrazing with sheep. But the main reason once more is greed mixed with a lack of compassion. Australian conservationists fear that, since the United States has lifted its ban on importing kangaroo skin products, the slaughter will escalate and begin endangering the kangaroo populations.[11]

The Ugandan, Iranian, Russian, and Australian slaughters of wildlife clearly are extreme examples of contemporary uncontrolled hunting. Perhaps the most distressing aspect of these affairs—and similar ones such as the much-publicized annual slaughter of baby seals in Canada, which is controlled—is that they bring home just how little compassion there is for animals in much of the human population. People may kill out of what they consider to be economic necessity or sport, but either kind of killing can be accompanied by a certain sympathy for the animals killed. Indeed, hunters and anglers often are also ardent conservationists—something that should be recognized even by people who find hunting morally reprehensible. Yet, obviously, many human beings still can commit mayhem on other species without a qualm.

THE WILDLIFE TRADE

Many species are under direct attack from humanity for other reasons than to provide food. Pressure toward extinction of such species indeed continues—and in many cases is even rising—in spite of much-heightened public awareness of endangered species and in spite of a proliferation of protective laws, particularly in developed countries. International trade in wildlife, for example, goes on at a level unsuspected by most people. Great numbers of animals are collected and shipped around the world for scientific and medical research alone. Both animals and plants are collected for display in zoos and botanic gardens, for the pleasure of private collectors, and for products that can be made from them.

As an example of how far-flung the trade for research animals has become, a few years ago we received a totally unsolicited offer from Nigeria to sell us a variety of animals for "research purposes." The accompanying list included ostriches, two kinds of geese, Marabou Storks, foxes, Crowned Cranes, two kinds of monkeys, baboons, and Chimpanzees.

Primates in particular often suffer depredations in the name of research. Collecting for zoos and laboratories has helped push Gorillas toward extinction—especially since large numbers have been killed in the process of capture or died in captivity before they could be displayed or experimented upon.[12]

One of the more preposterous and tragic examples involves the recent establishment, with the help of a French oil company, of the International Center for Medical Research in Franceville, Gabon. The center was established to study and help cure human infertility, deemed to be a serious problem in Gabon, where the prevailing view is that the country is underpopulated. The rate of natural population increase in Gabon in 1979 was 1.1 percent annually—a rate that, if continued, would double its population in 63 years. Its population density is very low by the standards of this overpopulated world, but it is not at all clear that further population increase could do anything but reduce its relatively high standard of living. Average per capita income in Gabon is almost as high as that of England—based on large resources of iron, manganese, uranium, and oil.[13]

In order to rescue Gabon from a "problem" that much of the world wishes it had, the new research center has erected a large primate facility. At the center, Gorillas and Chimpanzees will be studied to find an answer to the problem, although President Bong of Gabon has reportedly admitted that the infertility in the human population is due to an epidemic of gonorrhea. The primate facility is viewed as an outlet for baby Gorillas that become "available" as their mothers are shot by the Gabonese for food. According to one observer, in late 1979 six baby Gorillas had gone into the facility, and five had died because of the inexperienced staff.

As Dr. Shirley McGreal of the International Primate Protection League (IPPL) aptly pointed out: ". . . rabbits would have been better 'animal models' of human fertility, as gorillas and chimps breed so badly that they are getting close to extinction and can't compensate reproductively for human predation."[14] The situation is especially ironic since it is the pressure of expanding human populations that threatens Gorillas everywhere. Henry Heymann of the IPPL noted that in Gabon: ". . . the gorillas are being compelled to contribute their lives, health, freedom, and sanity to the expediting of their own demise. There is a resemblance to concentration camp prisoners being forced to dig their own graves before being murdered."[15]

So the direct pressures on the Gorilla persist in Gabon. They are openly hunted for food in a relatively rich country, and the hunting is aided and abetted by a crackpot "scientific" scheme.

The demand for great apes is high in medical research everywhere because of their close similarity to human beings, but their use today can be justified under only the tightest controls. Unfortunately, the quality of much medical research is poor, and many of the projects for which primates are imprisoned and sacrificed are without merit. Gabon's project does not stand alone in this regard. It is sad that a portion of the scientific community remains insensitive to the plight of endangered species, and even sadder that they are apparently without empathy for humanity's nearest relatives.

"Scientific" pressures are also put on endangered species by zoos, which all too often buy animals from unscrupulous animal dealers. The conditions under which the animals are obtained and shipped are often horrendous. For example, in August 1978, three Malay Tapirs, three Leopard Cats, fifty Stumptail Macaques, one Pileated Gibbon, one White-crested Gibbon, and thirty-eight White-handed Gibbons arrived at the Bangkok airport in six crowded cages. They were held for several days in "intense heat and insufferably cramped conditions" before being shipped to Belgium. The International Union for the Conservation of Nature and Natural Resources (IUCN) estimated that, because of the way these animals were captured, the forty captive gibbons, all young, represented the destruction of at least a hundred breeding groups.[16] The shipment was certainly inexcusable and probably illegal, and the animals were almost certainly bound for zoos.

There is also a substantial attrition of wild-animal species for collections outside of zoos. Very large numbers of freshwater and coral-reef fishes are collected for the aquarium trade. The numbers are not accurately known, but the magnitude of the flow can be guessed from a few statistics. In 1970 nearly 84 million living fishes were imported into the United States, and by 1979 the number had probably increased to about 250 million.[17]

Over 2 million reptiles were legally imported into the United States in 1970, and that number had doubled by 1979. Some of those reptiles were bound for private collections, but zoos probably still made up most of the trade. There is an additional flow of unknown dimensions of illegal imports, especially of rare snakes. Eight of the nation's top zoos were identified in 1977 as buyers of illegally imported reptiles. Dealers' catalogues list protected species for sale, and the poaching of rare snakes such as the

Arizona Ridge-nosed Rattlesnake is becoming something of a cottage industry in the southwestern United States.[18]

There is also extensive commercial trading and collecting of reptiles and amphibians in Italy. Each spring many tree frogs, tortoises, lizards, and snakes are collected in Italy and the Balkans and shipped into Central Europe for display in zoos or to be kept as pets. Wild populations of European Tortoises have been put in great jeopardy by collecting for the pet trade, and some European lizard and snake populations may also be in trouble. The Smooth Snake in England is already endangered, but it is still collected and offered for sale in pet shops. Tens of thousands of turtles and tortoises are imported by Great Britain annually for resale in the pet trade. Between 1967 and 1972, the United Kingdom received over 1.2 million specimens of the vulnerable Mediterranean Spur-thighed Tortoise from Morocco alone—and similar numbers are believed to go to continental Europe. It is thought that 80 percent die in the first year of captivity.[19]

The birds flowing into the United States and Europe to be caged and kept as pets number in the millions, and this doubtless constitutes a serious drain on many populations. Most wild birds do not thrive in captivity, and countless numbers die in the processes of capture and transport. For example, one of the most highly valued birds in the trade is the brilliant red Cock of the Rock, an inhabitant of the northern Andes. It is thought that fifty are killed for every one that arrives to grace a zoo's display. . . .[20]

The Fur Business

Perhaps the most widely known direct threat to terrestrial mammals comes from the hunting of them for one of their principal mammalian characteristics—their hair. Trade in animal pelts is a much bigger business than that of cacti, and it has proven even harder to suppress—not surprisingly, since many of the original owners of the skins are species that inhabit poor countries where the pressure to exploit them is understandably high.

The use of furs for clothing, rugs, tents, and the like is, of course, a tradition probably as old as *Homo sapiens* itself. Human beings have extracted a living from their immediate environs for most of the species' history, and any useful qualities made another species quite properly fair game. But the indiscriminate killing of a large number of mammals for their hides alone is a development of rather recent times—chiefly of the last century or two when economic conditions could support widespread trade in pelts.

Virtually no common mammal with a usable skin has escaped remorseless exploitation, and in the process common mammals have often been converted into uncommon mammals. Consider the cuddly Australian Koala—a creature that looks like a teddy bear and that many Americans think is called the "Qantas," thanks to the advertising campaigns of Australia's international airline.

In a total of about two years spent in Australia, we never saw a Koala outside a zoo or a reserve. It was not always so: the animals used to be abundant. But their skins were valuable, and they were mercilessly hunted from the earliest days of European invasion. By 1900 Koala numbers had been greatly decreased everywhere outside of the northeastern state of Queensland, although in the year 1908 it was still possible to ship almost 60,000 pelts through Sydney markets. In south-central Australia the Koala was exterminated soon after the end of World War I. Before then, one to two million skins were shipped out annually, frequently disguised with labels like "beaver," "skunk," "silver-gray possum," and "Adelaide chinchilla."

Queensland is the frontier state of Australia. It is noted for its cheerful and independent people, its unhappy aborigines, and its conservative and parochial politicians—sort of a down-under Texas. The state refuses to go on daylight saving time, and a standard quip from airline pilots is "We've just crossed the Queensland border—set your watch back one hour and ten years."

Queensland by 1927 was the last stronghold of the Koala. That year, in an event that Australian biologist A. J. Marshall called the most sordid episode in the history of the state,[21] Queensland declared open season on the Koala, even though the species' precarious position was well known. The state government licensed no fewer than ten thousand trappers and thus made itself accessory to the slaughter of over a half-million Koalas in a few months. Why did the Queensland government do it? For the same reasons that politicians often permit such atrocities to take place: votes and money. As Marshall put it: "Small landholders and farm workers wanted the money. And the government wanted their votes. Rural votes are often vital votes. These would have been alienated had the cabinet failed to proclaim the open season that a single hillbilly pressure group so eagerly wanted."

The Koala is unusual in that its numbers have been reduced much more by direct persecution than by habitat destruction. (There has been plenty of the latter, but suitable eucalyptus forests are still plentiful.)

Many other fur bearers have suffered both from being hunted for their skins and from the destruction of their habitats. And some of the most beautiful fur bearers, the great cats, have suffered additional assaults because of their own predatory habits.

The Snow Leopard, for example, used to range widely through the highlands of central Asia. Although human destruction of the Snow Leopard's habitat (and that of boar, deer, gazelles, wild goats, and its other prey) have undoubtedly had a negative effect, it is mainly threatened by hunters seeking its gorgeous pelt: the fur has a background color of pale gray tinged with cream and is marked with black rosettes. And the animal's protection is not made any easier when the cats include domestic animals in their diets.

The magnificent tigers are in deep trouble for the same combination of reasons. Moreover, like African Lions, tigers have the audacity to supplement their diets on occasion with the great exterminator itself: *Homo sapiens*. There are probably a few thousand Bengal Tigers left in its former range in India and adjacent countries, where they are especially hard-pressed by habitat destruction, concentrating the remaining individuals in ever smaller areas, ever closer to the people who fear them and want to kill them. Individuals are still poached, and as recently as 1979 skins were illegally imported into Great Britain.

The Caspian Tiger appears to be extinct, a victim of the destruction of the vegetation growing along rivers that were its habitat, in the course of the development of large-scale irrigation and agricultural schemes in the Soviet Union. Its demise was hastened by extermination squads of soldiers employed to remove the tigers as threats to people and domestic animals.

The Bali Tiger is also gone, and the Javan Tiger is at best barely hanging on by the tips of its claws. The Sumatran and Corbett's Tigers are doing better, the latter especially on reserves. There are perhaps three hundred wild individuals of the Siberian Tiger left. Its long-haired pelt is the most valued of tiger skins, and the Chinese greatly value the medicinal properties of various parts of its body. It has been heavily hunted, but its decline is blamed chiefly on the widespread destruction of the vast forests, especially in Manchuria, that were its home—and the destruction along with the forests of its natural prey. The status of the Chinese Tiger is unknown, but the species classically has been persecuted intensively, and little natural habitat remains. It seems likely that neither the Siberian nor the Chinese Tiger is long for this world outside of zoos.[22]

The Cheetah and the Lion were both once widely distributed in Asia, but few of either are left there now.[23] The Lion, for the moment, is relatively secure in Africa, but the Cheetah is in a precarious situation. The Cheetah is still poached for its fur, and it seems unlikely that the hunting will be totally controlled in the foreseeable future. But even if its fur were useless, it would still be endangered; the ecology of the Cheetah tends to make it vulnerable to extinction. This swift hunter, which can accelerate from zero to forty miles an hour in a few strides, exists naturally in the African savannahs at low densities—about one for every forty or fifty square miles. The daylight attacks in which it runs down its prey are conspicuous, and it is thus subject to loss of its captures to stronger predators, such as Spotted Hyenas, Leopards, and Lions.

Cheetah young are quite vulnerable. They follow their mothers on long cross-country treks where they fall prey to other predators. They also cannot benefit from a "baby-sitting" system of the sort that helps protect

Lion cubs. The Cheetah mother is usually solitary when she hunts, whereas a lioness living with a pride made up mostly of other females often has a surrogate available to ward off predators while she hunts.

The Cheetah's hunting habits and its relative weakness make it easy for herders to detect and kill it when it turns its attention to domestic animals. And as the savannah's game gives way more and more to herds of domestic animals, that shift occurs more and more frequently. The result is an increase in the hunting of Cheetahs as livestock predators.

At the same time, there is an increasing migration of farmers onto the grasslands. This leads to a habitat fragmentation that serves the widely dispersed Cheetahs badly.[24] Even large reserves are generally not capable of holding populations large enough to be safe from random extinctions and, in all likelihood, from loss of genetic variability. And natural migration between parks to permit restocking may become impossible, forcing heavy managment responsibilities on *Homo sapiens* even if the parks themselves survive.

The future of the Cheetah therefore depends on whether ways can be found both to alleviate the direct endangering from the predator control activities of herder and to arrest the fragmentation of the savannahs by cultivators—two very big tasks.

Endangering for Other Products

In addition to fur bearers, many animals have suffered, and continue to suffer, human predation for the nonedible products they can yield. In the Orient and in South America, butterflies are used to make decorative objects. Many a crocodile, alligator, and snake has been killed so that its skin could be made into shoes and handbags. The Cuban Crocodile, like so many of its relatives persecuted for its hide, persists in only two small swamps.[25] Several species of giant sea turtles are now endangered in part because their shells are used to make tortoiseshell products. Millions of birds, from ostriches to birds of paradise, have given their lives so stylish women could adorn themselves with their feathers.

Much of the pressure on elephants is generated by the continued depredations of ivory poachers. Zaire and some other African countries are hubs of an ivory trade that threatens elephants over the entire continent. The elephant populations of Kenya alone are estimated to have been reduced by two-thirds in only eight years. Poaching in Uganda accelerated during Idi Amin's reign and has continued unabated. Since 1972 the elephant population in Ruwenzori National Park has fallen from 3,000 to just 150 individuals.[26] The ivory trade is believed to account for the deaths of 50,000 to 150,000 elephants each year—up to 12 percent of the total African population. Each month C-130 cargo planes carry ivory shipments to South Africa, and ivory also leaves Africa through Burundi, the Congo, and the Central African Republic. But it is difficult to blame African villagers for being active as poachers when the sale of a large pair of tusks can bring in the equivalent of ten years' income![27]

The animal that has suffered most severely in recent years from killing for a product is that great browser of sub-Saharan Africa, the Black Rhinoceros. In recent years, that trade, in particular demand for the rhino's horn, has led to a catastrophic level of rhino poaching. Around 1970 about 20,000 Black Rhinos lived in Kenya. By 1980 the population was less than 10 percent of that—perhaps as few as 1,000. The sight of a Black Rhino on the Serengeti plain, wandering majestically, surmounted by tick birds, or wallowing like a huge pig in a mudhole, has been one of the most popular tourist attractions of Africa. Soon the memories and photographs of travelers may be the only places wild rhinos exist; the real ones will have been wiped out to "cure" the impotence of the ignorant rich.

PREDATOR CONTROL

A depressing amount of direct endangering of species is connected with predator control. Wherever human beings or their domestic livestock have become the prey of carnivores, *Homo sapiens* has quite reasonably tried to strike back. In early encounters, human beings faced animals like cave bears, lions, and tigers with clubs, spears, bows and arrows, large rocks, and pure courage. For a long time the battle was more or less even, but the invention of firearms changed the situation.

Wherever human beings had muskets and then rifles, the large predators were pushed back. The Grizzly Bear has been wiped out over much of the United States, including the state of California, where it ironically—and perhaps symbolically—is the state animal. The Wolf, victim of the most unjustly bad press of virtually any animal, has been exterminated over much of Europe and North America. That intelligent animal is anything but the vicious, treacherous beast it was once pictured—a point brought home to many in Farley Mowat's classic book *Never Cry Wolf.*[28] In Tasmania, the Wolf's marsupial namesake, the Thylacene Wolf, was similarly persecuted and driven back to inaccessible marginal areas for similar reasons.

Predator control programs, official or unofficial, contribute to the jeopardy of many species. The Bald Eagle, although strictly protected, is still gunned down by hunters in the United States. Eagles have even been pursued and shot down by men in helicopters.

Much effort in the United States goes into attempts to control the Coyote, a species in no danger whatever of extinction. Indeed, the Coyote thrives in the presence of *Homo sapiens* and has increased its range and its numbers. It seems to have evolved into a bigger, tougher, and smarter animal under the selection pressures of human attempts to suppress it. The biology of Coyotes, including an ability to increase their reproductive rate under duress, allows their populations to sustain enormous mortality and still persist.

In some areas, Coyotes may cause significant losses of sheep and lambs, but not to anything like the degree implied by popular western bumper stickers. Pressures from sheep-grazing interests once promoted broadcast use of chemical poisons against Coyotes—programs that resulted in great mortality in a wide variety of other wildlife until they were halted by executive order of the President in 1972. The effectiveness of these control programs against the Coyotes, however, is problematical. Very often they resulted in a larger Coyote population. Where they *were* successful, it sometimes was necessary to open ground squirrel control programs to keep the rodents from eating too much of the sheep's grass! The ground squirrels were previously controlled by—you guessed it—the Coyotes.

A sensible control program would involve attacking depredating individuals, not attempting to suppress all Coyotes over wide areas. It would also involve teaching sheepmen and others, especially those whose livestock graze on public land, where preserving wildlife is supposed to be one of its "many uses," that a certain level of predation is an expected cost of doing business. There certainly are ways to protect herds from predation, too, that do not require attempts to exterminate the predators. Maintaining one or two guard dogs with each flock is one simple and apparently effective method. The mere presence of such dogs often seems to be enough to discourage Coyotes from attacking a flock. But many sheepmen today think they should be free to graze their herds without protecting them in any way.[29]

Humanity has also attempted to exterminate populations and species of herbivores that attack domesticated plants. A major source of mortality for African Elephants has been control programs implemented to keep them from molesting farms. Entire populations have been exterminated in those programs. A large animal on an overpopulated island, the Ceylon Elephant has been pushed into the endangered category by hunting both for sport and for predator control. The elephants' depredations of plantations led the government to institute a bounty program in 1831. One celebrated hunter of the time, a Major Rogers, promptly killed more than fourteen hundred elephants, and the number of kills in general reached the point where the government had to cut the bounty from ten to seven shillings to save money. Today a couple of thousand individual elephants remaining in Sri Lanka are dependent on a few inadequate reserves for survival—which seems unlikely in the face of the expanding human population and expanding agriculture.[30]

In summary, *Homo sapiens* has a very long history of direct attacks on other species, some of which have resulted in extinction of the species under attack. People have hunted animals for food and other products for millennia, and probably at least contributed to the extinction of many large mammals well before the agricultural revolution. People have also killed—and still do kill—animals to prevent real or imagined threats to themselves or their domestic animals and crops.

Direct pressures against other species thus are obviously an important factor in extinctions. In many cases, however, such as the big cats, elephants, and rhinos, the direct hunting pressure has been augmented by damage or destruction of the ecosystem in which the animal lives—its habitat. Indeed, the *indirect* method of habitat destruction is by far the deadliest means by which humanity has pushed other organisms to extinction. And it is that indirect attack that holds the greatest threat to other forms of life in the future.

NOTES

1. W. Craig, "The expression of emotion in the pigeons. III. The Passenger Pigeon (*Ectopistes migratorius* Linn)," *Auk* 28:408, 1911.

2. I.L. Brisbin, "The Passenger Pigeon: A study in extinction," *Modern Game Breeding* 4:3–20, 1968.

3. The account of the Passenger Pigeon is based largely on Brisbin, op. cit., and Tim Halliday, *Vanishing Birds: Their Natural History and Conservation*, Holt, Rinehart, and Winston, New York, 1978. Halliday's book is beautifully written and illustrated and well documented.

4. T. Halliday, "The Extinction of the Passenger Pigeon *Ectopistes migratorius* and its relevance to contemporary conservation," *Biological Conservation* 17:157–162, 1980.

5. F.G. Roe, *The North American Buffalo: A Critical Study of the Species in the Wild State*, University of Toronto Press, Toronto, 1951.

6. *San Francisco Examiner and Chronicle*, October 5, 1975.

7. "I witnessed a massacre," *International Wildlife*, January–February 1980, p. 29.

8. Michael Weisskopf, "Iran's Wild Casualties," *Defenders*, April 1980.

9. "Creatures," *Audubon*, May 1980. Based on the book by an anonymous Russian bureaucrat (writing under the pseudonym Boris Komarov), *The Destruction of Nature in the Soviet Union* (N. F. Sharpe, White Plains, N. Y.).

10. Cited in Marshall, ed., *The Great Extermination: A Guide to Anglo-Australian Cupidity, Wickedness and Waste*, Heinemann, London, 1966, p. 19.

11. A. A. Burbidge, *The Status of Kangaroos and Wallabies in Australia*, Australian Government Publishing Service, Canberra, 1977; "New count method could determine kangaroos' future," *The Bulletin*, March 25, 1980; "Will U.S. encourage kangaroo slaughter?" *The Australian*, May 12, 1980. The ban was lifted in late 1980.

12. D. Cousins, "Man's exploitation of the Gorilla," *Biological Conservation* 13:287–296, 1978.

13. Gabon statistics from Population Reference Bureau, *World Population Data Sheet, 1979*.

14. Letter to us, February 6, 1980.

15. Letter to Russell Train, January 21, 1980.

16. *International Union for Conservation of Nature and Natural Resources (ICUN) Bulletin*, September 1978, p. 52.

17. 1970 statistics are from *Biological Conservation*, vol.4, no. 1, October 1971. The estimate for 1979 was obtained by extrapolation from the figure of over 300 million total wildlife

imports in that year; *Defenders*, February 1980. The figures in the following paragraphs are from the same sources.

18. A. S. Johnson, "The snaker's game," *Defenders*, February 1980; *IUCN Red Data Book*, 1975.

19. I. F. Spellerberg, "The amphibian and reptile trade with particular reference to collecting in Europe," *Biological Conservation* 10:221–232, 1976; *IUCN Red Data Book,*1975.

20. Tim Halliday, *Vanishing Birds: Their Natural History and Conservation* (New York: Holt, Rhinehart, and Winston, 1978), p. 44.

21. "On the disadvantages of wearing fur," in A. J. Marshall, ed., *The Great Extermination*, op. cit.

22. The information on the Snow Leopard and tigers is from Simon and Géroudet, *Last Survivors: The Natural History of Animals in Danger of Extinction*, World Publishing Company, New York, 1970, pp. 114–131; and *IUCN Bulletin*, May 1979, 136–137.

23. For example, see Kai Curry-Lindahl, *Let them Live: A Worldwide Survey of Animals Threatened with Extinction*, William Morrow, New York, 1972—a well-done survey of conditions about a decade ago, with good historical material.

24. Norman Myers, "The Cheetah in Africa under threat," *Environmental Affairs* 5:617–647, 1976.

25. *IUCN Red Data Book*, 1975.

26. *IUCN Bulletin*, April 1980.

27. *Sunday Nation*, Nairobi, Kenya, April 16, 1980; *IUCN Bulletin*, January/February 1980.

28. Available as a Dell paperback, New York, 1965.

29. Some of the information on Coyotes is from a seminar by R. Cassin, Department of Biological Sciences, Stanford University, June 5, 1980.

30. Information on the Ceylon Elephant is from Simon and Géroudet, *Last Survivors*, op. cit., pp. 132–139.

HOLMES ROLSTON, III

The Value of Species

INDIVIDUALS AND SPECIES

Many will be uncomfortable with the view that we can have duties to a collection. Feinberg writes, "A whole collection, as such, cannot have beliefs, expectations, wants, or desires. . . . Individual elephants can have interests, but the species elephant cannot."[1] Singer asserts, "Species as such are not conscious entities and so do not have interests above and beyond the interests of the individual animals that are members of the species."[2] Regan maintains, "The rights view is a view about the moral rights of individuals. Species are not individuals, and the rights view does not recognize the moral rights of species to anything, including survival."[3] Rescher says, "Moral obligation is thus always interest-oriented. But only individuals can be said to have interests; one only has moral obligations to particular individuals or particular groups thereof. Accordingly, the duty to save a species is not a matter of moral duty toward it, because moral duties are only oriented to individuals. A species as such is the wrong sort of target for a moral obligation."[4]

Holmes Rolston, III teaches philosophy at Colorado State University. His latest book is *Environmental Ethics* (Temple University Press, 1988).

Reprinted from Holmes Rolston, III, *Philosophy Gone Wild* (Prometheus Books, 1986) and "Duties to endangered species." *BioScience* 35 (1985): 718–726. © 1985 American Institute of Biological Sciences.

Even those who recognize that organisms, nonsentient as well as sentient, can be benefited or harmed may see the good of a species as the sum of and reducible to the goods of individuals. The species is well off when and because its members are; species well-being is just aggregated individual well-being. The "interests of a species" constitute only a convenient device, something like a center of gravity in physics, for speaking of an aggregated focus of many contributing individual member units.

But duties to a species are not duties to a class or category, not to an aggregation of sentient interests, but to a lifeline. An ethic about species needs to see how the species *is* a bigger event than individual interests or sentience. Making this clearer can support the conviction that a species *ought* to continue.

Events can be good for the well-being of the species, considered collectively, although they are harmful if considered as distributed to individuals. This is one way to interpret what is often called a genetic "load," genes that somewhat reduce health, efficiency, or fertility in most individuals but introduce enough variation to permit improving the specific form.[5] Less variation and better repetition in reproduction would, on average, benefit more individuals in any one next generation, since individuals would have less "load." But on a longer view, variation can confer stability in a changing world. A greater experimenting with individuals, although this typically makes individuals less fit and is a disadvantage from that perspective, benefits rare, lucky individuals selected in each generation with a resulting improvement in the species. Most individuals in any particular generation carry some (usually slightly) detrimental genes, but the variation is good for the species. Note that this does not imply species selection; selection perhaps operates only on individuals. But it does mean that we can distinguish between the goods of individuals and the larger good of the species.

Predation on individual elk conserves and improves the species *Cervus canadensis*. A forest fire harms individual aspen trees, but it helps *Populus tremuloides* because fire restarts forest succession without which the species would go extinct. Even the individuals that escape demise from external sources die of old age; their deaths, always to the disadvantage of those individuals, are a necessity for the species. A finite lifespan makes room for those replacements that enable development to occur, allowing the population to improve in fitness or adapt to a shifting environment. Without the "flawed" reproduction that permits variation, without a surplus of young, or predation and death, which all harm individuals, the species would soon go extinct in a changing environment, as all environments eventually are. The individual is a receptacle of the form, and the receptacles are broken while the form survives; but the form cannot otherwise survive.

When a biologist remarks that a breeding population of a rare species is dangerously low, what is the danger to? Individual members? Rather, the remark seems to imply a specific-level, point-of-no-return threat to the continuing of that form of life. No individual crosses the extinction threshold; the species does.

Reproduction is typically assumed to be a need of individuals, but since any particular individual can flourish somatically without reproducing at all, indeed may be put through duress and risk or spend much energy reproducing, by another logic we can interpret reproduction as the species keeping up its own kind by reenacting itself again and again, individual after individual. In this sense a female grizzly does not bear cubs to be healthy herself, any more than a woman needs children to be healthy. Rather, her cubs are *Ursus arctos,* threatened by nonbeing, recreating itself by continuous performance. A species in reproduction defends its own kind from other species, and this seems to be some form of "caring."

Biologists have often and understandably focused on individuals, and some recent trends interpret biological processes from the perspective of genes. A consideration of species reminds us that many events can be interpreted at this level too. An organism runs a directed course through the environment, taking in materials, using them resourcefully, discharging wastes. But this single, directed course is part of a bigger picture in which a species via individuals maintains its course over longer spans of time. Thinking this way, the life the individual has is something passing through the individual as much as something it intrinsically possesses. The individual is subordinate to the species, not the other way round. The genetic set, in which is coded the *telos,* is as evidently a "property" of the species as of the individual.

Biologists and linguists have learned to accept the concept of information in the genetic set without any subject who speaks or understands. Can ethicists learn to accept value in, and duty to, an informed process in which centered individuality or sentience is absent? Here events can be significant at the specific level, an additional consideration to whether they are beneficial to individuals. The species-in-environment is an interactive complex, a selective system where individuals are pawns on a chessboard. When human conduct endangers these specific games of life, duties may appear.

A species has no self. It is not a bounded singular. Each organism has its own centeredness, but there is no specific analogue to the nervous hookups or circulatory flows that characterize the organism. But, like the market in economics, an organized system does not have to have a controlling center to have identity. Having a biological identity reasserted genetically over time is as true of the species as of the individual. Individuals come and go; the marks of the species collectively remain much longer.

A consideration of species strains any ethic focused on individuals, much less on sentience or persons. But the result can be a biologically sounder ethic, though it revises what was formerly thought logically permissible or ethically binding. The species line is quite fundamental. It is more important to protect this integrity than to protect individuals. Defending a form of life, resisting death, regeneration that maintains a normative identity over time—all this is as true of species as of individuals. So what prevents duties arising at that level? The appropriate survival unit is the appropriate level of moral concern.

NOTES

1. Joel Feinberg, "The Rights of Animals and Unborn Generations," in W. T. Blackstone, ed., *Philosophy and Environmental Crisis* (Athens: University of Georgia Press, 1974), pp. 55–56.
2. Peter Singer, "Not for Humans Only," in K. E. Goodpaster and K. M. Sayre, eds., *Ethics and Problems of the 21st Century* (Notre Dame, Ind.: University of Notre Dame Press, 1979), p. 203.
3. Tom Regan, *The Case for Animal Rights* (Berkeley: University of California Press, 1983), p. 359.
4. Nicholas Rescher, *Unpopular Essays on Technological Progress* (Pittsburgh: University of Pittsburgh Press, 1980), p. 83.
5. G. R. Fraser, "Our Genetical 'Load.' A Review of Some Aspects of Genetical Variation," *Annuals of Human Genetics* 25 (1962), pp. 387–415.

MARTI KHEEL

Nature
and
Feminist Sensitivity

THE RULE OF REASON

Most of the literature within the field of environmental ethics may be seen as an attempt to establish rationally both hierarchies of value and universal rules of conduct based on such values. Most such literature presumes that reason alone will tell us which beings are of greatest value and, thus, what rules of conduct should govern our interactions with them. Singer refers to this idea when he states, "Ethics requires us to go beyond 'I' and 'you' to the universal law, the universalizable judgment, the standpoint of the impartial spectator or ideal observer or whatever we choose to call it."[1]

Interestingly, the field of environmental ethics is an outgrowth of two movements that were (and are) highly charged emotionally—i.e., the animal rights and environmental movements. Significantly, the members (mostly women)[2] of the early animal rights movement were often labeled "animal lovers" or "sentimentalists" in an attempt to belittle their concerns. But, as James Turner points out, "animal lovers were not ashamed to admit that their campaign to protect brutes from abuse was more the result of sentiment than of reason."[3]

Marti Kheel is co-founder of Feminists for Animal Rights and is a frequent contributor to professional journals in moral, political, and social philosophy.

Reprinted with permission from Marti Kheel, "The liberation of nature: A circular affair." *Environment Ethics* 7 (1985), pp. 141–49.

With the publication of Peter Singer's *Animal Liberation,* the animal liberation movement took a new direction. It was assumed that one of the reasons for the failure of the earlier movement was its appeal to emotion, rather than hard, logical, well-reasoned arguments. The new movement for animal rights (as well as environmental ethics) proudly grounds itself in rationality. As Peter Singer states, "Nowhere in this book, however, do I appeal to the reader's emotions where they cannot be *supported by reason.*"[4] Elsewhere Singer elaborates, "Ethics does not demand that we eliminate personal relationships and partial affections, but it does demand that when we act we assess the moral claims of those affected by our actions *independently of our feelings for them.*"[5] Dieter Birnbacher echoes this same idea when he states, "to be classed as moral, a norm must not express the contingent preferences of a certain individual or of a certain group, but must be issued from an interpersonal, *impartial* point of view and claim to be *rationally justifiable* to everyone."[6] In a similar vein, Paul W. Taylor states, "I hold that a set of moral norms (both standards of character and rules of conduct) governing human treatment of the natural world is a *rationally grounded* set if and only if, first, commitment to those norms is a practical entailment of adopting the attitude of respect for nature as an ultimate moral attitude, and second, the adopting of that attitude on the part of all *rational agents* can be *justified.*"[7]

The appeal to reason in ethics has a long philosophical tradition. One of its most notable proponents was Kant, who felt that an action was moral only if it was derived from a rationally grounded conception of the right or morally correct course of action. Kant went so far as to maintain that no action that springs from a natural inclination can have moral worth. Although most modern-day philosophers do not elevate reason to quite such heights, most still feel that any appeal to emotion is tantamount to having no argument at all.

THE LIMITS OF REASON

Although the literature in environmental ethics relies predominantly on the use of rational arguments, references to the limitations of rationality still manage to insinuate themselves. The frequent reference to an idea being "intuitive," "counterintuitive," or "reasonable" is, at least, a partial recognition of the significance of intuition or nonrational thought in moral decisions. Less frequent are direct references to the limitations of reason as in the statement by Alistair S. Gunn: "It may be that an environmental ethic involves a return to intuitionism, perhaps even a quasi-religious philosophical idealism."[8] In a similar vein, Tom Regan states, "How then, are we to settle these matters. I wish I knew. I am not even certain that they can be settled in a rationally coherent way, and hence the tentativeness of my closing remarks."[9]

Although often not explicitly stated, a significant portion of the literature does, in fact, rely on appeals to intuition or emotion. The argument from "marginal cases"[10] (i.e., "defective humans") is, perhaps, the most notable example of this occurrence. The argument from "marginal cases" concludes that if we do not wish to treat a marginal human being in a particular manner, there is no ethically defensible reason for treating at least some animals in a similar fashion. The proponents of this argument rely on our "intuition" or "feeling" that such behavior toward humans is wrong. Thus, Regan states, "Let us agree that there are certain immoral ways of treating (say) marginal beings; for example, suppose we agree that it is morally wrong to cause them gratuitious [sic] pain or arbitrarily to restrict them in their ability to move about as they will."[11] Why we should accord "marginal human beings," or even "non-marginal human beings," such rights is never established. The limitations of rational argument may, in fact, make it impossible to prove rationally why *anyone* or *anything* should have rights. Again, we fall back on the need to recognize and affirm the significance of feeling in our moral choices.

Rational arguments are also often used in the literature in emotionally selective ways. Thus, many writers fail to follow their arguments to their "rational" conclusion when this appears to be counterintuitive. It could be argued, for example, that the rational or logical extension of the arguments of the two major camps within environmental ethics would be to advocate the ultimate extinction of the human species. Callicott, for example, maintains that value distinctions should be established by ascertaining the importance of an organism to the stability of the biotic community. However, it is not at all clear that human beings contribute in any positive way to such stability, and a great deal of evidence suggests the reverse. In the words of James D. Hefferman, "If the integrity, stability, and beauty of the biotic community is the *summum bonum*, the best thing we can do is to find some ecologically sound way of disposing of the human race or at least drastically reducing the human population."[12] Similarly, it could be argued that the utilitarian goal of the minimization of suffering and pain could be most successfully implemented if human beings were thoughtful enough to become extinct.

The call to reason is also used by other writers as a means of learning our "natural place" within nature. Such writers argue that by understanding our "natural place" within nature we can learn what our moral actions should be. But, one might ask, why should *is* imply *ought*? Why should our natural place within nature dictate what it *should* be? To my knowledge, no philosopher to date has answered this question with a convincing "rational" argument, and I suspect that none will. Pragmatic arguments about how we will destroy all life on Earth unless we find our natural place within nature cannot persuade those who have no regard for life to begin with. Only those who *feel* their connection to all of nature to begin with will take an interest in its continuation. In more ways than one, the liberation of nature is a circular affair.

DISSOLVING THE DICHOTOMIES

What seems to be lacking in much of the literature in environmental ethics (and in ethics in general) is the open admission that we cannot even begin to talk about the issue of ethics unless we admit that we care (or feel something). And it is here that the emphasis of many feminists on personal experience and emotion has much to offer in the way of reformulating our traditional notion of ethics. Although this may appear at first to support the stereotypical divisions of our society which associate men with rationality and women with emotion, the emphasis on feeling and emotion does not imply the exclusion of reason. Rather, a kind of unity of reason and emotion is envisioned by many feminists.[13] As Carol McMillan puts it, ". . . to contrast thought and emotion by assuming that the latter is devoid of all cognition is to miss one of its crucial features."[14] Similarly, Mary Midgley states that "feeling and action are essential elements in morality, which concentration on thought has often made philosophers overlook. . . . In general, feelings, to be effective must take shape as thought, and thoughts, to be effective must be powered by suitable feelings."[15] In the words of Sarah Ruddick, "intellectual activities are distinguishable but not separable from disciplines of feeling. There is a unity of reflection, judgment and emotion."[16] Robin Morgan has used the term *unified sensibility* to describe this fusion of feeling and thought. In her words:

> How often have feminists called . . . for the 'peculiar blend of feeling and ratiocination' in our battles against the patriarchal dichotomization of intellect and emotion! It is the insistence on the connections, the demand for synthesis, the refusal to be narrowed into desiring less than everything—that is so much the form of metaphysical poetry and of metaphysical feminism. The unified sensibility.[17]

How, then, are we to attain such a "unified sensibility"? The difficulty lies in conceiving of something as alien to our usual conception of hierarchy and rules as what is proposed. The problem of unifying our own nature is compounded further when we, ourselves, are removed from the rest of nature. Emotion easily divides from reason when we are divorced from the immediate impact of our moral decisions. A possible step, therefore, in striving to fuse these divisions is to experience directly the full impact of our moral decision. If we *think*, for example, that there is nothing morally wrong with eating meat, we ought, perhaps, to visit a factory farm or slaughter house to see if we still *feel* the same way. If we, ourselves, do not want to witness, let alone participate in, the slaughter of the animals we eat, we ought, perhaps, to question the morality of indirectly paying someone else to do this on our behalf. When we are physically removed from the direct impact of our moral decisions—i.e., when we cannot see, smell, or hear their results—we deprive ourselves of important sensory stimuli which may be important in guiding us in our ethical choices.

Feminists have often emphasized the importance of personal experience in political and other seemingly impersonal matters. Its importance for ethical decisions is equally vital. This is, perhaps, the most practical implication of a feminist ethic: that we must involve ourselves as directly as possible in the *whole* process of our moral decisions. We must make our moral choices a circular affair.

Elizabeth Dodson Gray also highlights the importance of direct experience in moral decision making through an analogy with the situation faced by parents in making decisions about their children. In her words:

> The point is that we parents continually find some ground for making our decisions, grounds other than ranking our children in some hierarchy of their worth. What we perceive instead is that our children have differing needs, differing strengths, differing weaknesses. And occasions differ too. It is upon the basis of some convergence of all these factors that we make our decisions. And our decisions are always made within the overriding imperative that we seek to preserve the welfare of each of them as well as the welfare of the entire family.[18]

Carol McMillan adds weight to this notion by her statement that:

> The whole search in philosophy for universals, substances, essences, is a symptom of this preoccupation with the methods of science, of the craving for generality and the contemptuous attitude toward the particular case.... A refusal to grant that action based on natural inclination may sometimes be a legitimate way of responding to a moral difficulty obscures not only the nature of a moral difficulty but also the nature of goodness.[19]

In her book *In a Different Voice,* Carol Gilligan has argued that the emphasis on particularity and feeling is a predominantly female mode of ethical thought. As she puts it,

> The moral imperative that emerges repeatedly in interviews with women is an injunction to care, a responsibility to discern and alleviate the real and recognizable trouble of this world. . . . the reconstruction of the dilemma in its contextual particularity allows the understanding of cause and consequence which engages the compassion and tolerance repeatedly noted to distinguish the moral judgments of women.[20]

Men, on the other hand, she states, develop a sense of morality in which "relationships are subordinated to rules (stage four) and rules to universal principles of justice (stages five and six)."[21] According to Gilligan, "the rights conception of morality that informs [Lawrence] Kohlberg's principled level (stages five and six) is geared to arriving at an objectively fair or just resolution to moral dilemmas upon which all rational persons could agree. . . ."[22]

The problems entailed in implementing a female mode of ethical thought within a patriarchal society are obvious. With men building bigger and better bombs, rapidly depleting our natural resources, and torturing millions of animals in laboratories, one rightly worries what a particular individual's natural inclination might be. As Sara Ebenreck puts it, "If the answer to how to treat a tree or a field is dependent on what the person 'hears intuitively' from the field or tree, then—as John Kultgen points out—we must be open to the possibility that some people will hear a message which is 'rape us, despoil us, enslave us.' "[23]

It needs to be said in this context that men may respond in different ways to the call to ground our ethics in practical experience. Clearly, men do have a greater propensity toward violence as can be seen by their greater involvement in such violent activities as wars, violent crime, hunting, trapping, etc. Whether this propensity is biological or environmental or a combination of both is still an unanswered question. Whatever else we may conclude from this difference, however, it is difficult to escape the conclusion that in our dealings with nature, men have much to learn from women. Indeed, many men, including Buckminster Fuller, Lionel Tiger, Lyall Watson have concluded that "the only hope may be to turn the world over to women."[24]

Most nonhumans seem instinctively to take only what they need from the environment to survive. If humans ever had such an ability, we seem to have lost it.[25] The further divorced human beings are from this instinct or sensibility that nonhuman animals have, the more we seem to require rationality to act as its substitute. Interestingly, Aldo Leopold suggests that "ethics are possibly a kind of community instinct in-the-making."[26] Perhaps, then, we are fortunate in that the human capacity to destroy life, to ravage the Earth, and to otherwise wreak havoc on the world around us coexists with yet another capacity—namely, the capacity to question our right to do so.

It is only when our instincts have failed us that we turn to such concepts as rights. Thus, it is not surprising that the idea of individual rights and natural law emerged during the civil war in England, a time of great social upheaval.[27] The notion of *rights* can, in fact, be conceived of only within an antagonistic or competitive environment. The concept of competition is inherent in the very definition of rights. As Joel Feinberg states, "To have a right is to have a claim *to* something *against* someone."[28] The concept of rights is, thus, inherently dualistic. Unfortunately, however, we do live in a dualistic society where competition is a fact of life. The concept of rights in an expanded form to include all of nature may thus be a necessary tactical device within our current society.

CONCLUSION

Feminist spirituality has shown us how the concept of a patriarchal religion, which views God as a male figure of authority in the sky telling us how we should think or feel, does not speak to the needs of those who feel that their spirituality flows from within. In a similar vein, it may be argued, the concept of ethics as a hierarchical set of rules to be superimposed upon the individual does not address the needs of those people (perhaps, mostly women) who feel that their morality or inclinations toward nature reside within themselves.

For such people, an environmental ethic might be described in the words of Elizabeth Dodson Gray:

> Some day, perhaps, we shall have an identity that can enjoy the earth as friend, provider and home. When that happens, we will know that when the earth hurts, it will hurt us. Then, the environmental ethic will not just be in our heads but in our hearts—in the nerve endings of our sensitivity.[29]

With such a sensitivity we could perhaps, then dispense with the rigid, hierarchical rules of the past. If guidelines were to exist at all, they might simply flow from the desire to minimize human interference with the rest of nature.

In its highest form this sensitivity is, perhaps, simply love, for it is love that unifies our sensibilities and connects us with all of life. As Starhawk puts it,

> Love connects; love transforms. Loving the world, for what it is and our vision of what it could be, loving the world's creatures (including ourselves), caring for the stream, picking up the garbage at our feet, we can transform. We can reclaim our power to shape ourselves and our world around us.[30]

This sensitivity—the "unified sensibility"—cannot, however, be developed on only an abstract, rational plane any more than I can learn to love someone that I have never seen. It is a sensitivity that must flow from our direct involvement with the natural world and the actions and reactions that we bring about in it. If such direct involvement is often not a possibility for many of us, this does not mean that we should abandon the attempt to achieve the sensitivity described. Although in our complex, modern society we may never be able to fully experience the impact of our moral decisions (we cannot, for example, directly experience the impact that eating meat has on world hunger),[31] we can, nonetheless, attempt as far as possible to experience emotionally the knowledge of this fact.

What does all of this mean for environmental ethics as a field of study? How might the field of environmental ethics be changed by a recognition of the importance of feeling and emotion and personal experience in moral decision making? For one thing, writers in environmental ethics might spend less time formulating universal laws and dividing lines and spend more time using reason to show the limitations of its own thought. They might, for instance, show how seemingly "rational" rules and ideas are, in fact, based on distinct feelings. Few of us, for example, would relinquish the idea that we, as humans, are more important than a stone. Yet, by showing that such a thought is based, in fact, on a feeling and that it cannot be justified by rational thought alone, we may be able to detach from our egos long enough to see that we are, indeed, all part of a whole of which no part may rationally be said to be more important than another. Currently, those with power in our society use rationality as a means of enforcing their own morality. If it could also be shown that such rationality is, in fact, derived from particular feelings, we could then begin to genuinely assess those feelings and the morality that flows from them.

Environmental theorists also might begin to talk more openly about their experiences and feelings and their relevance to their ideas and actions. Rather than spending time trying to find a moral dividing line within nature, they might, instead, examine their own internal divisions (such as that between reason and emotion). In order to unite these dualities within themselves they might then attempt as far as possible to experience in practice the full implications of their own moral theories. In a similar vein, an appeal to their readers' emotions and sympathies might be considered more relevant in an argument for moral vegetarianism than an appeal to reason.

Finally, environmentl ethics might become more willing to recognize that the most fundamental questions about nature and the universe cannot, in the end, be answered rationally. Such an admission may not leave us with the sense of resolution and control that so many of us seem to hunger for, but it may, on the other hand, bring us closer to a feeling of the wonder of the universe and, perhaps, as a consequence, a greater appreciation of all of life.

NOTES

1. Peter Singer, *Practical Ethics* (Cambridge: University of Cambridge, 1979), p. 11.
2. The animal rights movement emerged from the humane movements of both England and the United States. According to Sydney Coleman, women made up such a large part of the humane movement that "were the support of the women of America suddenly withdrawn, the large majority of societies for the prevention of cruelty to children and

animals would cease to exist." Sydney Coleman, *Humane Society Leaders in America* (Albany, N. Y.: American Humane Association, 1924), p. 178.

3. James Turner, *Reckoning With the Beast* (Baltimore: Johns Hopkins University Press, 1980), p. 33.

4. Peter Singer, *Animal Liberation* (New York: Avon Books, 1975), p. xi. Italics added.

5. Peter Singer, *Practical Ethics*, p. 11.

6. Dieter Birnbacher, "A Priority Rule for Environmental Ethics," *Environmental Ethics* 4 (1980): 14.

7. Paul W. Taylor, "The Ethics of Respect for Nature," *Environmental Ethics* 3 (1981): 197.

8. Alistair S. Gunn, "Why Should We Care about Rare Species? *Environmental Ethics* 2 (1980): 203.

9. Tom Regan, *All That Dwell Therein*, (Berkeley: University of California Press, 1982), p. 202–03.

10. See, for example, Peter Singer, *Practical Ethics*, and Tom Regan, *All That Dwell Therein*.

11. Tom Regan, *All That Dwell Therein*, p. 119.

12. James D. Hefferman, "The Land Ethic: A Critical Appraisal," *Environmental Ethics* 4 (1982): 243.

13. Some of the ideas of Eastern religions also address the false division between reason and emotion. As Fritjof Capra points out (*The Tao of Physics* [New York: Bantam Books, 1984]), the notion of "enlightenment" (the awareness of the "unity and mutual interrelation of all things") is "not only an intellectual act, but is an experience which involves the whole person and is religious in its ultimate nature." The feminist notion of a "unified sensibility" may differ primarily from this notion of enlightenment in that feminists place less emphasis on withdrawal from the world (as in the inward activity of meditation) and more on a full participation in it.

14. Carol McMillan, *Women, Reason and Nature* (Princeton: Princeton University Press, 1982), p. 28.

15. Mary Midgley, *Heart and Mind* (New York: St. Martin's Press, 1981), pp. 12, 4.

16. Sara Ruddick, "Maternal Thinking," *Feminist Studies* 6, no. 2 (1980): 348.

17. Robin Morgan, "Metaphysical Feminism," in Charlene Spretnak, ed., *The Politics of Women's Spirituality* (Garden City, N. Y.: Anchor Press, 1982), p. 387.

18. Elizabeth D. Gray, *Green Paradise Lost*, (Wellesley, Mass.: Roundtable Press, 1979), p. 148.

19. Carol McMillan, *Women, Reason and Nature*, p. 28.

20. Carol Gilligan, *In A Different Voice* (Cambridge, Mass.: Harvard University Press, 1982), p. 100.

21. Ibid., p. 18. According to Lawrence Kohlberg, children undergo six stages of moral development, the sixth stage representing a fully mature moral being. Unfortunately, Kohlberg's study was based on interviews with boys only and ignores the significance and value of the different way in which women develop morally.

22. Ibid., p. 21–22.

23. Sara Ebenreck, "A Partnership Farmland Ethic," *Environmental Ethics* 5 (1983): 40.

24. Laurel Holliday, *The Violent Sex* (Guerneville, Calif.: Blue Stocking Books, 1978), p. 171.

25. Exceptions to this generalization may, perhaps, be found among certain tribal peoples such as the North American Indians.

26. Aldo Leopold, *A Sand County Almanac* (Oxford: Oxford University Press, 1966), p. 36.

27. See Raymond Polin, "The Rights of Man in Hobbes and Locke," in *Political Theory and the Rights of Man*, ed. D.D. Raphael (Bloomington: Indiana University Press, 1967) and S. F. Sapontzis, "The Value of Human Rights," *Journal of Value Inquiry* 12 (1978): 210–24.

28. Joel Feinberg, "The Rights of Animals and Unborn Generations," in *Responsibilities to Future Generations*, ed. Ernest Partridge (Buffalo, N.Y.: Prometheus Books, 1980), p. 139.

29. Elizabeth D. Gray, *Green Paradise Lost*, p. 85.

30. Starhawk, *Dreaming the Dark* (Boston: Beacon Press, 1982), p. 44.

31. Meat eating has been implicated by a number of writers as a major contributor to world hunger. It is estimated that eighty to ninety percent of all grain grown in America is used to feed animals, that seventeen times as much land is used as the amount needed to plant grains such as soybeans, and that "if we ate half as much meat, we could release enough food to feed the entire 'developing world.' " See Barbara Parham, *What's Wrong with Eating Meat?* (Denver, Colo.: Ananda Marga Publication, 1979), p. 38.

LILY-MARLENE RUSSOW

Why Do Species Matter?

SOME TRADITIONAL ANSWERS

There are, of course, some standard replies to the question "Why do species matter?" or, more particularly, to the question "Why do we have at least a *prima facie* duty not to cause a species to become extinct, and in some cases, a duty to try actively to preserve species?" With some tolerance for borderline cases, these replies generally fall into three groups: (1) those that appeal to our role as "stewards" or "caretakers," (2) those that claim that species have some extrinsic value (I include in this group those that argue that the species is valuable as part of the ecosystem or as a link in the evolutionary scheme of things), and (3) those that appeal to some intrinsic or inherent value that is supposed to make a species worth preserving. In this section . . . I indicate some serious flaws with each of these responses.

The first type of view has been put forward in the philosophical literature by Joel Feinberg, who states that our duty to preserve whole species may be more important than any rights had by individual animals.[1] He argues, first, that this duty does not arise from a right or claim that can properly be attributed to the species as a whole, and second, while we have

Lily-Marlene Russow teaches philosophy at Purdue University. She is a frequent contributor to professional journals in moral, political, and social philosophy.

Reprinted with permission from Lily-Marlene Russow, "Why do species matter?" *Environmental Ethics* 3 (1981), pp. 106–112.

some duty to unborn generations that directs us to preserve species, that duty is much weaker than the actual duty we have to preserve species. The fact that our actual duty extends beyond our duties to future generations is explained by the claim that we have duties of "stewardship" with respect to the world as a whole. Thus, Feinberg notes that his "inclination is to seek an explanation in terms of the requirements of our unique station as rational custodians of the planet we temporarily occupy."[2]

The main objection to this appeal to our role as stewards or caretakers is that it begs the question. The job of a custodian is to protect that which is deserving of protection, that which has some value or worth.[3] But the issue before us now is precisely *whether* species have value, and why. If we justify our obligations of stewardship by reference to the value of that which is cared for, we cannot also explain the value by pointing to the duties of stewardship.

The second type of argument is the one which establishes the value of a species by locating it in the "larger scheme of things." That is, one might try to argue that species matter because they contribute to, or form an essential part of, some other good. This line of defense has several variations.

The first version is completely anthropocentric: it is claimed that vanishing species are of concern to us because their difficulties serve as a warning that we have polluted or altered the environment in a way that is potentially dangerous or undesirable for us. Thus, the California condor whose eggshells are weakened due to the absorption of DDT indicates that something is wrong: presumably we are being affected in subtle ways by the absorption of DDT, and that is bad for us. Alternatively, diminishing numbers of game animals may signal overhunting which, if left unchecked, would leave the sportsman with fewer things to hunt. And, as we become more aware of the benefits that might be obtained from rare varieties of plants and animals (drugs, substitutes for other natural resources, tools for research), we may become reluctant to risk the disappearance of a species that might be of practical use to us in the future.

This line of argument does not carry us very far. In the case of a subspecies, most benefits could be derived from other varieties of the same species. More important, when faced with the loss of a unique variety or species, we may simply decide that, even taking into account the possibility of error, there is not enough reason to think that the species will ever be of use; we may take a calculated risk and decide that it is not worth it. Finally, the use of a species as a danger signal may apply to species whose decline is due to some subtle and unforseen change in the environment, but will not justify concern for a species threatened by a known and forseen event like the building of a dam.

Other attempts to ascribe extrinsic value to a species do not limit themselves to potential human and practical goods. Thus, it is often argued that each species occupies a unique niche in a rich and complex, but delicately balanced, ecosystem. By destroying a single species, we upset the balance of the whole system. On the assumption that the system as a whole should be preserved, the value of a species is determined, at least in part, by its contribution to the whole.[4]

In assessing this argument, it is important to realize that such a justification (a) may lead to odd conclusions about some of the test cases, and (b) allows for changes which do not affect the system, or which result in the substitution of a richer, more complex system for one that is more primitive or less evolved. With regard to the first of these points, species that exist only in zoos would seem to have no special value. In terms of our test cases, the David deer does not exist as part of a system, but only in isolation. Similarly, the Appaloosa horse, a domesticated variety which is neither better suited nor worse than any other sort of horse, would not have any special value. In contrast, the whole cycle of mosquitoes, disease organisms adapted to these hosts, and other beings susceptible to those diseases is quite a complex and marvelous bit of systematic adaption. Thus, it would seem to be wrong to wipe out the encephalitis-bearing mosquito.

With regard to the second point, we might consider changes effected by white settlers in previously isolated areas such as New Zealand and Australia. The introduction of new species has resulted in a whole new ecosystem, with many of the former indigenous species being replaced by introduced varieties. As long as the new system works, there seems to be no grounds for objections.

The third version of an appeal to extrinsic value is sometimes presented in Darwinian terms: species are important as links in the evolutionary chain. This will get us nowhere, however, because the extinction of one species, the replacement of one by another, is as much a part of evolution as is the development of a new species.

One should also consider a more general concern about all those versions of the argument which focus on the species' role in the natural order of things: all of these arguments presuppose that "the natural order of things" is, in itself, good. As William Blackstone pointed out, this is by no means obvious: "Unless one adheres dogmatically to a position of a 'reverence for all life,' the extinction of some species or forms of life may be seen as quite desirable. (This is parallel to the point often made by philosophers that not all 'customary' or 'natural' behavior is necessarily good).[5] Unless we have some other way of ascribing value to a system, and to the animals which actually fulfill a certain function in that system (as opposed to possible replacements), the argument will not get off the ground.

Finally, then, the process of elimination leads us to the set of arguments which point to some *intrinsic value* that a species is supposed to have. The notion that species have an intrinsic value, if established, would allow us to defend much stronger claims about human obligations toward threatened species. Thus, if a species is intrinsically valuable, we should try to preserve it even when it no longer has a place in the natural ecosystem, or when it could be replaced by another species that would occupy the same niche. Most important, we should not ignore a species just because it serves no useful purpose.

Unsurprisingly, the stumbling block is what this intrinsic value might be grounded in. Without an explanation of that, we have no nonarbitrary way of deciding whether subspecies as well as species have intrinsic value or how much intrinsic value a species might have. The last question is meant to bring out issues that will arise in cases of conflict of interests: is the intrinsic value of a species of mosquito sufficient to outweigh the benefits to be gained by eradicating the means of spreading a disease like encephalitis? Is the intrinsic value of the snail darter sufficient to outweigh the economic hardship that might be alleviated by the construction of a dam? In short, to say that something has intrinsic value does not tell us *how much* value it has, nor does it allow us to make the sorts of judgments that are often called for in considering the fate of an endangered species.

The attempt to sidestep the difficulties raised by subspecies by broadening the ascription of value to include subspecies opens a whole Pandora's box. It would follow that any genetic variation within a species that results in distinctive charcteristics would need separate protection. In the case of forms developed through selective breeding, it is not clear whether we have a situation analogous to natural subspecies, or whether no special value is attached to different breeds.

In order to speak to either of these issues, and in order to lend plausibility to the whole enterprise, it would seem necessary to consider first the justification for ascribing value to whichever groups have such value. If intrinsic value does not spring from anything, if it becomes merely another way of saying that we should protect some species, we are going around in circles, without explaining anything.[6] Some further explanation is needed.

Some appeals to intrinsic value are grounded in the intuition that diversity itself is a virtue. If so, it would seem incumbent upon us to create new species wherever possible, even bizarre ones that would have no purpose other than to be different. Something other than diversity must therefore be valued.

The comparison that is often made between species and natural wonders, spectacular landscapes, or even works of art, suggest that species might have some aesthetic value. This seems to accord well with our naive intuitions, provided that *aesthetic value* is interpreted rather loosely; most of us believe that the world would be a poorer place for the loss of bald eagles in the same way that it would be poorer for the loss of the Grand Canyon or a great work of art. In all cases, the experience of seeing these things is an inherently worthwhile experience. And since diversity in some cases is a component in aesthetic appreciation, part of the previous intuition would be preserved. There is also room for degrees of selectivity and concern with superficial changes: the variety of rat that is allowed to become extinct may have no special aesthetic value, and a bird is neither more nor less aesthetically pleasing when we change its name.

There are some drawbacks to this line of argument: there are some species which, by no stretch of the imagination, are aesthetically significant. But aesthetic value can cover a surprising range of things: a tiger may be simply beautiful; a blue whale is awe-inspiring; a bird might be decorative; an Appaloosa is of interest because of its historical significance; and even a drab little plant may inspire admiration for the marvelous way it has been adapted to a special environment. Even so, there may be species such as the snail darter that simply have no aesthetic value. In these cases, lacking any alternative, we may be forced to the conclusion that such species are not worth preserving.

Seen from other angles, once again the appeal to the aesthetic value of species is illuminating. Things that have an aesthetic value may be compared and ranked in some cases, and commitment of resources may be made accordingly. We believe that diminishing the aesthetic value of a thing for mere economic benefit is immoral, but that aesthetic value is not absolute—that the fact that something has aesthetic value may be overridden by the fact that harming that thing, or destroying it, may result in some greater good. That is, someone who agrees to destroy a piece of Greek statuary for personal gain would be condemned as having done something immoral, but someone who is faced with a choice between saving his children and saving a "priceless" painting would be said to have skewed values if he chose to save the painting. Applying these observations to species, we can see that an appeal to aesthetic value would justify putting more effort into the preservation of one species than the preservation of another; indeed, just as we think that the doodling of a would-be artist may have no merit at all, we may think that the accidental and unfortunate mutation of a species is not worth preserving. Following the analogy, allowing a species to become extinct for *mere* economic gain might be seen as immoral, while the possibility remains open that other (human?) good might outweigh the good achieved by the preservation of a species.

Although the appeal to aesthetic values has much to recommend it—even when we have taken account of the fact that it does not guarantee that all species matter—there seems to be a fundamental confusion that still affects the cogency of the whole argument and its application to the question of special obligations to endangered species, for if the value of a species is based on its aesthetic value, it is impossible to explain why an endangered species should be more valuable, or more worthy of preservation, than an unendangered species. The appeal to "rarity" will not help, if what we are talking about is species: each species is unique, no more or less rare than any other species: there is in each case one and only one species that we are talking about.[7]

This problem of application seems to arise because the object of aesthetic appreciation, and hence of aesthetic value, has been misidentified, for it is not the case that we perceive, admire, and appreciate a *species* —species construed either as a group or set of similar animals or as a name that we attach to certain kinds of animals in virtue of some classification scheme. What we value is the existence of individuals with certain characteristics. If this is correct, then the whole attempt to explain why species matter by arguing that *they* have aesthetic value needs to be redirected. This is what I try to do in the final section of this paper.

VALUING THE INDIVIDUAL

What I propose is that the intuition behind the argument from aesthetic value is correct, but misdirected. The reasons that were given for the value of a species are, in fact, reasons for saying that an individual has value. We do not admire the grace and beauty of the species *Panthera tigris;* rather, we admire the grace and beauty of the individual Bengal tigers that we may encounter. What we value then is the existence of that individual and the existence (present or future) of individuals like that. The ways in which other individuals should be "like that" will depend on why we value that particular sort of individual: the stripes on a zebra do not matter if we value zebras primarily for the way they are adapted to a certain environment, their unique fitness for a certain sort of life. If, on the other hand, we value zebras because their stripes are aesthetically pleasing, the stripes do matter.

The shift of emphasis from species to individuals allows us to make sense of the stronger feelings we have about endangered species in two ways. First, the fact that there are very few members of a species—the fact that we rarely encounter one—itself increases the value of those encounters. I can see turkey vultures almost every day and I can eat apples almost every day, but seeing a bald eagle or eating wild strawberries are experiences that are much less common, more delightful just for their rarity and unexpectedness. Even snail darters, which, if we encountered them every day would be drab and uninteresting, become more interesting just because we don't—or may not—see them every day. Second, part of our interest in an individual carries over to a desire that there be future opportunities to see these things again (just as when, upon finding a new and beautiful work of art, I will wish to go back and see it again). In the case of animals, unlike works of art, I know that this animal will not live forever, but that other animals like this one will have similar aesthetic value. Thus, because I value possible future encounters, I will also want to do what is needed to ensure the possibility of such encounters—i.e., make sure that enough presently existing individuals of this type will be able to reproduce and survive. This is rather like the duty that we have to support and contribute to museums, or to other efforts to preserve works of art.

To sum up, then: individual animals can have, to a greater or lesser degree, aesthetic value: they are valued for their simple beauty, for their awesomeness, for their intriguing adaptations, for their rarity, and for many other reasons. We have moral obligations to protect things of aesthetic value, and to ensure (in an odd sense) their continued existence; thus, we have a duty to protect individual animals (the duty may be weaker or stronger depending on the value of the individual), and to ensure that there will continue to be animals of this sort (this duty will also be weaker or stronger, depending on value).

NOTES

1. Joel Feinberg, "Human Duties and Animal Rights," in *On the Fifth Day: Animal Rights and Human Ethics,* Richard Knowles Morris and Michael W. Fox, eds. (Washington: Acropolis Books, 1978), p. 67.
2. *Ibid,* p. 68.
3. Cf. Feinberg's discussion of custodial duties in "The Rights of Animals and Future Generations," *Philosophy and Environmental Crisis,* pp. 49–50.
4. A similar view has been defended by Tom Auxter, "The Right Not to Be Eaten," *Inquiry* 22 (1979): 222–23.
5. William Blackstone, "Ethics and Ecology," *Philosophy and Environmental Crisis,* (Athens, Georgia: University of Georgia Press, 1974), p. 25.
6. This objection parallels Regan's attack on ungrounded appeals to the intrinsic value of human life as a way of trying to establish a human right to life. Cf. Tom Regan, "Do Animals Have a Right to Life?" *Animal Rights and Human Obligations,* p. 199.
7. There is one further attempt that might be made to avoid this difficulty: one might argue that species do not increase in value due to scarcity, but that our duties to protect a valuable species involves more when the species is more in need of protection. This goes part of the way towards solving the problem, but does not yet capture our intuition that rarity does affect the value in some way.

PART NINE
Epilogue

DESMOND STEWART

The Limits of Trooghaft

The Troogs took one century to master the planet, then another three to restock it with men, its once dominant but now conquered species. Being hierarchical in temper, the Troogs segregated *homo insipiens* into four castes between which there was no traffic except that of bloodshed. The four castes derived from the Troog experience of human beings.

The planet's new masters had an intermittent sense of the absurd; Troog laughter could shake a forest. Young Troogs first captured some surviving children, then tamed them as "housemen," though to their new pets the draughty Troog structures seemed far from house-like. Pet-keeping spread. Whole zoos of children were reared on a bean diet. For housemen, Troogs preferred children with brown or yellow skins, finding them neater and cleaner than others; this preference soon settled into an arbitrary custom. Themselves hermaphrodite, the Troogs were fascinated by the spectacle of marital couplings. Once their pets reached adolescence, they were put in cages whose nesting boxes had glass walls. Troogs would gaze in by the hour. Captivity—and this was an important discovery—did

Desmond Stewart is a novelist and short-story writer. His fiction includes the trilogy *A Sequence of Roles* (Chapman and Hall. 1965).

Reprinted from *Encounter* (London, February 1972), by permission of Anthony Sheil Associates, agents for Desmond Stewart.

not inhibit the little creatures from breeding, nor, as was feared, did the sense of being watched turn the nursing females to deeds of violence. Cannibalism was rare. Breeders, by selecting partners, could soon produce strains with certain comical features, such as cone-shaped breasts or cushion-shaped rumps.

The practice of keeping pets was fought by senior Troogs; the conservative disapproved of innovations while the fastidious found it objectionable when bean-fed humans passed malodorous wind. After the innovation became too general to suppress, the Troog elders hedged the practice with laws. No pet should be kept alive if it fell sick, and since bronchitis was endemic, pets had short lives. The young Troogs recognised the wisdom behind this rule for they too dislike the sound of coughing. But in some cases they tried to save an invalid favourite from the lethal chamber, or would surrender it only after assurances that the sick were happier dead.

Adaptability had enabled the Troogs to survive their travels through time and space; it helped them to a catholic approach to the food provided by the planet, different as this was from their previous nourishment. Within two generations they had become compulsive carnivores. The realisation, derived from pet-keeping, that captive men could breed, led to the establishment of batteries of capons, the second and largest human caste. Capons were naturally preferred when young, since their bones were supple; at this time they fetched, as "eat-alls", the highest price for the lowest weight. Those kept alive after childhood were lodged in small cages maintained at a steady 22 degrees; the cage floors were composed of rolling bars through which the filth fell into a sluice. Capons were not permitted to see the sky or smell unfiltered air. Experience proved that a warm pink glow kept them docile and conduced to weight-gain. Females were in general preferred to males and the eradication of the tongue (sold as a separate delicacy) quietened the batteries.

The third category—the ferocious hound-men—were treated even by the Troogs with a certain caution; the barracks in which they were kennelled were built as far as possible from the batteries lest the black predators escape, break in and massacre hundreds. Bred for speed, obedience and ruthlessness, they were underfed. Unleashed they sped like greyhounds. Their unreliable tempers doomed the few surreptitious efforts to employ them as pets. One night they kept their quarters keening in rhythmic sound; next day, they slumped in yellow-eyed sulks, stirring only to lunge at each other or at their keepers' tentacles. None were kept alive after the age of thirty. Those injured in the chase were slaughtered on the spot and minced for the mess bowl.

Paradoxically, the swift hound-men depended for survival on the quarry they despised and hunted: the fourth human caste, the caste most hedged with laws.

The persistence, long into the first Troog period, of lone nomadic rebels, men and women who resisted from remote valleys and caves, had perplexed the planet's rulers. Then they made an advantage out of the setback. The wits and endurance of the defeated showed that the Troogs had suppressed a menace of some mettle. This was a compliment and Troogs, like the gods of fable, found praise enjoyable. They decided to preserve a caste of the uncorralled. This fourth caste, known as quarry-men or game, were protected within limits and seasons. It was forbidden, for example, to hunt pre-adolescents or pregnant females. All members of the caste enjoyed a respite during eight months of each year. Only at the five-yearly Nova Feast—the joyous commemoration of the greatest escape in Troog history—were all rules abandoned: then the demand for protein became overpowering.

Quarry-men excited more interest in their masters than the three other castes put together. On one level, gluttonous Troogs found their flesh more appetising than that of capons. On another, academically minded Troogs studied their behavior-patterns. Moralising Troogs extolled their courage against hopeless odds to a Troog generation inclined to be complacent about its power. The ruins which spiked the planet were testimony to the rudimentary but numerous civilisations which, over ten millennia, men had produced, from the time when they first cultivated grains and domesticated animals till their final achievement of an environment without vegetation (except under glass) and with only synthetic protein. Men, it was true, had never reached the stage where they could rely on the telepathy that served the Troogs. But this was no reason to despise them. Originally Troogs, too, had conversed through sound hitting a tympanum; they had retained a hieroglyphic system deep into their journey through time; indeed, their final abandonment of what men called writing (and the Troogs "incising") had been an indirect tribute to men: telepathic waves were harder to decipher than symbols. It moved antiquarian Troogs to see that some men still frequented the ruined repositories of written knowledge; and though men never repaired these ancient libraries, this did not argue that they had lost the constructional talents of forbears who had built skyscrapers and pyramids. It showed shrewd sense. To repair old buildings or build new ones would attract the hound-men. Safety lay in dispersal. Libraries were a place of danger for a quarry-man, known to the contemptuous hound-men as a "book-roach." The courageous passion for the little volumes in which great men had compressed their wisdom was admired by Troogs. In their death throes quarry-men often clutched these talismans.

It was through a library that, in the fifth Troog century, the first attempt was made to communicate between the species, the conquerors and the conquered.

Curiosity was a characteristic shared by both species. Quarry-men still debated what the Troogs were and where they had come from. The first generation had known them as Extra-Terrestrials, when Terra, man's planet, was still the normative centre. Just as the natives of central America had welcomed the Spaniards as gods till the stake gave the notion of the godlike a satanic quality, millions of the superstitious had identified the Troogs with angels. But Doomsday was simply Troog's Day. The planet continued spinning, the sun gave out its heat and the empty oceans rolled against their shores. Living on an earth no longer theirs, quarry-men gazed at the glittering laser beams and reflected light which made the Troog-Halls and speculated about their tenants. A tradition declared that the first space vehicles had glowed with strange pictures. The Troogs, it was correctly deduced, had originally conversed by means analogous to language but had discarded speech in order to remain opaque, untappable. This encouraged some would-be rebels. They saw in precaution signs of caution and in caution proof of fallibility. A counter-attack might one day be possible, through science or magic. Some cynics pretended to find the Troogs a blessing. They quoted a long-dead writer who had believed it was better for a man to die on his feet when not too old. This was now the common human lot. Few quarry-men lived past thirty and the diseases of the past, such as cardiac failure and carcinoma, were all but unknown. But most men dreamed simply of a longer and easier existence.

The first human to be approached by a Troog was a short, stocky youth who had survived his 'teens thanks to strong legs, a good wind and the discovery of a cellar underneath one of the world's largest libraries. Because of his enthusiasm for a poet of that name, this book-roach was known to his group as "Blake." He had also studied other idealists such as the Egyptian Akhenaten and the Russian Tolstoy. These inspired him to speculate along the most hazardous paths, in the direction, for example, of the precipice-question: might not the Troogs have something akin to human consciousness, or even conscience? If so, might man perhaps address his conqueror? Against the backspace of an insentient universe one consciousness should greet another. His friends, his woman, laughed at the notion. They had seen what the Troogs had done to their species. Some men were bred to have protuberant eyes or elongated necks; others were kept in kennels on insufficient rations, and then, at the time of the Nova Feast or in the year's open season, unleashed through urban ruins or surrounding savannah to howl after their quarry—those related by blood and experience to Blake and his fellows. "I shall never trust a Troog," said his woman's brother, "even if he gives me a gold safe-conduct."

One Troog, as much an exception among his species as Blake among his, read this hopeful brain. It was still the closed season and some four months before the quinquennial Nova Feast. Quarry-men still relaxed in safety; the hounds sang or sulked; the Troogs had yet to prepare the lights and sounds for their tumultuous celebrations. Each morning Blake climbed to the Library. It was a long, rubbish-encumbered place with aisles still occupied by books, once arranged according to subject, but now higgledy-piggledy in dust and dereliction, thrown down by earthquake or scattered in the hunt. Each aisle had its attendant bust—Plato, Shakespeare, Darwin, Marx—testifying to a regretted time when men, divided by nationality, class or colour, suffered only from their fellows.

In the corner watched by Shakespeare, Blake had his reading place. He had restored the shelves to some order; he had dusted the table. This May morning a Troog's fading odour made him tremble. A new object stood on his table; a large rusty typewriter of the most ancient model. In it was a sheet of paper.

Blake bent to read.

Are you ready to communicate question.

Blake typed the single word: *yes.*

He did not linger but retreated in mental confusion to the unintellectual huddle round babies and potatoes which was his cellar. He half feared that he had begun to go mad, or that some acquaintance was playing him a trick. But few of his group read and no man could duplicate the distinctive Troog smell.

The days that followed constituted a continual seance between "his" Troog and himself. Blake contributed little to the dialogue. His Troog seemed anxious for a listener but little interested in what that listener thought. Blake was an earphone, an admiring confessor. Try as he feebly did, he got no response when he tried to evoke his woman, his children.

"Trooghaft, you are right," wrote the unseen communicator, attested each time by his no longer frightening scent, "was noble once." Blake had made no such suggestion. "The quality of being a Troog was unfrictional as space and as tolerant as time. It has become—almost human."

Then next morning: "To copy the habits of lower creatures is to sink below them. What is natural to carnivores is unnatural to us. We never ate flesh before the Nova; nor on our jouney. We adopted the practice from reading the minds of lower creatures, then copying them. Our corruption shows in new diseases; earlier than in the past, older Troogs decompose. It shows in our characters. We quarrel like our quarry. Our forms are not apt for ingesting so much protein. Protein is what alcohol was to humans. It maddens; it corrupts. Protein, not earth's climate, is paling our. . . ."

Here there was a day's gap before the typewriter produced, next morning, the word *complexion.* And after it, *metaphor.* Blake had learnt that the old Troog hieroglyphs were followed by determinants, symbols showing, for example, whether the concept *rule* meant tyranny or order. Complexion could only be used metaphorically of faceless and largely gaseous creatures.

To one direct question Blake obtained a direct answer: "How," he had typed, "did you first turn against the idea of eating us?"

"My first insight flashed at our last Nova Feast. Like everyone, I had been programmed to revel. Stench of flesh filled every Troog-Hall. Amid the spurt of music, the ancient greetings with which we flare still, the coruscations, I passed a meat-shop where lights pirouetted. I looked. I saw. Hanging from iron hooks—each pierced a foot-palm—were twenty she-capons, what you call women. Each neck was surrounded by a ruffle to hide the knife-cut; a tomato shut each anus. I suddenly shuddered. Nearby, on a slab of marble, smiled a row of jellied heads. Someone had dressed their sugar-hair in the manner of your Roman empresses: 'Flavian Heads.' A mass of piled up, tong-curled hair in front, behind a bun encoiled by a marzipan fillet. I lowered myself and saw as though for the first time great blocks of neutral-looking matter: 'Paté of Burst Liver.' The owner of the shop was glad to explain. They hold the woman down, then stuff nutriment through a V-shaped funnel. The merchant was pleased by my close attention. He displayed his Sucking Capons and Little Loves, as they call the reproductive organs which half of you split creatures wear outside your bodies."

"Was this," I asked in sudden repugnance, "Trooghaft?"

Encouraged by evidence of soul, Blake brought to the Troog's notice, from the miscellaneous volumes on the shelves, quotations from his favourite writers and narrative accounts of such actions as the death of Socrates, the crucifixion of Jesus and the murder of Che Guevara. Now in the mornings he found books and encyclopaedias open on his table as well as typed pages. Sometimes Blake fancied that there was more than one Troog smell; so perhaps his Troog was converting others.

Each evening Blake told Janine, his partner, of his exploits. She was at first sceptical, then half-persuaded. This year she was not pregnant and therefore could be hunted. For love of her children, the dangers of the Nova season weighed on her spirits. Only her daughter was Blake's; her son had been sired by Blake's friend, a fast-runner who had sprained his ankle and fallen easy victim to the hounds two years before. As the Nova Feast approached, the majority of the quarry-men in the city began to leave for the mountains. Not that valleys and caves were secure; but the mountains were vast and the valleys remote one from another. The hound-men preferred to hunt in the cities; concentrations of people made their game easier.

Blake refused to join them. Out of loyalty Janine stayed with him.

"I shall build," the Troog had written, "a bridge between Trooghaft and Humanity. The universe calls me to revive true Trooghaft. My Troog-Hall shall become a sanctuary, not a shed of butchers."

Blake asked: "Are you powerful? Can you make other Troogs follow your example?"

The Troog answered: "I can at least do as your Akhenaten did."

Blake flushed at the mention of his hero. Then added: "But Akhenaten's experiment lasted briefly. Men relapsed. May not Troogs do likewise?" He longed for reassurance that his Troog was more than a moral dilettante.

Instead of an answer came a statement:

"We can never be equals with *homo insipiens*. But we can accept our two species as unequal productions of one universe. Men are small, but that does not mean they cannot suffer. Not one tongueless woman moves, upside-down, towards the throat-knife, without trembling. I have seen this. I felt pity, *metaphor*. Our young Troogs argue that fear gives flesh a quivering tenderness. I reject such arguments. Why should a complex, if lowly, life—birth, youth, growth to awareness—be sacrificed for one mealtime's pleasure?"

Although Blake recognised that his Troog was soliloquising, the arguments pleased him. Convinced of their sincerity, Blake decided to trust his Troog and remain where he was, not hide or run as on previous occasions. There was a sewer leading from his refuge whose remembered stench was horrible. He would stay in the cellar. On the first day of the Nova Feast he climbed as usual to his corner of the library. But today there was no paper in the typewriter. Instead, books and encyclopaedias had been pulled from the shelves and left open; they had nothing to do with poetry or the philosophers and the stench was not that of his Troog. Sudden unease seized him. Janine was alone with the children, her brother having left to join the others in the mountains. He returned to his cellar and, as his fear already predicted, found the children alone, wailing in one corner. The elder, the boy, told the doleful tale. Two hound-men had broken in and their mother had fled down the disused sewer.

Blake searched the sewer. It was empty. His one hope, as he too hid there, lay in his Troog's intervention. But neither the next day nor the day after, when he stole to the library, watching every shadow lest it turn to a hound-man, was there any message. This silence was atoned for on the third morning.

"If we still had a written language, I should publish a volume of confessions." The message was remote, almost unrelated to Blake's anguish. He read, "A few fat-fumes blow away a resolution. It was thus, the evening of the Nova Feast's beginning. Three Troog friends, *metaphor*, came to my Hall where no flesh was burning, where instead I was pondering these puny creatures to whom we cause such suffering. 'You cannot exile yourself from your group; Trooghaft is what Troogs do together.' I resisted such blandishments. The lights and sounds of the Nova were enough. I felt no craving for protein. Their laughter at this caused the laser beams to buckle and the lights to quiver. There entered four black hound-men dragging a quarry-female, filthy from the chase, her hands bound behind her. I was impassive. Housemen staggered under a great cauldron; they fetched logs. They placed the cauldron on a tripod and filled it with water; the logs were under it."

Blake shook as he read. This was the moment for his Troog to incarnate pity and save his woman.

"They now unbound and stripped the female, then set her in the water. It was cold and covered her skin with pimples.

"Again laughter, again the trembling lights and the buckling lasers.

"We, too, have been reading, brother. We have studied one of their ways of cooking. *Place the lobster*—their name for a long extinct sea-thing —*in warm water. Bring the water gently to the boil. The lobster will be lulled to sleep, not knowing it is to be killed. Most experts account this the humane way of treating lobster.*

"The logs under the cauldron gave a pleasant aroma as they started to splutter. The female was not lulled. She tried to clamber out: perhaps a reflex action. The hound-men placed an iron mesh over the cauldron."

Blake saw what he could not bear to see, heard the unhearable. The Troog's confession was humble.

"The scent was so persuasive. 'Try this piece,' they flashed, 'it is so tender. It will harden your scruples.' I hesitated. Outside came the noise of young Troogs whirling in the joy of satiety. A Nova Feast comes only once in five years. I dipped my hand, *metaphor*"—(even now the Troog's pedantry was present)—"in the cauldron. If one must eat protein, it is better to do so in a civilised fashion. And as for the humanity, *metaphor,* of eating protein—I should write Trooghaft—if we ate no capons, who would bother to feed them? If we hunted no quarry, who would make the game-laws or keep the hound-men? At least now they live, as we do, for a season. And while they live, they are healthy. I must stop. My stomach, *metaphor,* sits heavy as a mountain."

As Blake turned in horror from the ancient typewriter, up from his line of retreat, keening their happiest music, their white teeth flashing, loped three lithe and ruthless hound-men. All around was the squid-like odour of their master.